THE RHETORICAL FOUNDATIONS OF SOCIETY

THE RHETORICAL FOUNDATIONS OF SOCIETY

ERNESTO LACLAU

VERSO

London • New York

First published by Verso 2014
© Ernesto Laclau 2014

1 3 5 7 9 10 8 6 4 2

Verso
UK: 6 Meard Street, London W1F 0EG
US: 20 Jay Street, Suite 1010, Brooklyn, NY 11201
www.versobooks.com

Verso is the imprint of New Left Books

ISBN-13: 978-1-78168-170-1 (PBK)
ISBN-13: 978-1-78168-171-8 (HBK)
eISBN-13: 978-1-78168-218-0 (US)
eISBN-13: 978-1-78168-527-3 (UK)

British Library Cataloguing in Publication Data
A catalogue record for this book is available from the British Library.

Library of Congress Cataloging-in-Publication Data
A catalog record for this book is available from the Library of
Congress.

Typeset in Minion Pro by Hewer Text UK Ltd, Edinburgh, Scotland
Printed and bound by CPI Group (UK) Ltd, Croydon, CR0 4YY

Contents

Introduction

This volume collects several essays written over the last fifteen years. Although they respond to several conjunctures and contexts, there is a common thread running throughout them: all of them are contributions to the construction of a political ontology which can respond to the challenges presented by the post-Marxist and post-structuralist situation within which we are operating. The moment of a systematic presentation of such an ontology lies somewhere in the future, and I do not claim that this volume has such a status. But the essays that follow represent steps – some of them not inessential – in that direction. As an introduction to them, I would like to say something about the initial historical context in which my intellectual and political project took shape, as well as about the main theoretical stages which have structured its formulation.

In order to understand the initial context of my theoretical intervention, we have to go back to the troubled history of the Argentina of the 1960s. In 1955 a conservative military coup had overthrown the popular Peronist government and a more or less institutionalized dictatorship had been established, which lasted for the following eighteen years – I say *more or less institutionalized* because periods of formal liberal governments (elections, and so on) alternated with others of direct military rule; but *dictatorship*, anyway, because even when civilian governments were in office, they had been elected on the basis of the proscription of Peronism – by far the majority mass party in the country. In the 1960s this institutionalized dictatorship began to show increasing fissures and fractures and, as a result, the Peronist resistance, at the beginning confined to the working-class districts of the main cities, started spreading to wider sectors of the population.

This is the process of what in the Argentina of that time was called 'the nationalization of the middle classes'. The Argentinean middle classes had traditionally been liberal – of the Right or the Left – but in the 1960s they were increasingly hegemonized by a national-popular agenda. (In the Argentine political jargon 'liberal' is not opposed to 'conservative' but to 'national-popular'.) The backbone of classical Peronism, as it had been constituted in the 1940s, had been the trade-union movement. During the Peronist government, the strongest industrial trade-unions of Latin America had been formed, with the active support of the state. Their epicentre was the triangle consti-tuted by the newly industrialized cities of Buenos Aires, Rosario and Córdoba. Not surprisingly, intervening in the trade-unions' organiza-tion, by deposing the current union authorities and replacing them with military interventors, was one of the first measures taken by the military government.

It was the exclusive character of this dominant working-class connotation that started to become less obvious in the 1960s. On the one hand, the crisis of the liberal oligarchic regime led to the margin-alization of large sections of the middle classes, whose mobilization gave to Peronism a mass dimension that far exceeded its initial social limits. The student movement, for instance, which had traditionally been anti-Peronist, became increasingly dominated by various shades of the Peronist Youth. On the other hand, the majority sections of the trade-union movement, increasingly bureaucratized, developed a corporatism leading to constant transactions and semi-agreements with the new military government installed in 1966, entirely at odds with the new wave of radicalization that swept society in the late 1960s and early 1970s. This opened the way to the so-called *setent-ismo* ('spirit of the 1970s') and the emergence of a new, national-popular Left entirely different from the traditional, liberal Left. It was pretty obvious to most militants that we were participating in new mass processes that far exceeded the limits of any narrow 'classism'.

Dealing with those limits, however, was not a straightforward enterprise. Although we were active in several movements inside or on the periphery of the newly radicalized Peronism, from the theo-retical point of view most of us considered ourselves Marxists, and the Marxist texts advocated exactly the strict 'classist' orientation from which we were trying to free ourselves. The *Communist Manifesto* already gave us an image of class struggle under capitalism as domi-nated by the increasing centrality of the antagonism between wage labour and capital. A process of proletarianization, it was thought, was extinguishing the middle classes and the peasantry, so that the last antagonism of history would be a showdown between the capital-ist bourgeoisie and a vast proletarian mass. This thesis of a progressive simplification of the social structure under capitalism was the back-bone of classical Marxism, and is particularly visible in the over-economistic texts of the Second International. An example: in a discussion with the Bavarian social-democratic leader von Vollmar, Kautsky asserted that the task of the socialists was not to defend all oppressed people, but only the working class, because it was the exclusive bearer of the future of humanity.

Very quickly, we became aware that such an impasse was not only facing us, Argentinians, who were experiencing it. The 1960s and 1970s were two profoundly creative decades for left-wing thought. Those are the years of the Cuban Revolution – which by no stretch of imagination can be conceived in terms of working-class centrality; of Fanon's great books on anti-colonial subjectivities; even of Mao's assertion of 'contradictions within the people', so that the notion of 'the people', which would have been anathema for classical Marxism, was given revolutionary legitimacy. These are also the years of mass mobilizations of students, marginal groups and various minorities, in both the US and Europe. We were faced with an explosion of new identities and with complex logics of their articulation that clearly called for a change of ontological terrain.

So how to deal with that situation? There were, at first sight, two roads that I resolutely refused to take. The first was to stick to Marxist categories, turning them into a reverentially hypostasized dogma while, at the same time, empirically developing political action with only a loose connection with those categories. This is the road that many people, both in Communist and Trotskyist movements, chose at the time, but I was never in the least tempted to follow it. The second was the symmetrical opposite: to reduce Marxism to a sclerotic dogma, unconnected to the issues of the present, and to start anew with a different type of discourse, entirely ignoring the field of Marxist discursivity. I also refused to take this route. I was convinced that a great intellectual tradition never dies that way, through some sort of sudden collapse.

I tried to engage myself in a different kind of intellectual operation. I found very illuminating the distinction, established by Husserl, between 'sedimentation' and 'reactivation'. Sedimented ideas are those crystallized forms that have broken their link with the original intuition from which they proceeded, while reactivation is the revelation of that forgotten link, so that the forms can be seen *in status nascens*. The

Spinozan distinction between *natura naturans* and *natura naturata* (nature as the source of natural things, and nature as the display of things proceeding from that source) moves, to some extent, in the same direction. I could not, of course, simply adopt the Husserlian distinction without introducing into it a basic change. For Husserl, the reactivating process leads to a transcendental subject that is the absolute source of meaning; for me, it leads to an instance of radical contingency in which many other decisions could have been taken. If so, reconstructing the contingent character of the decision becomes primordial, and this can only be done by revealing the fields of inchoate thoughts – that is, of alternative decisions that could have been taken and that the contingent road chosen had obliterated. This is the analytic method that I have systematically followed since those early days: whenever I have found in the Marxist (and more generally, socialist) texts some theses that clashed with my experience or intuition, I tried to reconstruct the historical contexts and the intellectual operations through which such theses were formulated. In all cases I found that those theses were the result of a *choice*, and that the discarded alternatives continued operating in the background and re-emerged with the inevitability of the return of the repressed. In this way, I think that we managed to establish an area of interdiscursivity within Marxist and socialist texts that makes possible a better appreciation of their inner plurality. A first formulation of our conclusions can be found in *Hegemony and Socialist Strategy*, which I wrote with Chantal Mouffe almost thirty years ago.

In this interrogation of the Marxist and socialist tradition in the late 1960s and early 1970s there were two authors who had an important influence in helping me to shape my outlook: Althusser and Gramsci. From Althusser, what came as a highly enlightening notion was his thesis that class contradictions are always *overdetermined*. This means that there are not simple class contradictions, constituted at the level of the relations of production and represented then at other levels, but instead a plurality of antagonisms, not all of them reducible to class contradictions, which establish between them relations of inter-determination. This was a clear advance in the direction of what we were seeking: on the one hand, a variety of antagonisms constituted political subjectivities, which escaped a direct class determination; on the other, if the relation between these different agents was one of *over*determination, what was necessary was to establish the exact meaning of that 'over'.

Althusser's notion of 'overdetermination' comes clearly from psychoanalysis, but he advanced very little in the attempt at translating all the intricacies and nuances of Freudian logics into the political field. The more his reflection advanced, however, the more difficult it was to proceed without defining with precision the nature of the 'over', for it was increasingly clear that a simple determination – as in the classical duality base/superstructure – would no longer do the trick. In a first moment, there was the attempt to introduce the political and ideological instances within the very notion of 'mode of production', but this led to all kinds of theoretical impasses. So, in a second moment, there was the attempt to refer the unities of concrete social analysis to the wider category of 'social formation'. Thus, Étienne Balibar asserts:

> [T]he concept of mode of production certainly designates in Marx, even at an abstract level, the complex *unity* of determinations concerning the base and the superstructure. But we cannot by any means *deduce* either the mode of this constitution or the process of functioning and historical tendencies of the social relations under consideration, or the laws of combination of the different aspects of class struggle . . . from these formal characteristics – that is, on the basis of a comparison between different possible forms. That is why one cannot *invent* historically 'possible' modes of production.[1]

The problem is that, the more we move away from the notion of simple determination, the more imperative it becomes to establish relational logics of a new type – which clearly exceed what is thinkable in a Marxist universe. Again: what was increasingly needed was a displacement of the general ontological terrain. The Althusserian school was to some extent groping in that direction with its assertion that Marxism was grounded on two theoretical disciplines: historical materialism and dialectical materialism – an obscure recognition of the fact that there is no overlap between the ontic and the ontological orders (an overlap which is necessarily to be found in all theories postulating a simple and direct determination).

But still more important, at the time, than the influence of Althusser was my reading in depth of the work of Gramsci. Gramsci

---

1 Etienne Balibar, *Cinq études du matérialisme historique* (Paris: Francois Maspero, 1979), pp. 231–2, translation is my own.

provided a new arsenal of concepts – war of position, collective wills, intellectual and moral leadership, organic intellectuals, integral state and, especially, hegemony – which made it possible to advance in the understanding of collective identities in ways that no other Marxist of his time – or indeed of ours either – even approached. Let us take, for instance, a central issue: the interrelations between the social and the political in connection with the question of universality. For Hegel, bureaucracy – understood as the ensemble of state apparatuses – was the locus of universality; it was the 'universal class'. Civil society was, on the contrary, the realm of particularism, designed as the 'system of needs'. Marx, as is well known, asserted, against Hegel, that there is nothing universal in the state, for it is an instrument of the dominant class. The moment of universality had to be transferred to civil society itself – the universal class being the proletariat. But, with an iron logic, this led to the view that a reconciled society required the withering away of the state. As I have tried to show in other works, Gramsci's intervention takes its distance from both Hegel and Marx. He agrees with Marx, against Hegel, that the place of emergence of the universal does not involve a separate sphere, but cuts across the barrier separating state and civil society. But he agrees with Hegel, against Marx, that the construction of a universal class (which, in fact, was no longer a class but a collective will) was a *political* construction out of heterogeneous elements. Where Marx spoke of a 'withering away' of the state, Gramsci speaks about the construction of an 'integral state'. It was this construction that he called 'hegemony'. So it became increasingly clear to me that the building up of a hegemonic nexus posed a series of theoretico-political issues that pointed, at the same time, to a new agenda for reflection.

This agenda turned around the following central issues:

1. If the articulation between the social (understood in a broad sense, including the economy) and the political was itself going to be political, the classical triad of levels – economic, political, ideological – had to be drastically rethought. Althusser himself, as we have seen, had tried to some extent to advance in that direction, with his attempt to include the political and the ideological dimensions within the very notion of 'mode of production'. And Balibar, with his attempt of moving the centre of concrete analysis from the mode of production to the social formation, took a new

and bolder step in that direction. This salutary turn, however, left a problem unsolved: How is a social formation structured? If it is going to be a meaningful *totality* and not a heteroclite addition of elements, some reconceptualization of the internal links between the latter would have to take place – the links having ontological priority over the articulated elements. It was at this point of the argument that it became progressively clear to me that the Gramscian notion of hegemony had all the potential to address the questions concerning the nature of this articulating role. The centrality of the mode of production in social analysis had to be replaced by that of 'hegemonic formation'.

2. Thus, this turn involved giving the political, in some way, a privileged ontological place in the articulation of the social whole. But it was evident that this was impossible without deconstructing the category of 'the political'. The political had been considered, in the type of theorization that I inhabited, as a *level* of the social formation, and it was obvious that, theoretically, we would not have advanced a single step if we left untouched the identity of the political as a level and simply attributed to it the role of determination in the last instance. It was with this last notion that I was taking issue, before this role was attributed to one instance or the other. So the questions about the political were taking shape in my mind in the following terms: How must the political be conceived so that something like a hegemonic operation becomes thinkable?

3. This also involved two other interrelated questions. First: If the hegemonic link has a grounding role within the social and if it is, as a link, more primary than the *levels* resulting from it and the agents constituted by it, how do we determine its ontological status? Second: In its hegemonic dimension (and I think we can safely equate hegemony with the political), politics should be conceived as the process of instituting the social. So: What are the experiences in which this instituting moment shows itself – in which the political becomes visible, as it were, in *status nascens*?

The essays that follow are attempts to deal, in different ways, with various aspects of these three main issues. I will not try to summarize their conclusions. I think they are explicit enough. I just want to mention, at this point, some of the other authors whose works I have found particularly helpful in shaping my theoretical perspective.

From Barthes, I learned how linguistic categories should not be seen as merely regional but, if properly redefined, as extensible to the ensemble of social life. Derrida's deconstruction showed me how to break into sedimented forms of apparent necessity and discover the kernel of contingency that inhabits them. From Wittgenstein's 'language games', I took the notion that the link between words and actions is more primary than the separation between them (which is a purely artificial and analytical operation). This was highly illuminating for understanding the internal structuration of hegemonic formations. Finally, many aspects of Lacan's work were for me of capital importance – in particular, the logic of the *objet a*, whose deep homology with Gramsci's hegemony I saw immediately.

Finally, let me say something about the status of these essays. Although they have a variety of occasional origins, I have tried to return in each of them to my main thesis concerning the hegemonic character of the social link and the ontological centrality of the political. This led to inevitable reiterations of the main argument. But I have preferred to keep them as they were originally published, in order to show something about the various contexts within which our hegemonic theoretical approach developed. So what the reader will find in the different chapters are reformulations, with small changes, of the main thesis concerning hegemonic logics. But these reformulations are arrived at starting from different theoretical contexts (rhetorical, psychoanalytical, philosophical, semiotic). This contextual diversity tries to capture some of the many facets that the hegemonic approach to politics can illuminate, while showing, at the same time, the productivity that these various contextual references can have for an understanding of the political. The only alternative would have been to unify all of them in a single text. But that would have been a different project from the one I had in mind when I planned this volume.

A few words just before closing this introduction. Over the last fifteen years we have seen the emergence of a set of new phenomena in the political and social fields that corroborate the two main theses around which my political reflection was structured. The first concerns the dispersion and proliferation of social agents. Gone are the days in which emancipatory political subjectivities were confined to social class identities. On the contrary, the present world scene, especially since the beginning of the economic crisis in 2008, shows us the expansion of forms of protest that escape any obvious institutional domestication (movements like the *indignados* in Spain and other similar movements in Europe, the Occupy Wall Street movement in the US, the *piqueteros* in Argentina, various forms of new social protest in the Middle East and Northern Africa, and so on). These mobilizations tend to operate in a way that overflows the channelling abilities of existing institutional frameworks. This is the horizontal dimension of 'autonomy', and it exactly corresponds to what, in my work, I have called 'equivalential logics'. But my second thesis is that the horizontal dimension of autonomy will be incapable, left to itself, of bringing about long-term historical change if it is not complemented by the vertical dimension of 'hegemony' – that is, a radical transformation of the state. Autonomy left to itself leads, sooner or later, to the exhaustion and dispersion of the movements of protest. But hegemony not accompanied by mass action at the level of civil society leads to a bureaucratism that will be easily colonized by the corporative power of the forces of the status quo. To advance both in the directions of autonomy and hegemony is the real challenge to those who aim for a democratic future that gives real meaning to the frequently advocated 'socialism of the twenty-first century'.

CHAPTER 1

The Death and Resurrection
of the Theory of Ideology

I

In a recent essay on theories of ideology,[1] Slavoj Žižek describes contemporary approaches by distributing them around the three axes identified by Hegel: *doctrine, belief* and *ritual* – that is, 'ideology as a complex of ideas (theories, convictions, beliefs, argumentative proce-dures); ideology in externality, that is, the materiality of ideology, the Ideological State Apparatus; and finally, the most elusive domain, the "spontaneous" ideology at work at the heart of social existence itself.'[2] He gives as an example the case of liberalism: '[L]iberalism is a doctrine (developed from Locke to Hayek) materialised in rituals and apparatuses (free press, elections, markets, etc and active in the "spon-taneous" (self-)experience of subjects as "free individuals".'[3] In the three cases Žižek finds an essential symmetry of development: at some stage the frontier dividing the ideological from the non-ideo-logical is blurred and, as a result, there is an inflation of the concept of ideology that loses, in that way, all analytical precision. In the case of ideology as a 'system of ideas', the unity of that system depends on the possibility of finding a point external to itself from which a *critique* of ideology might proceed – for example, by showing through a *symp-tomal reading* the *true* interests to which a given ideological configuration responded. But, as Žižek illustrates with examples taken from the works of Barthes, Paul de Man, Ducrot, Pêcheux, and from my own, it is precisely the assumption of this 'zero level' of the ideo-logical of a pure extra-discursive reality that constitutes the ideological misconception par excellence. In the case of 'Ideological State

---

1 'The Spectre of Ideology', Introduction to Slavoj Zizek, ed., *Mapping Ideology* (London/New York: Verso, 1994), pp. 1–33.
2 Ibid., p. 9.
3 Ibid.

Apparatuses' – or, in the Foucauldian version, the disciplinary proce-
dures operating at the level of micro-power – we find symmetrical
versions of the same *petitio principii*: does not the *unity* of the State
Apparatuses require the very cement of the ideology they supposedly
explain? Or, in the case of the disciplinary techniques: Does not their
dispersion itself require the constant recomposition of their articulation, so that we have to appeal to a discursive medium that makes the
very distinction between the ideological and the non-ideological
collapse? And the case is even clearer when we move to the realm of
beliefs: here, from the very beginning, we are confronted with a
supposedly 'extra-ideological' reality whose very operation depends
on mechanisms belonging to the ideological realm:

> [T]he moment we take a closer look at those allegedly extra-ideolog-
> ical mechanisms that regulate social reproduction, we find ourselves
> knee-deep in the . . . obscure domain in which reality is indistin-
> guishable from ideology. What we encounter here, therefore, is the
> third reversal of non-ideology into ideology: all of a sudden we
> become aware of a For-itself of ideology at work in the very In-itself
> of extra-ideological actuality.[4]

Here Žižek correctly detects the main source of the progressive abandonment of 'ideology' as an analytical category: 'this notion somehow
grows' too strong; it begins to embrace everything, including the very
neutral, extra-ideological ground supposed to provide the standard by
means of which one can measure ideological distortion. That is to say,
is it not the ultimate result of discourse analysis that the order of
discourse as such is inherently 'ideological'?[5] We see, thus, the logic
governing the dissolution of the terrain classically occupied by the
theory of ideology. The latter died as a result of its own imperialistic
success. What we are witnessing is not the decline of a theoretical
object as a result of a narrowing of its field of operation, but rather the
opposite: its indefinite expansion, consequent on the explosion of the
dichotomies that – within a certain problematic – confronted it with
other objects. Categories such as 'distortion' and 'false representation'
made sense as long as something 'true' or 'undistorted' was considered

4   Ibid., pp. 14–15.
5   Ibid., p. 16.

to be within human reach. But once an extra-ideological viewpoint becomes unreachable, two effects necessarily follow: first, discourses organizing social practices are both incommensurable and on an equal footing with all others; and, second, notions such as 'distortion' and 'false representation' lose all meaning.

But where does this leave us? Are we supposed to put aside entirely notions such as 'distortion', 'false consciousness', and so on? The difficulty is that if we simply do so, we enter into a vicious circle whereby the conclusions of our analysis negate its premises. Let us for a moment consider the reasons for the decline of the 'critique of ideology' approach – as expressed in its purest terms by classical Marxism, and prolonged today by Habermas's regulative ideal of undistorted communication. The bedrock of such a critique is to postulate access to a point from which – at least tendentially – reality would speak without discursive mediations. The full positivity and graspability of such a point gives a rationale to the whole critical operation. Now, the critique of this approach starts from the negation of such a metalinguistic level, from showing that the rhetorico-discursive devices of a text are irreducible and that, as a result, there is no extra-discursive ground from which a critique of ideology could proceed. (This does not mean, of course, that ideological critique is impossible – what is impossible is *a critique of ideology as such*; all critiques will necessarily be intra-ideological.)

What is not usually perceived, however, is that this critique of the 'critique of ideology' can advance in two different directions that lead to contradictory results. The first leads to what we could call a new positivism and objectivism. If we entirely do away with the notion of 'distortion' and assert that there are only incommensurable 'discourses', we merely transfer the notion of a full positivity from an extra-discursive ground to the plurality of the discursive field. This transference retains entirely the idea of a full positivity. In the same way that we have a naturalistic positivism, we can have a semiotic or a phenomenological one. If, on the other hand, what we are asserting is that the very notion of an extra-discursive viewpoint is the ideological illusion par excellence, the notion of 'distortion' is not abandoned but is instead made the cornerstone of the dismantling of any metalinguistic operation. What is new in the latter is that what now constitutes a distorted representation is the very notion of an extra-discursive closure. I will discuss later the ways in which the concept of 'distortion' has to be reformulated in order to fulfil this new role. Let us just say for the time being that this reformulation is the starting point for a possible re-emergence of a notion of ideology that is not marred by the stumbling blocks of an essentialist theorization.

Let us concentrate for a moment on the Althusserian theory of ideology. Ideology is, for Althusser, *eternal*. The mechanisms producing the subject through misrecognition are inscribed in the very essence of social reproduction. We have no hope of escaping the mirroring game involved in ideological interpellation. For him, however, ideology constitutes itself as an object through its opposition to science: the determination of the distortion brought about by ideological representations and the alienated character of the subject depend on the analyst's knowledge of what social reproduction actually is – a knowledge that includes an understanding of the mirroring mechanism. We *know* that History is a process without a subject, precisely because we are able to go scientifically beyond subjective alienation.

This leaves us, however, with an apparently intractable problem. Everything depends on what is being misrecognized – or, rather, on the nature and extent of the misrecognition. If what is misrecognized is a *particular* type of social relation, we could easily imagine a different one in which no misrecognition at all occurs. This is what was assumed by the classical notion of emancipation. But what Althusser argues is different: it is that we are dealing with a *necessary* misrecognition that is independent of any type of social configuration. In this case, however, what is misrecognized is the principle of social structuration as such, the closure operated by any symbolic system. This launches us into a new problem: if closure *as such* requires misrecognition (in other words, its opposite) it is the very idea of closure that constitutes the highest form of misrecognition. Either misrecognition is reducible to an objective function by a neutral gaze, or that gaze is not neutral but part of the universal misrecognition – in which case what presents itself as the opposite of misrecognition belongs to the essence of the latter. I can maintain a strong frontier between closure (the auto-reproduction of social relations) and the necessary forms of misrecognition accompanying it only insofar as there is a metalinguistic vantage point from which closure *shows* itself without any subjective passage through misrecognition. But if that vantage point proves to be illusory, misrecognition *contaminates* closure; and, given that misrecognition, distortion, is universal, its other (closure, self-transparency) becomes the main form of misrecognition. In that case, distortion is constitutive of social objectivity. But what might be a form of distortion that remains such while the distinction between the distortion and what is distorted is obliterated? This is the next problem that we have to address.

II

The notion of a constitutive distortion is apparently a *contradictio in adjecto*. A distortion, it seems, cannot be constitutive: it is only if there is a more primary meaning which is not itself distorted that a distortive effect can become visible at all. But does this conclusion exhaust all the logical possibilities that a relation of distortion opens? Let us consider the matter carefully. It is certainly inherent to all distortion that a 'primary' meaning is presented under a 'false' light. The operation this presentation involves – concealment, deformation, or whatever – is something that we can leave indeterminate for the time being. What is essential to distortion is, first, that a primary meaning is presented as something different from what it is, and, second, that the distortive operation – not only its results – has to be somehow visible. This last point is crucial: if the distortive operation does not leave any traces in its result, it will fully succeed in constituting a new meaning. But what we are dealing with is a constitutive distortion. That is, we are both positing an originary meaning (as is required by any distortion) and withdrawing it (for the distortion is constitutive). In that case, the only logical possibility of pulling together these two apparently antinomic dimensions is if the original meaning is illusory and the distortive operation consists precisely in creating that illusion – that is, projecting into something that is essentially divided the illusion of a fullness and self-transparency that it lacks. Let us say something about *what* is being projected, and about the visibility of the projection as such.

In my previous discussions I have used three necessarily interrelated notions – 'originary meaning', 'self-transparency' and 'closure'. It is time to say something more about the nature of this link. Something is originary insofar as it does not have to go outside itself in order to constitute what it is; it is self-transparent insofar as its internal dimensions are in a relation of strict solidarity between themselves; and it is closed in itself as far as the ensemble of its 'effects' can be determined without going beyond its original meaning. As we see, each of these notions (without exactly being synonymous with the other two) requires the latter's presence in order to actualize its own meaning. And it is precisely this full meaning that is dislocated by the postulation of a constitutive distortion: in the first and third cases, both the 'originarity' and internality of the 'effects' are upset by discursive mediation, and the opacity of the internal dimensions of the self-enclosed entity interrupts its self-transparency.

This would only show, however, that *dislocation* is constitutive, and that the very notion of a metaphysical closure has to be put into question.[6] But the notion of *distortion* involves something more than mere dislocation – namely, that a *concealment* of some sort takes place in it. Now, as we have seen, what is concealed is the ultimate dislocation of what presents itself as a closed identity, and the act of concealment consists in projecting onto that identity the dimension of closure that it ultimately lacks. This has two chief consequences:

1. The first is that that dimension of closure is something that is actually absent – if it was ultimately present there would be *revelation* rather than *projection*, and no concealment would be involved. In that case what we are dealing with is, *the presence of an absence*, and *the ideological operation par excellence consists of attributing that impossible role of closure to a particular content that is radically incommensurable with it*. In other terms: the operation of closure is impossible but at the same time necessary – impossible because of the constitutive dislocation lying at the heart of any structural arrangement; necessary because, without that fictitious fixing of meaning, there would not be meaning at all.[7] Here we can start seeing the way in which ideology as 'misrepresentation' might be *eternal*: not, as Althusser thought, because the alienation of the subject is the necessary complement of an objective History whose meaning might be located elsewhere, but because the notion of

---

6   This is what many currents of contemporary thought have shown, from later Wittgensteinian philosophy to deconstruction. My own contributions to this task can be found in *New Reflections on the Revolution of Our Time* (London: Verso, 1990) and in several of the essays collected in *Emancipation(s)* (London: Verso, 1996).

7   Closure is the condition of meaning insofar as, all identities being purely differential, they need the system in order to constitute themselves as identities.

that 'objective meaning' is itself the very form of misrepresentation through which any identity acquires its fictitious coherence. The crucial point is to realise that it is this dialectics between necessity and impossibility that gives ideology its terrain of emergence.

2. This dialectics creates in any ideological representation – and at this stage it should be clear that ideology is *one* of the dimensions of *any* representation – an insurmountable split that is strictly constitutive. On the one hand, closure as such, being an impossible operation, cannot have a content of its own and only shows itself through its projection in an object different from itself. On the other hand, this particular object, which at some point assumes the role of incarnating the closure of an ideological horizon, will be deformed as a result of that incarnating function. Between the particularity of the object that attempts to fulfil the operation of closure and this operation, there is a relationship of mutual dependency in which each of the two poles is required, and at the same time, each partially limits the effects of the other. Let us suppose that, at some point in a Third World country, nationalization of the basic industries is proposed as an economic panacea. Now, this is just a technical way of running the economy, and if it remains so it will never become an *ideology*. How does the transformation into the latter take place? Only if the particularity of the economic measure starts to incarnate something more and different from itself – for instance, the emancipation from foreign domination, the elimination of capitalist waste, the possibility of social justice for excluded sections of the population, and so on; in short, the possibility of constituting the community as a coherent whole. That impossible object – the fullness of the community – appears here as depending on a particular set of transformations at the economic level. This is the ideological effect *strictu senso*: the belief that there is a particular social arrangement that can bring about the closure and transparency of the community.[8] There is ideology whenever a particular content shows itself as more than itself. Without this dimension of horizon we would have ideas or systems of ideas, but never ideologies.

---

8   But let us remember that this illusion is a necessary one. The argument should be understood as presenting ideology as a dimension of society that cannot be suppressed, not as a critique of ideology.

With this we have answered our first question: what an ideological distortion projects on a particular object is the impossible fullness of the community.[9] In order to address the second – how the operation of distortion becomes visible – we have to explore further the dialectics of incarnation/deformation to which I have just alluded. Let us start with deformation. If what I have said above is correct, the deformation inherent in a process of ideological (mis)representation consists in making a certain content equivalent to a set of other contents. In our example: an economic measure becomes equivalent to other historical transformations leading to a process of global human emancipation. Let us be clear that equivalence does not mean identity: each of these transformations retains something of its own identity, but the purely privative character of the identity is weakened through its participation in the equivalential chain. This is so because, as far as the equivalential chain is concerned, each of these transformations – without entirely dropping its own particularity – is an equivalent name for the absent fullness of the community. The only thing we can say is that the relationship between particular and equivalential identities is unstable: everything depends on which function – representing a content *within* the community or representing the latter as an absent fullness – will prevail. And the same applies to the dimension of incarnation: representing the fullness of the community cannot entirely do away with the particularity of the content through which the incarnation takes place; for, in the case that such a doing away was complete, we would arrive at a situation in which incarnated meaning and incarnating body would be entirely commensurable with each other – which is the possibility that we are denying *ex hypothesi*. We see here what it is that makes possible the visibility of the distortive operation: the fact that neither of the two movements in which it is based can logically reach its *ad quem* term.

I have so far spoken – largely for analytical reasons – of two dimensions that I have called 'incarnation' and 'deformation'. The distinction is certainly valid from an analytical point of view, for 'incarnation' refers to an absent fullness using an object different from

---

9   This communitarian reference only applies, of course, to social and political ideologies, which are the ones with which we are primarily concerned. But in other types of ideology the pattern is similar. A scientific paradigm, for instance, can present itself as incarnating the fullness of the pure principle of scientificity. A scientific theory thus becomes an ideology when it becomes a horizon. Darwinism would be a good example.

itself as a means of representation, while 'deformation' refers to a relation of equivalence between particular objects. But the relevance of
the distinction is limited by the fact that an incarnation in the sense
that I have described can only proceed through equivalential deformation. To assume the opposite – that is, the incarnation of an
impossible object in a particular body, which did not pass through an
equivalential relationship between particularities – would involve
attributing a new meaning arbitrarily to an old term, with the result
that between the two meanings there would be a simple relation of
equivocality, in the Aristotelian sense. But in that case, as the new
meaning would be fully constituted and entirely independent of the
old, the absent fullness would have found a *direct* form of representation, a presence of its own, and, as a result, would not be absent after
all but very much present. This would make any relation of incarnation impossible.[10] If the relation of incarnation *is*, on the contrary,
possible, and if what is to be incarnated is an impossible object, the
incarnating body cannot be the transparent medium through which a
fully constituted meaning receives expression. The dilemma is clear:
the incarnating body has to express something different from itself;
but as this 'something different' lacks an identity of its own, its only
means of *constitution* are the contents belonging to the incarnating
body. It is clear that these two requisites can only be made compatible
if some deformation of those contents takes place. This is exactly what
happens in an equivalential relation. The specificity of equivalence is
the destruction of meaning through its very proliferation. Let us
suppose that I try to define the meaning of a term through equivalential enumeration – for example, 'welfare of the people'. I can say that
health, housing, education, and so on, constitute an equivalential
chain giving us a notion of what people's welfare is. It is clear that such
a list can be indefinitely expanded. This expansion consists, apparently, of an enrichment of meaning, but what is achieved through this
enrichment is its exact opposite: if I have to specify what all the links
of the equivalential chain have in common, then the more the chain
expands, the more the differential features of each of the links will

---

10   If this is possible, however, in the Christian conception of incarnation, it is
because what is incarnated is not an absent fullness but an object entirely constituted
prior to the act of incarnation, as opposed to one depending on that act for its
constitution.

have to be dropped in order to keep alive what the equivalential chain attempts to express.

This could be put in slightly different terms by saying that each of the links of the equivalential chain names something different from itself, but that this naming only takes place insofar as the link belongs to the chain. And for the reasons previously mentioned, the more extended the chain, the more that naming will prevail over the particularistic references of the individual links. It is for this reason that I have spoken of the destruction of meaning through its very proliferation. This allows us to understand the precise relationship between 'empty' and 'floating' signifiers – two terms that have had a considerable currency in contemporary semiotic and post-structuralist literature. In the case of a floating signifier, we would apparently have an overflowing of meaning, while an empty signifier, on the contrary, would ultimately be a signifier without a signified. But if we analyze the matter more carefully, we realize that the floating character of a signifier is only the phenomenal form of its emptiness. A signifier like 'democracy', for instance, is certainly a floating one: its meaning will be different in liberal, radical anti-fascist and conservative anti-communist discourses. But how is this floating structured? In the first place, for the floating to be possible, the relationship between signifier and signified has already to be a loose one – if the signifier was strictly attached to one and only one signified, no floating could take place. So, the floating requires a tendential emptiness. But, in the second place, the pattern of the floating requires, first, that the floating term be differently articulated to discursive chains that oppose each other (otherwise there would be no floating at all), and, second, that, within these discursive chains, the floating term function not only as a differential component but as an equivalential one in relation to all the other components of the chain. If 'democracy' is presented as an essential component of the 'free world', the fixing of the meaning of the term will not occur purely by constructing for it a differential position, but by making of it one of the names of the fullness of society that the 'free world' attempts to achieve – and this involves establishing an equivalential relation with all the other terms within that discourse. 'Democracy' is not synonymous with 'freedom of the press', 'defence of private property' or 'affirmation of family values'. But what gives its specific ideological dimension to a discourse on the 'free world' is that each of these discursive components is not closed within its own differential particularity, but functions also as an alternative name for the equivalential totality that its relations constitute. Floating a term and emptying it are thus two sides of the same discursive operation.

All this leads to an inevitable conclusion: understanding the workings of the ideological within the field of collective representations is synonymous with understanding this logic of simplification of the social field that we have called 'equivalence', and its two central operations: 'floating' and 'emptying'. I will illustrate these propositions with three historical examples of the configuration of ideological spaces, and then conclude with more general considerations on the contradictory movements that govern the operation of ideological closure.

III

My first example comes from Michael Walzer's *Thick and Thin*.[11] He begins the book by recalling having seen on TV news in 1989 a picture of a demonstration in Prague:

> It is a picture of people marching in the streets of Prague; they carry signs, some of which say, simply, 'Truth' and others 'Justice'. When I saw the picture, I knew immediately what the signs meant – and so did everyone else who saw the same picture. Not only that: I also recognized and acknowledged the values that the marchers were defending – and so did (almost) everyone else. Is there any recent account, any post-modernist account, of political language that can explain this understanding and acknowledgement? How could I penetrate so quickly and join so unreservedly in the language game or the power play of a distant demonstration? The marchers shared a culture with which I was largely unfamiliar; they were responding to an experience I had never had. And yet, I could have walked comfortably in their midst. I could carry the same signs.[12]

It is on the basis of this experience that Walzer distinguishes between thick and thin morality.[13] The first represents the complete set of

---

11   Michael Walzer, *Thick and Thin: Moral Argument at Home and Abroad* (Notre Dame/London: University of Notre Dame Press, 1994).

12   Ibid., p. 1.

13   Walzer takes his notion of 'thickness' from Clifford Geertz's *The Interpretation of Cultures* (New York: Basic Books, 1973).

moral principles of a group, and is embedded in the totality of its cultural practices. It varies from time to time and from place to place. Thin morality, on the contrary, constitutes an ultimate core of moral principles which make possible transcultural evaluations and understanding – as in the case of the Prague demonstration. Walzer's problem is: How do we account for this transcultural core?

Walzer's treatment of the problem is highly illuminating. He rejects all easy solutions that would transform thin morality into an a priori core to be specified independently of more comprehensive moral frameworks. Thus, he rejects the Habermasian view, according to which '[m]inimal morality consists in the rules of engagement that bind all the speakers; maximalism is the never-finished outcome of their arguments.'[14] As he shows, this view presupposes rules of engagement that are far from minimal, and that minimalism would be an initial core out of which maximalism would later grow. But, for Walzer, this view is wrong: morality always starts from being thick. 'Morality is thick from the beginning, culturally integrated, and it reveals itself thinly only on special occasions, when moral language is turned to special purposes.'[15] If this is so, it follows that minimalism is not an Esperanto embedded in maximalism, that it cannot substitute for maximalism, and that it can never be foundational, for – thin morality not being a content specifiable a priori – 'it is not the case that different groups of people discover that all of them are committed to the same set of ultimate values.'[16] But this does not mean that thin morality is shallow: on the contrary, its principles constitute a morality 'close to the bone': 'In moral discourse thinness and intensity go together, whereas with thickness comes qualification, compromise, complexity and disagreement.'[17]

In that case, what is the actual content of thin morality? Walzer thinks he can give an answer to that question. I quote his answer in full:

It is possible, nonetheless, to give some substantial account of the moral minimum. I see nothing wrong with the effort to do that so long as we understand that it is necessarily expressive of our own

14   Walzer, *Thick and Thin*, p. 12.
15   Ibid., p. 4.
16   Ibid., p. 18.
17   Ibid., p. 6.

thick morality. There is no neutral (unexpressive) moral language. Still, we can pick out from among our values and commitments those that make it possible for us to march vicariously with the people in Prague. We can make a list of similar occasions (at home, too) and catalogue our responses and try to figure out what the occasions and the responses have in common. Perhaps the end product of this effort will be a set of standards to which all societies can be held – negative injunctions, most likely, rules against murder, deceit, torture, oppression, and tyranny.[18]

Now, I find this answer disappointing. It looks as if Walzer, in spite of his insightful argumentation, has not finally resisted the temptation of giving to thin morality a *positive content* – something against which the whole movement of his thought militates. For the problem that remains unanswered is the following: if the whole operation depends on picking out from our commitments and values those which are to be the content of thin morality, the meaning of the operation depends upon who does the picking. If Walzer's argument is correct – as I think it is – and there is no neutral picking out, the distinction between thin and thick morality can only be internal to a particular thick culture, and is likely to be different in different cultures. But the problem is partly obscured by the deceptive obviousness of terms such as 'deceit', 'torture', 'oppression' and 'tyranny' – to which we could add 'truth' and 'justice'. It seems evident that nobody would favour 'tyranny', 'deceit' and 'injustice'. Ergo, the universality of the agreement apparently makes it the ideal candidate to give thin morality a content. It is here that the misunderstanding lies. What I will attempt to show is that, by agreeing to oppose 'injustice', 'deceit' or 'tyranny', we have not agreed about anything whatsoever. At this point my argument dovetails with my previous remarks on floating and empty signifiers.

Let us go back to the Prague demonstration. People carried signs saying 'truth' and 'justice'. Before asking ourselves about an ultimate thin core, an anterior question has to be answered: Does either of the terms assert anything different from the other? Two terms can exist within a discursive structure in two opposite types of relation: a relation of *combination* if they are constituted through differentiation from each other, and a relation of *substitution* if they can replace each other within

---

18   Ibid., pp. 9–10.

the same signifying context. As we have seen, the latter is a case of a relation of equivalence. Although, in an equivalence, the differential meaning of its components does not entirely collapse, all the terms of the equivalence point, through their differential bodies, to something other than themselves – what I have called an 'absent fullness'. What we have to determine is the meaning of 'truth' and 'justice' on the placards of the demonstrators: Were they primarily interested in differentiating 'truth' from 'justice', or were they using them as equivalent terms to express the good of the community, denied by the fallen regime? I think there can be no doubt: they were doing the latter. But, in that case, if the only content of the demonstrators' discourse was 'truth' and 'justice' – as these are empty signifiers pointing to the absent fullness of the community – agreeing with them about the positive value of those signifiers would be the same as agreeing about nothing. The Chinese invasion of Tibet was called by its perpetrators 'the peaceful liberation', and it is clear that agreeing with them that 'liberation' and 'peace' are good things does not involve any support for their action.

But, of course, the discourse of the demonstrators was not only about 'truth' and 'justice'. The chain of equivalences through which the empty signifier 'justice' circulated was far more complex, and included, as Walzer rightly points out, things such as 'an end to arbitrary arrests, equal and impartial law enforcement, the abolition of the privileges and prerogatives of the party elite – common, garden variety justice'.[19] The crucial question, however, is whether we can move to all these specifications without abandoning the terrain of thin morality, or whether, by entering into that terrain, we are moving towards contextual, thick morality. In other words: What is the relation, for instance, between 'arbitrary arrests' and 'injustice'? Can we deduce the injustice of arbitrary arrests from a mere analysis of the category of 'injustice'? Or does the construction of 'arbitrary arrests' as unjust require some further contextual specifications? I think that the latter is the case – that, irrespective of how much we want arbitrary arrests to be seen as unjust, historical and contextual conditions have to coalesce for the articulation between the two terms to be established, and that these conditions are not just thrown up by the mere circulation of 'justice' as an empty signifier within a discursive context. If this is so, and if thin morality must have a richer content than mere agreement about the

---

19   Ibid., p. 2.

positive character of some empty terms, thin morality is as contextual as thick (although, of course, its contexts are different). Thin morality is not a core to be isolated analytically, but the result of an historical construction. It requires the prolongation of equivalential logics beyond the limits of given communitarian contexts. This of course means that the contents of thin morality, far from being permanent, are perpetually renegotiated.

The crucial point is that, if my argument is accepted, we are dealing not with a stable and minimal content – with some sort of 'original position' *à la* Rawls – but with *attributing* to a particular content the function of representing (or incarnating) the absent fullness of the community, one of whose names is 'justice'. But, as we know, this incarnation – which involves making a given particularity the expression of something different from itself – is possible only to the extent that a particular content enters into a relation of equivalence with other particularities. As we know, the effect of the logic of equivalence is to impoverish meaning: this explains how thinness can proceed out of thickness. In a world in which processes of globalization constantly transgress the limits of particular communities, the historical conditions are created for the development of ever more extended chains of equivalence and, in this way, for thinness to expand. The production of social identities is the result, in the contemporary world, of the crossing of contradictory logics of contextualization and decontextualization: if the crisis of stable universal values opens the way for an increasing social diversity (contextualization), then thin morality (decontextualization) also becomes increasingly important.

But this operation of attributing the function of representing the absent fullness of the community to a chain of particular contents is ideological in the strict sense of the term (and it should be clear from everything I have said that this assertion does not involve any pejorative connotation). A chain of particular contents represents an impossible object – this is, a first distortion, what I have called incarnation; but this incarnation is only possible (as a second distortion) insofar as an equivalential relation weakens the differential character of each link of the chain. We can also see clearly why the distortion has to be constitutive: because the object to be represented is, at the same time, impossible and necessary. The illusion of closure is something we can negotiate with, but never eliminate. Ideology is a dimension that belongs to the structure of all possible experience.

IV

In order to clarify my argument, let us take some examples from an entirely different historical experience, but one that depends on extending the logic of equivalence to its extreme limit: I am referring to mysticism. I have spoken about the need for representing an object – a fullness – which, by definition, transcends all representation. This is, at its purest, the problem of the mystic. He aspires to give expression to direct contact with God – in other words, with something that is strictly ineffable because it is incommensurable with anything that exists. He is the *deus absconditus*, a mystical Nothing. For the great monotheistic religions there is an unsurpassable abyss between the Creator and the *ens creatum*: 'Mysticism does not deny or overlook the abyss; on the contrary, it begins by realising its existence, but from there it proceeds to a quest for the secret that will close it in, the hidden path that will span it.'[20] The mystical Nothing is not an empty place; in some sense it is the fullest of all places, although that fullness, precisely for being so, transcends the limits of the sayable. It is on this basis that Gershom Scholem establishes a distinction between allegory and symbol:

> If allegory can be defined as the representation of an expressible something by another expressible something, the mystical symbol is an expressible representation of something which lies beyond the sphere of expression and communication, something which comes from a sphere whose face is, as it were, turned inward and away from us . . . The symbol 'signifies' nothing and communicates nothing, but makes something transparent which is beyond all expression. Where deeper insight into the structure of the allegory uncovers fresh layers of meaning, the symbol is intuitively understood all at once – or not at all . . . It is a 'momentary totality' which is perceived intuitively in a mystical *now* – the dimension of time proper to the symbol.[21]

Now, how is it possible to express the inexpressible? Only if a certain combination of terms is found in which each is divested of its particular meaning – if each of them does not *express* but *destroys* the differential character of that meaning. We already know the way in

---

20   Gershom Scholem, *Main Trends in Jewish Mysticism* (New York: Schocken, 1995), p. 8.
21   Ibid., p. 27.

which this can be achieved: through equivalence. I will take as an example one of the cases studied by Scholem: the litany *haadereth vehaemunah lehay olamim*, to be found in the 'Greater Hekhaloth' and included in the liturgy of the High Holidays. I quote its beginning:

> Excellence and faithfulness – are His who lives for ever
> Understanding and blessing – are His who lives for ever
> Cognition and expression – are His who lives for ever
> Grandeur and greatness – are His who lives for ever
> Magnificency and majesty – are His who lives for ever
> Counsel and strength – are His who lives for ever' etcetera[22]

The other attributes of Him who lives for ever are lustre and brilliance, grace and benevolence, purity and goodness, unity and honour, crown and glory, precept and practice, sovereignty and rule, adornment and permanence, mystery and wisdom, might and meekness, splendour and wonder, righteousness and honour, invocation and holiness, exultation and nobility, song and hymn, praise and glory.

The analysis of this prayer by Scholem is revealing. He stresses the fact that the mystical effect of the prayer is obtained by an equivalential reiteration that destroys any differential meaning of the attributes of the Lord. He asserts:

> [T]he climax of sublimity and solemnity to which the mystic can attain in his attempt to express the magnificence of his vision is also the *non plus ultra* of vacuousness. Philipp Bloch, who was the first to be deeply impressed by the problem presented by these hymns, speaks of their 'plethora of purely pleonastic and unisonous words which do not in the least assist the process of thought but merely reflect the emotional struggle'. But at the same time, he shows himself aware of the almost magical effect of this vacuous and yet sublime pathos on those who are praying when, for example, hymns composed in this spirit are recited on the Day of Atonement.[23]

And, referring to the litany quoted above, he says that it 'is a classic example [in its original language] of an alphabetical litany which fills

22   Ibid., p. 58.
23   Ibid.

the imagination of the devotee with splendid concepts clothed in magnificent expression; the particular words do not matter.[24]

It could not be clearer. The enumeration does not enrich our conceptual knowledge of the attributes of God, for the only meaning that each of these attributes keeps in the enumeration is the positive value that those terms have in ordinary language – and from this point of view they are all strictly equivalent. The addition of them all in a way that destroys their differentiated meanings is the means of expressing the inexpressible. As in the case of 'truth' and 'justice' on the placards of the Prague demonstrators, each of the terms is an alternative name of something that lacks any direct form of represen-tation. The difference is, of course, that in the Prague case the enumeration was not indefinite, because there was an attempt to link the empty signifiers 'truth' and 'justice' to contents like 'the end of arbitrary arrests', and so on, which retain their particular meanings, while the mystical discourse attempts to go beyond *all* particular meaning, expanding the enumeration indefinitely.[25]

In the literature on mysticism there is a frequent distinction between introvertive and extrovertive experiences, the first being purely internal experiences of going beyond all differences and multi-plicity, while the extrovertive mystic, in the words of W. T. Stace, 'using his physical senses, perceives the multiplicity of external material objects – the sea, the sky, the houses, the trees – mystically transfigured so that the One, or the Unity, shines through them'.[26] Let us quote three passages from Eckhart, taken from Stace's book. The first illustrates an experience of the introversive type, while the second and third refer us back to extrovertive mystical experiences. The first is as follows:

> [T]he human spirit scales the heavens to discover the spirit by which the heavens are driven . . . Even then . . . it presses on further into the vortex, the source in which spirit originates. There the spirit in knowing has no use for number, for numbers are of use only in time,

24   Ibid., p. 59.
25   The question that remains is whether the mystical discourse really succeeds in carrying out this universal weakening of meaning through equivalence. It is perhaps possible that, after all, it remains a residual element of particularism that cannot be eliminated. I will return to this question below.
26   W. T. Stace, *Mysticism and Philosophy* (Philadelphia/New York: J. B. Lippincott, 1960), p. 61.

in this defective world. No one can strike his roots into eternity without being rid of the concept of number . . . God leads the human spirit into the desert, into his own unity which is pure One.[27]

The extrovertive texts assert the following: 'All that a man has here externally in multiplicity is intrinsically One. Here all blades of grass, wood and stone, all things are One. This is the deepest depth.'[28] 'Say Lord, when is a man in mere understanding? I say to you "when a man sees one thing separated from another". And when is he above mere understanding? That I can tell you: "When he sees all in all, then a man stands above mere understanding".'[29]

Extrovertive mysticism presents no problem for us: we are confronted with a pure relation of equivalence. Blades of grass, wood and stone cancel out their differences and become alternative names of something that is beyond them but that can only be named through them. But introverted mysticism is apparently different, for it looks as if the passage through equivalence was not necessary, and as if a pure beyond, although ineffable, could be experienced in a direct way. In that case, closure could finally take place – not, evidently, at the level of representation, but at the level of an ineffable experience. But I would suggest that this conclusion is deceptive. Although I cannot entirely prove the point here, my hypothesis is that, even in introspective mysticism, the experience of the One requires the appeal to something particular that is less than the Absolute. As we have seen, for Eckhart no one 'can strike his roots into eternity without being rid of the concept of number'. The decisive question is whether, once we have got rid of that concept, the One is experienced as unmediated fullness, as undistorted presence, or whether that which we have got rid of is an internal component of the experience of the One. In that case, what is less than the Absolute contaminates the very experience in which the Absolute discloses itself. I think the second to be the case – that in order to be experienced as Absolute, the Absolute requires constant reference to what is less than itself. Now, the concept of number enters into this picture not in its own specific particularity, but as an

---

27 Ibid., p. 99.
28 Ibid., p. 63.
29 Ibid., p. 64.

instance of a being that is 'other than the One'. And this 'being other than the One' is something that only shows itself insofar as they are all equated in their contraposition to the Absolute. So the relation of equivalence between particularities is required for the experience of even an introvertive mysticism.

V

The thesis I am trying to defend is that this double movement found in its most extreme form in mysticism – that is, incarnation and deformation of particular contents through the expansion of equivalential logics – is at the root of *all* ideological processes, political ideologies included. To show its operation in a field entirely different from that of mystical experiences, I will refer to the way in which Georges Sorel's conception of myth is structured.

Sorel's work takes place in the period of the so-called 'crisis of Marxism' at the turn of the nineteenth century – that is, in a historical climate where the conviction that the operation of the inevitable laws of capitalism was leading to a proletarian revolution had been seriously eroded. Croce's rejection of historical positivism, for instance, had led him to assert the inanity of any unifying interpretation of the historical process and, consequently, the impossibility of grounding social action in any kind of scientific certitude. For him, any action was, as a result, the effect of a subjective conviction.

These two themes – the impossibility of unifying historical events by conceptual means, and the grounding of historical action in conviction and will – are certainly present in Sorel, but he gives them a new twist and invests them with a new meaning, viewing them in terms of a far more radical historical possibility. Here we find the cornerstone of Sorel's thought in its mature stage: social processes do not involve only displacements in the relation of forces between classes, because a more radical and constitutive possibility is always haunting society – the dissolution of the social fabric and the implosion of society as a totality. Society not only suffers domination and exploitation – it is also threatened with decadence, with the only-too-real possibility of its radical non-being. This distinctive possibility opens the way to a new and peculiar logic in the relation between groups. There are three capital moments in this logic.

1. The first is that the opposition which dominates Sorel's vision of the social is not primarily the one between bourgeoisie and proletariat, but rather that between decadence and the full realization of society. If the proletariat as a social force receives historical priority, this is because it is seen as the main instrument to confront decadence. But, crucially, it is not the actual victory of the proletariat against the bourgeoisie that will bring about 'grandeur' and arrest decadence, but the very fact of the open confrontation between the two groups. Without confrontation there is no identity; social identities require conflict for their constitution. Sorel thus sees in Marxism not a scientific doctrine explaining the objective laws of capitalism, but a finalistic ideology of the proletariat, grounded in class struggle. Social relations, left to themselves, are simply a 'mélange'. Only the will of determined social forces gives a consistent shape to social relations, and the determination of that will depends on the violent confrontations between the groups.

2. But if the historical justification of the action of the proletariat is given by its being the only force capable of opposing the decadence of civilization, that justification is indifferent to the *contents* of the proletarian programme, and depends entirely on the contingent ability of those contents to bring about an effect that is external to themselves. There is no ethical justification intrinsic to socialism. This has two chief consequences. The first is that all social identity or social demand is constitutively split: it is, on the one hand, a particular demand; but, on the other hand, it can also be the bearer, the incarnation, of social 'grandeur', as opposed to decadence. Between particular contents and the absent fullness of society the same relation is established that has been discussed throughout this essay. 'Grandeur' and 'decadence' do not have intrinsic contents of their own, but are the empty signifiers of a fullness of society (or its opposite, its corruption or non-being) which could be actualized by the most heterogeneous social forces. So – and this is the second consequence – it is enough that the working class show itself as a limited historical actor, closed in its corporative demands and incapable of incarnating society's will to fullness, for its claims to lose all legitimacy. The political trajectory of Sorel is a living example of the contingency of the relation between working-class demands and 'grandeur': he

passed from being a theoretician of revolutionary syndicalism to allying himself with a fraction of the monarchist movement, and ended his career by supporting the Third International. The diffusion of Sorelian themes in antagonistic social movements, from Bolshevism to fascism, is an even more telling example of the ambiguous possibilities that his démarche opened.

3. But there is something more – and more important – in the logic of Sorel's critique of bourgeois society. If it is the moment of violence as such, and not the victory of either of the two poles of the confrontation, that enables the prevention of social decadence, it is the reproduction of violence as an end in itself that constitutes the real objective. This means, on the one hand, that proletarian violence can become an instrument of the regeneration of the bourgeoisie itself, insofar as the latter will develop its own violence in order to respond to that of the proletariat. But, on the other hand, proletarian violence will be a non-violent violence – one addressed to nothing in particular, having become its own end. Aristotle distinguished between actions that are mere instruments for the achievement of an end (such as walking to the corner to buy a newspaper) and those that constitute their own end (walking to promenade oneself). Now, this distinction can easily be deconstructed – even the most instrumental of actions develops abilities in the actor that become part of his identity, and whose reproduction becomes partly its own end. In Sorel, this logic is taken to its ultimate conclusion: the action (violence) is increasingly separated from its own contents, and exclusively judged by the effect it has on the identity of the actors.

This split in the signification of *any* historical action can be seen at work in the three basic contrapositions that structure Sorel's thought: force/violence, utopia/myth, political strike/general proletarian strike. The important point is that the second term of each of these contrapositions differs from the first because of the equivalential relation that each of its internal components establishes with the others. Let us, firstly, examine force/violence. Force is always concrete; it is *particular* force as developed, for instance, in class-dominated societies. And the dominated groups also use force when they try either to obtain concessions or to displace the ruling elites from power, in order to establish a new system of domination. A force is always concrete; it is entirely absorbed by its own differentiated particularity. Violence is, on the contrary, addressed not to this or that system of domination, but to the form of domination a such. It is the (impossible) event bringing about the reconciliation of society with itself. Each instance of violence against domination as such is equivalent to all the others; the particularity of each struggle expresses, through that particularity, a content strictly differentiated from each particular instance.

Utopia/myth: while a utopia is an intellectual construction, the blueprint of a fully achieved (and in principle achievable) society, myth is an ensemble of equivalential images capable of galvanizing the imaginary of the masses, thus launching them into collective action:

> [M]en who are participating in a great social movement always picture their coming action as a battle in which their cause is certain to triumph. These constructions, knowledge of which is so important for historians, I propose to call myths; the syndicalist 'general strike' and Marx's catastrophic revolution are such myths . . . I now wish to show that we should not attempt to analyse such group of images in the way that we analyse a thing into its elements, but that they must be taken as a whole, as historical forces, and that we should be especially careful not to make any comparison between accomplished fact and the picture people had formed for themselves before action.[30]

That is, the contraposition between utopia and myth is grounded not only in the different nature of their particular contents – neater and intellectualistic in one case, more imprecise and diffuse in the other – but in their entirety different functions: the contents of the myth are substitutable by each other (that is why they have to be taken as a whole), as they all symbolize an absent fullness, and their efficacy has to be measured by their equivalential mobilizing effects, not by the success of their differentiated literal contents. For Croce, the impossibility of a fully rational action meant that an ungrounded decision was at the root of the constitution of a historical will. The absent rationality had to be substituted by an emotional identification, which explains the creative role of passion in History. This is exactly the function of myth in Sorel, for whom passion played the central role in the constitution of the will.

---

30   Georges Sorel, *Reflections on Violence* (London: Allen & Unwin, 1925), p. 22.

Finally, the two types of strike. Here the same duality is repeated. While the political strike aims at particular objectives within a system of domination, the proletarian strike target is the abolition of domination as such. But, again, the proletarian strike being a myth, it is not an actual event, separated from actual political strikes, but a dimension that unifies, in an equivalential way, a variety of struggles and actions over a whole historical period. Whether a concrete event belongs to either the political or the proletarian action is something that is, in the last instance, undecidable and always open to a plurality of readings and strategico-discursive interventions.

As we can see, the same duality resulting from the equivalential logics operating both in the Prague demonstration and in mysticism is to be found at the root of these Sorelian distinctions. While, in the case of force, the particularity of the aim gives the struggle its entire meaning, with violence the concrete struggle is just the occasion for a more general confrontation, which shows itself through the equivalence of that concrete struggle with others, governed by different aims. While, in the case of utopia, each of its dimensions can be analytically distinguished by their particular function within the whole, with myth each of its distinctive features becomes the equivalential symbol of all the others. Finally, while, in the case of the political strike, the struggle is entirely exhausted when its aim is achieved, with the proletarian strike each of the partial confrontations is the pretext for keeping alive and training the proletariat as a revolutionary agency. In the case of the second term of each of the distinctions, the particularity is the means of representation for something transcending it.

VI

Let us now generalize these conclusions, and bring them to bear upon a theory of ideology. The crisis of the notion of 'ideology' was linked to two interconnected processes: the decline of social objectivism and the denial of the possibility of a metalinguistic vantage point allowing the unmasking of ideological distortion. From the first point of view, 'ideology' had been considered as a *level* of the social whole – as in the Marxist trinity of the economic, the political, and the ideological. But this conception declined once it was understood that ideological mechanisms were essential to the structuration of both the political and the economic levels. This led to an inflation of the concept of ideology, referred to at the beginning of this chapter, and finally, when it was perceived that it had lost all analytic value, to its abandonment. Other terms, such as 'discourse', were less ambiguous and better adapted to express a conception of the social link that transcended both objectivism and naturalism.

The history of the second conception of ideology, which related to notions such as false or distorted consciousness, has been different, for, although the metalinguistic operation of unmasking was no longer considered possible, distorting mechanisms, as we have seen, were given increasing attention insofar as they were linked to the creation of the illusion of closure indispensable to the constitution of the social link. It is the study of the mechanisms making this illusion possible that constitutes the specific field of a contemporary theory of ideology.

I have said before that these mechanisms invert the forms of representation of an object, which is simultaneously necessary and impossible. This is at the root of the constitutive distortion that explains the ideological operation. It consists, as we have seen, in a double process according to which, between closure as an impossible operation and the particularity of the object incarnating it, there is a mutual dependency in which each pole partially limits the effects of the other. I have said enough about the way in which equivalence deforms and weakens the particularity of each of its links. What must be added now is what happens from the other angle: the effects on the structuration of the chain of what remains of those particularities. These remainders are absolutely essential for any equivalence, for, if they were to vanish, the chain would collapse into simple identity.

Let us take as an example the particular demands that, according to Walzer, give content to 'justice' for the Prague demonstrators: the end of arbitrary arrests, equal and impartial law enforcement, and so on. As we have seen, 'justice', as an empty signifier, is not *necessarily* associated with any of these demands. But, as it has no form of representation of its own, once incarnated in certain demands it becomes in some way imprisoned by them, and is not able to circulate freely. The remainders of particularity (of the links of the chain) limit its possible displacements. Even more: a chain of equivalences can in principle expand indefinitely, but once a set of core links has been established, this expansion is limited. Some new links would simply be incompatible with the remainders of particularity that are already part of the chain. Once the 'end of arbitrary arrests' has become one of the names of 'justice', the 'prevalence of the will of the people over all legal restrictions' cannot without difficulty enter into the same system of equivalences. This does not mean that the particularistic remainder of the 'end of arbitrary arrests' will be always the same – on the contrary, new equivalential links can modify the meaning of 'arbitrariness' or of 'arrest'; but the important point is that deformation does not operate unimpeded. There is a resistance of meaning that operates in the opposite direction.

It is through the operation of this double and contradictory movement that the illusion of closure is discursively constructed. This shows us the theoretical (and impossible) conditions under which the end of the ideological could take place. It could only happen if either of the two movements that we have specified could reach its ultimate extreme and fully eliminate the operativity of the other. It would occur if the distortion became actual dissolution, and the equivalence, identity: in that case everything would become an undifferentiated One, and the project of the mystic would have succeeded. But it would also happen if the equivalential logic were eliminated, and the remainder of particularity grew to dominate the totality of the object. This is the dream of the various versions of the 'end of ideology', generally associated with the ideal of pure, non-political, administrative practices. In both cases, closure would not be an illusion but a reality. But both are impossible dreams, ensuring that we will continue living in an ideological universe.

CHAPTER 2

On the Names of God

I

God is nameless for no one can either speak of him or know him . . .
Accordingly, if I say that 'God is good', this is not true. I am good, but
God is not good! In fact, I would rather say that I am better than God,
for what is good can become better and what can become better can
become the best! Now God is not good, and so he cannot become
better, he cannot become the best. These three are far from God:
'good', 'better', 'best', for he is wholly transcendent . . . Also you should
not wish to understand anything about God, for God is beyond all
understanding . . . If you understand anything about him, then he is
not in it, and by understanding something of him you fall into ignorance, and by falling into ignorance, you become like an animal since
the animal part in creatures is that which is unknowing.[1]

If God is nameless, it is due to His absolute simplicity, which excludes
from itself any differentiation or representational image:

You should love God non-mentally, that is to say the soul should
become non-mental and stripped of her mental nature. For as long as
your soul is mental, she will possess images. As long as she has images,
she will possess intermediaries, and as long as she has intermediaries,
she will have no unity or simplicity. As long as she lacks simplicity, she
does not truly love God, for true love depends upon simplicity.[2]

The only true attribute of God is Oneness, because it is the only attribute that is not determinate. If I say that God is good, 'goodness' is a
determination that implies the negation of what differs from it, while

---

1 Meister Eckhart, *Selected Writings* (London: Penguin, 1994), Sermon 28
(DW 83, W 96), pp. 236–7.
2 Ibid., p. 238.

God is the negation of the negation. Oneness, as a non-attribute that involves no difference, and therefore no negation, is thus the only thing that we can predicate about Him:

> 'Oneness is purer than goodness and truth. Although goodness and truth add nothing, they do nevertheless add something in the mind: when they are thought, something is added. But oneness adds nothing, where God exists in himself, before he flows out into the Son and the Holy Spirit . . . If I say that God is good, then I am adding something to him. Oneness on the other hand is a negation of negation and a denial of denial. What does 'one' mean? One is that to which nothing has been added.[3]

If we call God 'Lord', or 'father', we are dishonouring Him, because those names are incompatible with Oneness – a Lord requires a servant, and a father, a son. So, 'we should learn that there is no name we can give God so that it might seem that we have praised and honoured him enough, since God is "above names" and is ineffable'.[4] It seems necessary to conclude, with Dionysius the Areopagite, that 'the cause of all that is intelligible is not anything intelligible'. This paves the way for the mystical way, the *via negativa*. God is

> not soul, not intellect,
> not imagination, opinion, reason and not understanding,
> not logos, not intellection,
> not spoken, not thought,
> not number, not order,
> not greatness, not smallness,
> not equality, not inequality,
> not likeness, not unlikeness,
> not having stood, not moved, not at rest.[5]

What we are presented with here, through all these negations, is a certain manipulation of language by which something ineffable gets

3   Ibid., Sermon 17 (DW 21, W 97), p. 182.
4   Ibid., Sermon 5 (DW 53, W 22), p. 129.
5   Pseudo-Dionysius Areopagite, 'Mystical Theology', in *The Divine Names and Mystical Theology*, trans. John D. Jones (Milwaukee, WI: Marguette University Press, 1980), p. 221.

expressed. This is a generalized tendency within mysticism: a distortion of language that deprives it of all representative function is the way to point to something beyond all representation. In some primitive texts – those related, for instance, to Merkabah mysticism – this effect is obtained by giving each organ of the body of the Creator, in their descriptions, such an enormous length that all visual representation becomes impossible. As Scholem points out, 'the enormous figures have no intelligible meaning or sense-content, and it is impossible really to visualise the "body of the shekinah" which they purport to describe; they are better calculated, on the contrary, to reduce every attempt at such a vision to absurdity'.[6] In a highly intellectualized discourse such as that of Eckhart the devices are, obviously, much more sophisticated – they rely on the redemptive nature of language, according to which 'words come from the Word'. But, in any case, it is a distortion of the normal use of language that is at stake. What is involved in such a distortion?

Let us concentrate for a moment on the series of negations through which Dionysius attempts to approach the (non-)essence of the Divinity. In the first place, all the contents that are negated are part of an enumeration that has no internal hierarchy or structure. They are in a purely paratactic relation with each other. In the second place, the enumeration is an open one: many more contents – actually, all representational content – could have been part of the same enumeration. Now this enumerative operation is crucial to produce the effect of meaning that Dionysius is looking for. If he had just said, for instance, that God is not 'imagination', the possibility would always have existed that He is something else, endowed with a positive content. It is only the location of 'imagination' in an enumerative chain with 'opinion', 'logos', 'number', 'intellection', and so on, as well as the open character of the enumeration, that guarantees that God can be identified with the 'ineffable'. But, in that case, the enumeration is not just an enumeration in which each of its terms would express the fullness of its own isolated meaning (as when we say, for instance, that the United States was visited last year by many British, French and Italian people). In the case of the Dionysius text, each of the terms of the enumeration is part of a chain which, *only when it is taken as a*

6   Gershom Scholem, *Major Trends in Jewish Mysticism* (New York: Schocken, 1995), p. 64.

totality, expresses the non-essence of that Who is the Cause of All Things. That is, we are dealing with a peculiar type of enumeration, one whose terms do not simply coexist alongside one another, but instead can replace each other because they all, within the enumerative arrangement, express the same thing. This is the type of relation I call *equivalence*.

It could perhaps be objected that this possibility of an equivalential substitution is simply the result of the negative character of each of the terms of Dionysius's enumeration. But I do not think that this is the case. If the only thing that we had in the succession of negative terms was the negation of which they are bearers, the possibility of expressing the ineffable would be lost. For, if all we are saying is that God is not A, not B and not C, this by itself does not exclude the possibility that He is D, E or F. That is, if we focus exclusively on the *not* of the negation, there is no way of meaningfully constructing the open-ended dimension of the enumeration (on which the possibility of expressing the 'ineffable' depends). We are apparently dealing with two contradictory requirements: we want to maintain the ineffable character of the experience of the divinity, and we want at the same time to show through language such an ineffable presence. As I said, no pure concentration on the *not* will help us to meet these two requirements. However, the enumeration of Dionysius has another dimension, for what he is saying is not that God is 'not imagination' – paragraph – 'not logos' – paragraph, and so on. What he is actually saying is, first, that God is something that goes *beyond* the specific meaning of terms such as 'imagination', 'logos', 'intellection', and so on; and, second, that this transcendence, this going beyond the specific meanings of these terms, is shown through the equivalence that the terms establish between themselves. For it is clear that an equivalential enumeration – as distinct from a purely additive one – destroys the particularized meanings of its terms as much as a succession of negations. I can perfectly replace 'not imagination', 'not logos', and 'not intellection' by the equivalential succession 'imagination', 'logos', and 'intellection'. In both cases I would be saying exactly the same, for if I have to concentrate – in order to establish the equivalence – on what 'imagination', 'logos', and 'intellection' have in common, I have to drop most of the particularized meanings of each of these terms; and if the chain of equivalence is extended enough, it can become the way of expressing something that exceeds the representational content of all its links – in other words, the 'ineffable'. The advantage of eliminating the *not* from the enumera-tion is that, in that way, its equivalential character becomes more ostensible, and its infinitude – its open-ended nature – becomes fully visible. When I enumerate 'not-A', 'not-B', 'not-C', and so on, I can incorporate D to that chain, in the fullness of its positive meaning, without any further requirement. But if I have the equivalence between the positive terms A, B and C, I cannot incorporate D into that chain without the added requirement of reducing D to what it has in common with the three previous terms.

So, from this analysis, we can conclude that saying that God is something different from any particular attribute that we can predicate of Him, and saying that he expresses Himself through the *totality* of what exists,[7] is to say exactly the same thing. Likeness (= equivalence) between things is the way in which God – actualizes Himself? – expresses Himself? Listen to Eckhart:

> God gives to all things equally and so, as they flow forth from God, all things are equal and alike. Angels, men and women and all creatures are equal where they first emerge from God. Whoever takes things in their first emergence from God, takes all things as equal . . . If we take a fly as it exists in God, then it is nobler in God than the highest angel is in itself. Now all things are equal and alike in God and are god. And this likeness is so delightful to God that his whole nature and being floods through himself in this likeness . . . It is a pleasure for him to pour out his nature and his being into this likeness, since likeness is what he himself is.[8]

Insofar as the experience of the ineffability of God passes through the equivalence of contents that are less than Him, He is both beyond those contents and, at the same time, fully dependent on them for His actualization. Indeed, the more he is 'beyond', the more extended is the chain of equivalences on which His actualization depends. His very transcendence is contingent upon an increased immanence. To

---

7   This, of course, is where various mystical currents start to diverge. Is the experience of the Oneness of God Himself, or that of an expression of God? For our argument in this chapter, the debate around dualism, monism and pantheism is not really relevant. Let me just say in passing that, from the point of view of the logic of the mystical discourse, pantheism is the only ultimately coherent position.

8   Eckhart, *Selected Writings*, Sermon 16 (DW 12, W 57), pp. 177–8.

quote Eckhart again: 'God is in all things. The more he is in things, the more he is outside them: the more in, the more out and the more out, the more in.'[9] As David says in Browning's 'Saul':

> Do I task any faculty highest, to imagine success?
> I but open my eyes – and perfection, no more and no less,
> In the kind I imagined, full-fronts me, and God is seen God
> In the star, in the stone, in the flesh, in the soul and the clod.[10]

Now, if God is present 'in the star, in the stone, in the flesh, in the soul and in the clod', it is clear that mystical experience does not lead to an actual *separation* from things and daily pursuits but, on the contrary, to a special way of joining them, so that we see in any of them a manifestation of God's presence. According to Eckhart,

> [t]hose who are rightly disposed truly have God with them. And whoever truly possesses God in the right way, possesses him in all places: on the street, in any company, as well as in a church or a remote place or in their cell. No one can obstruct this person, for they intend and seek nothing but God and take their pleasure only in him, who is united with them in all their aims. And so, just as no multiplicity can divide God, in the same way nothing can scatter this person or divide them for they are one in the One in whom all multiplicity is one and is non-multiplicity.[11]

---

9   Ibid., Sermon 4 (DW 30, W 18), p. 123.

10   Jacob Korg, ed., *The Poetry of Robert Browning* (Indianapolis/New York: Bobbs-Merrill, 1971), p. 286. The following are some other examples of a theme that is quite common in mystical literature. Julian of Norwich refers to a small thing that she is beholding, the size of a hazelnut: 'In this little thing I saw three properties. The first is that God made it: the second, that God loveth it: the third that God keepth it. And what beheld I in this? Truly, the Maker, the Lover and the Keeper' (*The Revelation of Divine Love of Julian of Norwich*, trans. James Walsh [London: Burns & Oates, 1961], p. 60). In his diary, George Fox sees in everything existing the 'hidden unity in the Eternal Being'. Commenting on that passage, Evelyn Underhill says: '"To know the hidden unity in the Eternal Being" – know it with invulnerable certainty, in the all embracing act of consciousness with which we are aware of the personality of those we truly love – it is to live at its fullest the Illuminated Life, enjoying "all creatures in God and God in all creatures"' (Evelyn Underhill, *Mysticism: A Study in the Nature and Development of Man's Spiritual Consciousness* [New York: E. P. Dutton], p. 309).

11   Eckhart, 'The Talks of Instruction', *Selected Writings*, p. 9.

This experience of daily involvement as one in which multiplicity is not denied but lived as the variegated expression of a transcendent unity is the distinctive mark of the 'unitive life' required by the mystical consciousness. Eckhart gives two metaphoric examples of what it is to live multiplicity in unity. The first is the case of somebody who is thirsty: his thirst will accompany all the activities in which he is engaged, irrespective of their variety. The other refers to somebody who is in love: his or her feeling will taint the multifarious pursuits of that person's daily life.

A last important aspect to be considered is mystical *detachment*, whose inner structure is most revealing for our purposes. The detachment in question cannot be that of an anchorite, who lives a segregated existence, for the mystic is not refusing involvement in daily life. The mystic should be fully engaged and, at the same time, strictly detached from the world. How is this possible? As we know, actually existing worldly things – Browning's star, stone, flesh, soul and clod, Julian's small thing like a hazelnut – can be considered from two perspectives: either in their isolated particularity, in which each of them lives a separate existence, or in their equivalent connection, in which each of them shows the Divine essence. So, the mystic has to love each instance of his worldly experience as something through which the Divinity shows itself; however, as it is not the particular experience in its own naked particularity that shows God but instead its equivalential connection with everything else, it is only the latter connection, the contingency of the fact that it is *this* experience rather than any other one that I am having at the moment, that brings me closer to the Divinity. Essential detachment and actual involvement are two sides of the same coin. It is like the formation of the revolutionary will of a subordinated class: every participation in a strike, in an election, in a demonstration, does not count so much as the particular event concerned, but as a contingent instance in a process that transcends all particular engagement: the education of the class, the constitution of its revolutionary will. On the one hand, the latter transcends all particular engagement and, in that sense, requires the class to be detached from them; on the other hand, however, without a serious engagement in the particular event there is no constitution of the revolutionary will. Paradoxically, it is the detached nature of what is invested in the particular action, its purely contingent link with it, that guarantees that the involvement in that action is going to be a serious one. Let us hear Eckhart for the last time:

We must train ourselves not to seek or strive for our own interests in anything but rather to find and to grasp God in all things . . . All the gifts which he has granted us in heaven or on earth were made solely in order to be able to give us the one *gift*, which is himself. With all other gifts he simply wants to prepare us for that gift, which is himself . . . And so I tell you that we should learn to see God in all gifts and works, neither resting content with anything nor becoming attached to anything. For us there can be no attachment to a particular manner of behaviour in this life, nor has this ever been right, however successful we may have been. Above all, we should always concentrate upon the gifts of God, and always do so afresh.[12]

We may draw two important conclusions from our brief exploration of mysticism. The first concerns the specific problems involved in naming God. Since He is God the ineffable, we could use whatever name we want to refer to Him, as long as that name is not granted any determinate content. Eckhart says that, precisely for that reason, it is best just to say 'God', without attributing anything to Him. So the name of God, if we are not going to soil His sublime reality (and our experience of it) has to be an empty signifier, a signifier to which no signified can be attached. And this poses a problem to us. Is 'God' such an empty signifier, or is this name already an *interpretation* of the sublime, of the absolute fullness? If the second is the case, to call the sublime 'God' would be the first of the irreverences. In other words, while the mystical experience underlies an ineffable fullness that we call 'God', that name – God – is part of a discursive network that cannot be reduced to that experience. And, in fact, the history of mysticism has provided a plethora of alternative names to refer to that sublimity: the Absolute, Reality, the Ground, and so on. There have even been some mystical schools – such as certain currents of Buddhism – that have consequently been atheistic. If the mystical experience is really going to be the experience of an absolute *transcendens*, it has to remain indeterminate. Only silence would be adequate. To call it 'God' is already to betray it, and the same would be the case for any other name we might choose. Naming 'God' is a more difficult operation than we would have thought.

---

12   Ibid., p. 40.

Let us now move to my second conclusion. As we have seen, there is an alternative way of naming God, which is through the self-destruction of the particularized contents of an equivalential chain. We can refer to God by the names of 'star, stone, flesh, soul and clod', for, insofar as they are part of a universal chain of equivalences, each can be substituted by any of the others. Ergo, they would all be indifferent terms to name the totality of what exists – namely, the Absolute. Here we are confronted, however, with a different problem from that of naming God in a direct way – or, perhaps, with the same problem seen from another angle; for if that operation could be achieved, we would accomplish something more than obtaining a universal equivalence: we would have destroyed the equivalential relation and made it collapse into simple identity. Let us consider the matter carefully. In a relation of equivalence the particular meanings of its terms do not simply vanish; they are partially retained, and it is only in some respects that the substitution of one term by the others operates. There are some currents of Hindu mysticism that have advocated a total collapse of differences into undifferentiated identity, but Western mysticism has always played around the Aristotelian–Thomist notion of analogy, grounded in an equivalence that is less than identity. A mystic like Eckhart was trying to think 'unity in difference', and that is why the analogical relation of equivalence was crucial in his discourse. The universe of differences had to be brought into unity without the differential moment being lost. But it is here that we find a problem, for if the equivalence becomes absolutely universal, the differential particularism of its links necessarily collapses. We would have an undifferentiated identity in which any term would refer to the totality; but in that case the totality – the Absolute – could be named in an immediate, direct way, and its transcendent dimension, which is essential to the mystical experience (and discourse) would have been lost. If, on the other hand, the equivalence remains an equivalence and does not collapse into identity, it will be *less* than universal. In that case, as it remains an equivalence, it will be able to be the means of representation of something transcending it; but, as the chain will be less than universal, 'clod', 'flesh' and 'stone' will not only be the transparent medium of expression of the Absolute, but also its jailers: the remainder of particularity will be back with a vengeance – as it cannot be eliminated, it will transform the mystical intervention, from a free walk into the Absolute, into the attribution of an absolute value to a particularity entirely incommensurable with it.

If we put together these two conclusions, the result is only one: God cannot be named; the operation of naming Him, either in a direct way or indirectly, through the equivalence of contents that are less than Him, involves us in a process by which the residue of particularity that the mystical intervention tries to eliminate proves to be irreducible. In that case, however, the mystical discourse points in the direction of a dialectics between the particular and the Absolute that is more complex than it claims to be, and which we have now to explore.

II

Let us concentrate for a moment on this double impossibility around which the mystical discourse is organized, and see whether it belongs exclusively to the field of mystical experience or should rather be conceived as the expression, in mystical clothes, of something belonging to the general structure of all possible experience. Naming God is impossible, we said, because, being the absolute *transcendens*, He is beyond all positive determination. If we radicalize the logical implications of this impossibility, we see that even the assumption that God is an entity, even the assumption of Oneness - if Oneness is conceived as the unicity of an entity - is something that is already an undue interpretation, because it is to attribute a content to that which is beyond any possible content. If we remain within the realm of discourse, of the *representable*, the 'sublime' - the 'numinous', as Rudolph Otto calls it - is that which is radically not representable. So, unless we espouse the rationalistic assumption that there is nothing in experience that cannot be translated into a positive representational content, this impossibility - as the limit of all representation - will not simply be a logical impossibility, but an experiential one. A long tradition has given a name to it: the experience of finitude. Finitude involves the experience of fullness, of the sublime, as that which is radically lacking - and is, in that sense, a necessary beyond. Let us remember the way in which Lacan described the imaginary identification that takes place at the mirror stage: it presupposes a constitutive lack; it is the primary identification that functions as a matrix for all the subsequent secondary ones - so the life of the individual will be the vain search for a fullness from which he is going to be systematically deprived. The object that would bring about that ultimate fullness is the beyond of which the mystic claims he is having a direct experience. As such, it is something that accompanies *all* possible experience. The historical importance of the mystical discourse is that, by radicalizing that 'beyond', it has shown the essential finitude that is constitutive of all experience; its historical limit has been, in most cases, its having surrendered to the temptation of giving a positive content to that 'beyond' – the positive content being dictated not by mystical experience itself, but by the religious persuasion of the mystic. This can be seen most clearly in the argument about God showing Himself in everything existing. If the argument is admitted in all its implications, we should conclude that actions we would call immoral express God as much as all the others. This is a conclusion that was accepted by some extreme mystical sects: as far as I live in God, I am beyond all moral limitations. But in most cases the mystic accepts conventional religious morality. It is clear, however, that the latter is not dictated by mystical experience, but by the positive religion to which the mystic belongs.

Let us move to the other side of what we have called the double impossibility of structuring the mystical discourse: the representation of the 'beyond' through a chain of equivalences. As we have seen, the condition of this form of representation of the Absolute is that the equivalence does not collapse into unity (for in that case we would be dealing with a *direct* representation, and the dimension of 'beyond' would be lost). To have a *true* equivalence, the differential particularity of its terms has to be weakened, but not entirely lost. What are the effects of the remaining particularity? The main one is to place limits on those links that can become part of the equivalential chain. Let us suppose, for instance, that we have in a relation of equivalence 'chastity', 'daily prayer' and 'charity'. If the equivalence collapsed into identity – that is, if all differential meaning were obliterated – there would be no obstacle to 'free love' becoming part of the chain. But if the chain is a chain of *equivalences*, the particular meanings would not have been entirely eliminated and, in that sense, 'chastity' would resist the incorporation of 'free love' into the chain. The differential meanings are a limitation but, at the same time, a condition of possibility of the equivalence. However, the equivalence is, as we have seen, a condition of representation of the 'beyond'. As the equivalence requires partial retention of the differential meanings of its terms (which involves placing limits on its expansion), the only possible conclusion is that the very constitution of the 'beyond' is not indifferent to the differential contents whose equivalence is the condition of its representation.

The consequences of this sequence are momentous for the structuration of the mystical experience (in other words, for the possibility of an absolutely empty signifier that would represent a realm beyond all particularism and difference). For the only possible conclusion is that there is no possibility of a realm beyond differences that is not ancillary to an operation of reintroducing difference. That remainder of difference and particularism cannot be eliminated and, as a result, necessarily contaminates the very content of the 'beyond'. Here we have a process that can be described in either way: either as a 'materialization' of God, giving Him a differential content that is His very condition of possibility, or as the deification of a particular set of determinations that are invested with the function of incarnating the Absolute. But both ways show the same deadlock: a pure expression of the Divine essence, which proved to be impossible through straight naming, is no more possible when we use, in an indirect way, a chain of equivalences. We see here why a mystic like Eckhart has to rely on the contents of a positive religion: because the mystical experience, left to itself, is incapable of providing those differential remainders that are nevertheless its condition of possibility.

In this way, mystical discourse reveals something belonging to the general structure of experience: not only the separation between the two extremes of radical finitude and absolute fullness, but also the complex language games that it is possible to play on the basis of the contamination of each of them by the other. It is to the strategies made possible by this unavoidable contamination that I now want to refer. I will give two examples – one from the field of politics, the other from ethics.

As I have argued in my work, 'hegemony' is the key concept to thinking politics.[13] I understand by 'hegemony' a relationship by which a particular content assumes, in a certain context, the function of incarnating an absent fullness. For instance, in a society suffering deep social disorganization, 'order' can be seen as the positive reverse of a situation of generalised *anomie*. The initial situation, to which 'order' is

---

13   The original formulation of this argument is to be found in Ernesto Laclau and Chantal Mouffe, *Hegemony and Socialist Strategy* (London: Verso, 1985). I have developed various dimensions of the hegemonic relationship (especially in what refers to the relationship's fullness/particularity) in the essays collected in *Emancipation(s)* (London: Verso, 1996).

opposed, is the experience of deprivation, finitude and facticity. Now, once this experience takes place at different points within the social fabric, all of them will be lived as equivalent to each other, since, beyond their differences, all of them will point to a common situation of dislocation and incompletion. So fullness as the positive reverse of this situation of constitutive lack is that which would bring about the completion of the community. But a second dimension emerges here. We know that a relation of equivalence weakens differential meaning: if we have to concentrate on what all differences have in common (which is that to which the equivalence points), we have to move in the direction of a 'beyond' all differences, which will be tendentially empty. 'Order' cannot have a particular content, given that it is the simple reverse of all situations lived as disordered. Like mystical fullness, political fullness needs to be named by terms deprived, as much as possible, of any positive content. Where the two begin to diverge is at the point where mysticism deploys all kinds of strategies to have the ultimately unavoidable positivity of content reduced to a minimum, while a hegemonic practice will make of that ultimate impossibility its *raison d'être*: far from increasing the gap between fullness and differential content, it will make of a certain particular content the very name of the fullness. The 'market economy', for instance, will be presented in some discourses as the *only* content that can bring about the fullness of the community and, as such, as the very name of that fullness. At that point, however, a third dimension comes into operation. We pointed out earlier that the condition of an equivalential relation is that the differential meanings, although weakened, do not disappear, and that they place limits on the possibility of an indefinite expansion of the chain of equivalences. Now, these limits are obviously more important in a political discourse than in a mystical one, given that the former tries to establish a stable articulation between fullness and difference. Once 'market economy' has become, in a discourse, the name of the fullness of the community, some equivalences will become possible, while some others will be more or less permanently excluded. This situation is certainly not fixed, as discursive configurations are submitted to deforming pressures – some equivalences, for instance, can change the meaning of 'market' – but the decisive point is that, if the function of representing the fullness deforms the particular content which assumes that function, that particular content reacts by limiting the indeterminacy of the equivalential chain.

My second conclusion concerns ethics. There has been a lot of discussion in recent years about the consequences, for moral engagement, of 'postmodernity' and, in a more general sense, of the critique of philosophical essentialism. Does the questioning of an absolute ground not deprive moral commitments of any foundation? If everything is contingent, if there is no 'categorical imperative' that would constitute a bedrock of morality, are we not left with a situation in which 'anything goes' and, consequently, with moral indifference and the impossibility of discriminating between ethical and unethical actions? Let us see what are the theoretical preconditions of this conclusion. I think that we have here to distinguish between two issues. The first concerns the possibility of a serious moral engagement with *any kind* of action (leaving aside for the moment their actual contents). What the critique of essentialism implies is that there is no way of morally discriminating, a priori, between particular courses of action – not even in the sense of establishing a minimal content for a categorical imperative. But this does not logically imply that serious moral commitments could not be attached to engagements taken by less than aprioristically dictated courses of action. To conclude the opposite would be the same as saying that only the particularity of a course of action conceived *as particularity* could be the source of a serious moral engagement. But this is exactly what the whole of mystical experience is denying. Let us remember what we saw earlier about the dialectics between *detachment* and *engagement* in Eckhart. It is only insofar as I experience my contact with the Divinity as an absolute, beyond all particularised content, that I can give to my particular courses of action their moral seriousness. And if we generalise in the way I indicated earlier, it is only if I experience the absolute as an utterly empty place that I can project into contingent courses of action a moral depth that, left to themselves, they lack. As we can see, the 'postmodern' experience of the radical contingency of any particular content claiming to be morally valid is the very condition of that ethical overinvestment that makes possible a higher moral consciousness. As in the case of 'hegemony', we have here a certain 'deification' of the concrete whose ground is, paradoxically, its very contingency. Serious moral engagement requires a radical separation between moral consciousness and its contents, so that no content can have any aprioristic claim to be the exclusive beneficiary of the engagement.

Let us now move to the second issue. Even if we grant that this gap between the experience of the absolute as an empty place and the engagement with the particular contents that are going to incarnate it becomes a permanent one, does this not leave us entirely guideless as to what are the *right* incarnating contents? Certainly, it does. This lack of guidance is what I earlier called facticity, finitude. If there was an aprioristic logic linking the experience of the absolute to particular contents, the link between the incarnated absolute and its incarnating content would have become a necessary one, and the absolute would have lost its dimension of beyond. In that case we would be able to name God in a direct way, or at least to claim to have a discursive mastery of His essence, as Hegel did in his *Logic*. To claim the opposite does not mean that *any* content, at any moment, can be an equal candidate for the incarnation of the absolute. This is only true *sub species aeternitatis*. But historical life takes place in a terrain that is less than eternity. If the experience of what I have referred to in terms of the dual movement 'materialization of God'/'deification of the concrete' is going to live up to its two sides, neither the absolute nor the particular can find a final peace with the other. This means that the construction of an ethical life will depend on keeping open the two sides of this paradox: an absolute that can only be actualized by being something less than itself, and a particularity whose only destiny is to be the incarnation of a 'sublimity' transcending its own body.

CHAPTER 3

Articulation and the Limits of Metaphor

I

In a well-known essay,[1] Gerard Genette discusses the question of the interdependence between metaphor and metonymy in the structure of Proust's narrative. Following the path-breaking work of Stephen Ullmann,[2] he shows how, in addition to the central role traditionally granted to metaphor in Proust's work, there are other semantic movements of a typically metonymic nature whose presence is, however, necessary, for metaphor to succeed in its figural effects. A hypallage such 'sécheresse brune des cheveux' ('the brown dryness of hair') – instead of 'sécheresse des cheveux bruns' ('the dryness of brown hair') – would be a typical example of such metonymic displacements. Genette, however, insists from the very beginning that it is not a simple question of recognizing the coexistence of both metaphor and metonymy in the Proustian text, but of showing how they require each other, how without the one shading into the other neither of them could play the specific role expected of them in the constitution of a narrative economy. In his words, '[F]ar from being antagonistic and incompatible, metaphor and metonymy sustain and interpenetrate each other, and to give its proper place to the second will not consist in drawing a concurrent list opposed to that of metaphors, but rather in showing the relations of "coexistence" within the relation of analogy itself: the role of metonymy within metaphor'.[3]

Genette gives several examples of such interconnection. Thus, he refers to the numerous cases in which 'bell tower' (*clocher*) is metaphorically (analogically) related to 'ear [of wheat or corn]' (*épis*), or to 'fish', depending on the environment of the church – rural in the first

---

1 'Métonymie chez Proust', in Gérard Genette, *Figures III* (Paris: Seuil, 1972), pp. 41–63.
2 Stephen Ullmann, *Style in the French Novel* (Cambridge: CUP, 1957).
3 Genette, 'Métonymie chez Proust', p. 42.

case, and maritime in the second. This means that the spatial relation of contiguity is the source of metaphoric analogical effects. 'Ear–bell tower' (or *église–meule*) in the middle of the fields, 'fish–bell tower' near the sea, 'purple–bell tower' over the vineyards, '*brioche*-bell tower' at the time of the sweets, 'pillow–bell tower' at the beginning of the night – there is clearly in Proust a recurrent, almost stereotyped stylistic scheme, which one could call chameleon–bell tower (*clocher– caméléon*). Thus there is a sort of resemblance by contagion. The metaphor finds its support in a metonymy. Quoting Jean Ricardou, Genette enunciates the principle: 'qui se ressemble s'assemble (et réciproquement)'.[4]

Many more examples of this essential solidarity between contigu- ity and analogy are given: that between autochthonous dishes and *vin du pays*; between paintings and their geographical framework; between the desire for peasant women and their rural milieu; between relatives; between images succeeding each other in diegetic meta- phors; between landscapes and their reflection in the glass doors of a bookshelf, and so on. In all these cases we see that, without the mutual implication between metaphor and metonymy, it would be impossi- ble to ensure the unity of a discursive space. Proust himself was only partially aware of this mutual implication, and tended to privilege its metaphorical side. As Genette says,

> The indestructible solidarity of writing, whose magic formula Proust seems to be looking for ('only metaphor can give a sort of *eternity* to style', he will say in his article on Flaubert) cannot only result from the horizontal link established by the metonymical trajectory; but one cannot see how it could result from just the vertical link of the metaphoric relation either. Only the crossing of one by the other can subtract the object of the description, and the description itself from 'time's contingencies', that is, from all contingency; only the mutual crossing of a metonymic net and a metaphoric chain ensures the coherence, the necessary cohesion of *text*.[5]

Let us see how this crossing takes place. Central to it is the structure of 'involuntary memory'. Apparently we have, in the mechanism of

---

4   Ibid., p. 45.
5   Ibid., p. 60.

reminiscence, the case of a pure metaphor, devoid of any metonymic contamination (the taste of the madeleine, the position of the foot on the uneven pavement, and so on). But the punctual character of that analogical memory is immediately overflown. As Genette shows, it is only retroactively that the analysis finds that reminiscence starts from an analogy which it would isolate as its 'cause': 'In fact, the real experience begins, not by grasping an identity of sensation, but by a feeling of "pleasure", of "happiness", which first appears without the notion of its cause.'[6] Although the examples in *Swann* and in *Le Temps Rétrouvé* differ in their unfolding, the essential point is, in both cases, that the chain of reminiscences goes, in a metonymic way, far beyond the original analogy (in Swann, the cup leads to the reminiscence of the room, from the room to the house, then to the village, and from there to the whole region): '[It is essential here] to note that this first explosion [the analogic detonator] is always accompanied also and necessarily, by a kind of chain reaction which proceeds, not by analogy but by contiguity, and which is very precisely the moment in which the metonymic contagion (or, to use Proust's term, the *irradiation*) substitutes the metaphoric evocation.'[7]

For Genette it is this crossing between metaphor and metonymy that ensures that there is a narrative. If we had only had the metaphoric dimension, *À la recherche du temps perdu* would not have been a novel but a succession of lyrical moments without any temporal chaining. So he concludes:

> Without metaphor Proust (approximately) says, there are no true memories; we add for him (and for everybody): without metonymy, there is no chaining of memories, no *history*, no novel. For it is metaphor that retrieves lost Time, but it is metonymy that reanimates it, that puts it back in movement: that returns it to itself and to its true 'essence', that is its own escape and its own Search. So here, only here – through metaphor but *within* metonymy – it is here that the Narrative (*Récit*) begins.[8]

A few remarks before taking leave of Genette. He has illuminated very well the relation of mutual implication between metaphor and

---

6   Ibid., p. 56.
7   Ibid.
8   Ibid., p. 63.

metonymy which alone creates the unity of the text. That mutual implication thus has *totalizing* effects. He quotes, for example, the following passage from Proust:

> I threw myself down on the bed; and, just as if I had been lying in a berth on board one of those steamers which I could see quite near me and which at night it would be strange to see stealing slowly through the darkness, like shadowy and silent but unsleeping swans, I was surrounded on all sides by pictures of the sea.[9]

And Genette comments: 'One remarks here the explicit concurrence of the metaphoric relation (*comme si*) and of the metonymic one (*près de moi*); and the second metaphor is also itself metonymic, grafted into the first (*navires = cygnes*)'.[10]

The question that remains to be posed, however, is that concerning the kind of unity that the articulation of metaphor with metonymy manages to constitute. Granting – as I think one should – that such a unity is vital to the coherence of a text, there are several possibilities as to how to conceive the interaction between these two dimensions. Genette does not, certainly, suggest that such an interaction should be conceived as the adjustment of the pieces of a clockwork mechanism, and the very terms that he uses (*recoupement*, *croisée*) suggest that he has something considerably more complex in mind. He does not, however, advance very much in determining the specific nature of that *recoupement* – largely, I think, because his main concern is to show the *presence* of both tropes in the Proustian text. Discussing Jakobson's distinction between metonymy as the prosaic dimension of discourse and metaphor as the poetic one, he asserts that 'one should consider Proustian writing as the most extreme attempt towards this mixed stage, fully assuming and activating the two axes of language, which it would certainly be laughable to call "poem in prose" or "poetic prose", and which constitute, absolutely and in the

---

9   "*Je me jetais sur mon lit; et, comme si j'avais été sur la chouchette d'un de ces bateaux que je voyais assez près de moi et que la nuit on s'étonnerer de voir se déplacer lentement dans l'obscurité, comme des cygnes assombris et silentieux mais qui ne dorment pas, j'étais entouré de tous côtés des images de la mer.*" Marcel Proust, *In Search of Lost Time, Volume II: Within a Budding Grove*, trans. C. K. Scott Moncrieff and Terence Kilmartin, rev. D. J. Enright (New York: Random House, 1992), p. 524.

10   Ibid., p. 51, n. 5.

full sense of the term, the Text'.[11] For the issues that we are going to discuss in this chapter, it is crucial to determine precisely the logics involved in the articulation of axes of that 'mixed stage'.

II

Genette is clearly conscious that his use of the categories 'metaphor' and 'metonymy' is somewhat idiosyncratic, for it goes beyond what canonical rhetoric would have ascribed to them. There is in Proust, for instance, a marked preference for 'continuous metaphors' (*métaphores suivies*). 'There are very rarely in his work those fulgurant rapprochements suggested by a single word, the only ones for which classical rhetoric reserved the name metaphor.'[12] In many cases the analogical comparisons take place in a continuous way, occupying several pages of the text. But it might also seem abusive to call metonymy a contiguity of memories that does not involve any relation of substitution. However, as Genette points out,

> it is the nature of the semantic relation that is at stake, and not the form of the figure . . . Proust himself has given an example of such an abuse by calling metaphor a figure which, in his work, is most frequently a comparison explicit and without substitution, so that the effects of contagion to which we have referred are nearly the equivalent, on the axis of contiguity, of what Proustian metaphors are on the axis of analogy – and are, in relation to metonymy *stricto sensu*, what Proustian metaphors are vis-à-vis classical metaphors . . . The signal-sensation becomes very quickly in Proust a sort of *equivalent* of the context to which it is associated, as the '*petite phrase*' of Vinteuil has become, for Swann and Odette, 'as the national air of their love': that is, its emblem.[13]

This passage is crucial. Genette speaks, on the one hand, of an 'abusive' use of rhetorical categories; but, on the other, he describes such an abuse as a transgression involving a movement from the *form* of the figure to a *semantic* relation which, while implicit in that form, goes clearly beyond those formal limits. So the following questions arise:

---

11   Ibid., p. 61.
12   Ibid., p. 55.
13   Ibid., p. 58.

1. If the semantic relations underlying both metaphor and metonymy transcend their rhetorical form, are not those relations anchored in signification as such, beyond classical rhetorical limits, or, alternatively, could not signification be seen as a generalized rhetoric? In other words, could that 'rhetoricity' be seen not as an abuse but as constitutive (in the transcendental sense) of signification?

2. In that case, is it enough to conceive that 'beyond' of the rhetorical form as simply 'semantic' – which would necessarily attach it to the level of the signified? Would not the relationship signifier/signified involve a dialectic that takes us beyond semantics, to a materiality of the signifier which inscribes rhetorical displacements in the very structure of the sign? (Let us think in Freud's 'verbal bridges'.)

3. Why are those displacements rhetorical in nature – dominated by the basic metaphor/metonymy opposition?

4. How to conceive of that opposition? Does it involve a relation of complementarity or, rather, a mutual limitation of their effects, so that metonymy establishes the limits of metaphor, and vice versa?

One way of dealing with these questions would be to turn our attention to a theoretical approach that explicitly tries to link rhetorical categories to the structural dimensions of signification as such. I am referring to the famous essay by Roman Jakobson, 'Two Aspects of Language and Two Types of Aphasic Disturbances'.[14] Jakobson's starting point is that aphasia, being a disturbance in language use, 'must begin with the question of what aspects of language are impaired in the various species of such a disorder'.[15] Such interrogation could not be answered 'without the participation of professional linguists familiar with the patterning and functioning of language'.[16]

As Jakobson points out, any linguistic sign presupposes its arrangement through two different operations: *combination and contexture*, whereby a sign acquires its location, in accordance with syntactic rules in an orderly succession with other signs; and *selection and substitution*, whereby a sign can be replaced by others in any given structural

---

14   Roman Jakobson, 'Two Aspects of Language and Two Types of Aphasic Disturbances', in Morris Halle and Roman Jakobson, *Fundamentals of Language* (The Hague: Mouton, 1956).

15   Ibid., p. 69.

16   Ibid.

location. This distinction corresponds to the two axes of language identified by Saussure: the syntagmatic and the paradigmatic (which he called associative). Combination and substitution were, for Saussure, the only two kinds of operation regulating the relations between signs. Starting from these two dimensions, Jakobson identifies two aphasic disturbances. The first, *similarity disorder*, is related to the impossibility of substituting terms, while the ability to combine them remains unimpaired; in the second – *contiguity disorder* – that ability to combine words is what is affected. Quite apart from aphasic disorders, there is, according to Jakobson, a propensity in each language user to rely primordially on one or the other pole of language:

> In a well known psychological test, children are confronted with some noun and told to utter the first verbal response that comes into their heads. In this experiment two opposite linguistic predilections are invariably exhibited: the response is intended either as a substitute for, or as a complement to, the stimulus . . . To the stimulus *hut* one response was *burnt out*; another, *is a poor little house*. Both reactions are predicative; but the first creates a purely narrative context, while in the second there is a double connection with the subject *hut*: on the one hand, a positional (namely, syntactic) contiguity, and on the other a semantic similarity.[17]

From these two axes of language – the paradigmatic and the syntagmatic, substitution and combination – Jakobson moves to the rhetorical field: metonymy would correspond to combination, and metaphor to substitution. And this alternative is not purely regional, but regulates human behaviour as a whole: 'in manipulating these two kinds of connection (similarity and contiguity) in both their aspects (positional and semantic) – selecting, combining and ranking them – an individual exhibits his personal style, his verbal predilections and preferences.'[18]

> The bipolar structure of language (or other semiotic systems) and, in aphasia, the fixation on one of these two poles to the exclusion of the other, require systematic comparative study. The retention of either

---

17   Ibid., pp. 90–1.
18   Ibid., p. 91.

of these alternatives in the two types of aphasia must be confronted with the predominance of the same pole in certain styles, personal habits, current fashions, etc.[19]

This argument is, for Jakobson, at the basis of a wider cultural interpretation. In verbal art, we have that in poetry, where lyric privileges the metaphorical axis, as in romanticism and symbolism, while in realist art, whose epitome is the novel, metonymic displacements prevail. We have here again, in different terms, the argument that we have already found in Genette: Proust's major work is a novel, and not a paratactic succession of lyrical moments, because metaphors are grounded in metonymic connections. For Jakobson this alternative applies equally to non-verbal art: in cubism, the succession of synecdoches is essentially metonymic, while in surrealism the quasi-allegorical images lean towards metaphor. And, in film, the plurality of angles and close-ups in Griffith's production is metonymic in nature, while in Charlie Chaplin and Eisenstein a metaphoric substitution of images structures the narrative. Indeed, any semiotic system can, for Jakobson, be understood in terms of the metaphoric/metonymic alternative.

The great merit of Jakobson's analysis is to have brought rhetorical categories to their specific location within linguistic structure – that is, to have shown that it is the latter that is at the root of all figural movements. Metaphor and metonymy, in that sense, are not just some figures among many, but the two fundamental matrices around which all other figures and tropes should be ordered. So the classification of rhetorical figures ceases to be a heteroclite enumeration of forms, and presents a clear structure anchored in their dependence on the fundamental dimensions of language. But the transition from these dimensions to their specific rhetorical investment requires some further considerations, which I will summarize in the next few pages.

1. There is, in the first place, the question of the transition from the axis of combination – the syntagmatic dimension – to metonymy. Because, although a tropological movement along that dimension can only be conceived in metonymical terms, there is nothing in combination, considered in isolation, requiring that such a movement should take place. One can perfectly imagine a combination

---

19   Ibid., p. 93.

of terms following syntactic rules that would not involve any metonymic displacement. There is a zero-degree of the tropological as far as combination is concerned. I can perfectly well say 'sécheresse des cheveux bruns' instead of 'sécheresse brune des cheveux'. If so, the figural would be something added to signification from outside, not an integral part of signification, and we would be back to the classical vision of the rhetorical as an adornment of language. So if we want to establish a more intimate connection between tropes and signification, we have to find a way of undermining the very possibility of a rhetorically neutral zero-degree.

2. This way is quickly found once we move from 'combination' to the second axis: 'substitution/selection'. For here, unlike on the axis of combination, there is no zero-degree: substitution (again, considered in isolation) is not submitted to any a priori syntactic rule. Saussure himself says it: 'While a syntagm immediately summons the idea of an order of succession and of a determinate number of elements, the terms of an associative family do not present themselves in either a definite number or in a determinate order'.[20] So the axis of substitution, *which is also constitutive of language*, subverts the very principle of structural locations on which the syntagmatic succession is grounded. Saussure's diagram of the ensemble of possibilities opened by substitution (Fig. 3.1) is most revealing.

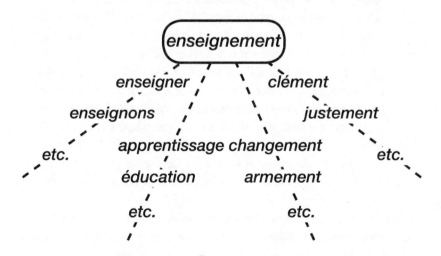

20   Ferdinand de Saussure, *Cours de linguistique générale* (Paris: Payot, 1980), p. 174.

One of these possibilities is particularly important for my argument: the impossibility of confining substitution (and, as a result, tropological transgression) to the order of the signified. Saussure asserts: 'There is either double community of sense and form, or community of only either sense or form. Any word can evoke anything susceptible of being associated with it one way or another.'[21] This is why I asserted before that the 'beyond' the rhetorical form cannot be confined to *semantic* associations. One possibility is that rhetorical movements do not only take place at the level of the signified but also at that of the signifier. (In Freud's 'Rat Man', there is displacement from 'rat' to *Spielratten* (gambling) and thus the father (a gambler) is incorporated into the 'rat complex'.)

3. Where do these considerations leave us as far as the relationship metaphor/metonymy is concerned? The main conclusion is that the notions of 'analogy' and 'contiguity' which are, respectively, the defining grounds of the two tropes, far from being entirely different in nature, tend, on the contrary, to shade one into the other. Why so? Because both of them are transgressions of the same principle, which is the differential logic associated to the syntagmatic axis of the signifying system. The only distinction it is possible to establish between these figures is that, in the case of metonymy, the transgression of the structural locations that define the relations of combination is fully visible, while in metaphor, analogy entirely ignores those structural differentiations – associations, as Saussure shows, can move in the most divergent directions. In one sense it can be said that metaphor is the *telos* of metonymy, the moment in which transgression of the rules of combination has reached its point of no return: a new entity has come into existence which makes us forget the transgressive practices on which it is grounded. But without those transgressive practices which are essentially metonymic, the new metaphoric entity could not have emerged. As Genette shows in the case of Proust, analogy is always grounded in an originary contiguity.

A conclusion can be drawn here that will be important for my political analysis: contiguity and analogy are not essentially different from each other, but the two poles of a continuum. Let me give an example

---

21   Ibid., p. 174.

I have discussed elsewhere.[22] Let us suppose that there is a neighbourhood where there is racist violence and the only force capable of confronting it in that area are the trade-unions. We would think that, normally, opposing racism is not the natural task of the trade-unions, and that if it is taken up by them in that place it is by a contingent constellation of social forces. That is, such a 'taking up' derives from a relation of contiguity – that its nature is metonymic. But let us imagine that this 'taking up' continues for a long period of time – in that case, people would become accustomed to it and would tend to think that it is a normal part of trade-union practice. So what was a case of contingent articulation becomes a part of the central meaning of the term 'trade-union' – 'contiguity' shades into 'analogy', 'metonymy' into 'metaphor'. Anticipating what I will discuss presently, we can say that this is inherent to the central political operation that I call 'hegemony': the movement from metonymy to metaphor, from *contingent* articulation to *essential* belonging. The name – of a social movement, of an ideology, of a political institution – is always the metaphorical crystallization of contents whose analogical links result from concealing the contingent contiguity of their metonymical origins. Conversely, the dissolution of a hegemonic formation involves the reactivation of that contingency: the return from a 'sublime' metaphoric fixation to a humble metonymic association.

4. With this conclusion, however, we have only established: a) that the metaphoric/metonymic distinction has a matricial priority over other tropes – which means it is possible, one way or the other, to reduce them to that matrix; and b) that such a matricial distinction does not refer simply to opposites, but to the two poles of a continuum. But to assert that rhetoricity is inherent to signification requires one more step: to show that, without a tropological displacement, signification could not find its own ground. I have tried to prove this point elsewhere, and I will not repeat it here.[23] Let us just say that this proof requires a demonstration that signification, to be possible, requires its own closure – and that such a

22   Ernesto Laclau, 'The Politics of Rhetoric', in Tom Cohen, J. Hillis Miller, Andrzej Warminski and Barbara Cohen, *Material Events: Paul de Man and the Afterlife of Theory* (Minneapolis, MN: Minnesota University Press 2001), pp. 229–53. See Chapter 4 of this volume.

23   See 'Why do Empty Signifiers Matter to Politics?', in *Emancipation(s)* (London: Verso, 1996); and *On Populist Reason* (London: Verso, 2005), Chapter 4.

closure, because it involves the representation of an object that is both impossible and necessary, leads to the discursive production of empty signifiers. An empty signifier, as I have tried to show, is not just a signifier without a signified – which, as such, would be outside signification – but one signifying the blind spot inherent to signification, the point where signification finds its own limits, but which, if it is going to be possible at all, has to be represented as the meaningless precondition of meaning. In psychoanalytic terms, it would be the moment of the Real – the moment of distortion of the Symbolic, which is the precondition for the symbolic to constitute itself as totality. Now, if the representation of something unrepresentable is the very condition of representation as such, this means that the (distorted) representation of this condition involves a *substitution* – that is, it can only be tropological in nature. And it is not a substitution to be conceived as a replacement of positive terms: it will involve giving a name to something that is essentially 'nameless', to an empty place. That is what gives *catachresis* its centrality. And as any figural movement involves saying something more than what can be said through a literal term, catachresis is inherent to the figural as such – it becomes the trade mark of 'rhetoricity' as such.

5. Let us go back, at this point, to the question of the ground of the metaphoric/metonymic continuum. Such a ground is given, as I have indicated, by the opposition of *any* tropological movement to the differential logic of combination inherent in the syntagmatic pole of signification. The difference between analogy and contiguity is that, although both, through their substitutions, subvert such a differential logic, the visibility of what is subverted is very much present in the case of metonymy, while it tends to disappear in the case of metaphor. But if this subversion of combinatorial locations is inherent to rhetoricity, and rhetoricity is one of the dimensions of signification, this means that the latter can only be conceived as an endless process of successive institutions and subversions of different locations. That is why orthodox structuralism has always tended to emphasize the syntagmatic pole of language at the expense of the paradigmatic one. But the ambiguity created by the operation of the two opposed logics of combination and substitution did not go entirely unnoticed, even in the work of Saussure. As Joan Copjec has pointed out,

'Emphasizing the "synchronic perspective" of the linguist and his community, Saussure eventually decided to give priority to the contemporaneous system of signifiers operating at some (hypothetical) moment: the present. Forgetting for his own purposes his important stipulation that meaning must be determined retroactively, that is, forgetting the diachronic nature of meaning, he ultimately founded the science of linguistics on the systematic totality of language. Thus, the structuralist argument ceased to be that the final signifier S_2 determines that which has come before, S_1, and became instead that S_2 determines S_1 and S_1 determines S_2; that is, reciprocal oppositions stabilize meanings between coexistent terms; and differential relations no longer threaten the transvaluation of all preceding signifiers.'[24]

But if we incorporate the diachronic perspective that Saussure himself enunciated but forgot about, the consequence is clear: S_2 can be the ground of the system only as far as it does not have a precise, particular location within it. The same argument can be presented in terms of set theory: what names the set cannot be part of it. What the rhetorical turn would add to this argument is that the term naming the set would be one of the particular elements of that set that splits its own identity between its own particularity and its role of signifying the totality. It is this double role that is at the root of all topological displacement.

6. Rhetoricity, as a dimension of signification, has no limits in its field of operation. It is coterminous with the very structure of objectivity. This is, first of all, connected with the notion of 'discourse' that I have used in my work, which is not exclusively or primarily linked to speech or writing, but to any signifying practice. This entails that it is equivalent to the social production of meaning – that is, to the very fabric of social life. There is no possibility of any strict separation between signification and action. Even the most purely constative of assertions has a performative dimension, and, conversely, there is no action that is not embedded in signification. For the same reason, there cannot

24   Joan Copjec, 'Sex and Euthanasia of Reason', in *Read my Desire* (Cambridge, MA: MIT Press, 1995), pp. 205–6.

be any stark separation between signification and affect, given that the latter is only constituted through a differential cathecting of the various components of a signifying chain. As in Wittgenstein's 'language games', words and actions (to which we should add affects) are part of an interdependent network. This means that linguistic categories such as the signifier/signified and syntagm/paradigm distinctions – if properly theorized – cease to belong to a regional discipline and come to define relations operating in the very terrain of a general ontology.

But, secondly, if signification could close itself in syntagmatic terms – if paradigmatic relations of substitution could themselves be reabsorbed by combinatorial rules – the role of rhetoric could not be ontologically constitutive. The structuralist closure of the relation of mutual determination between S_1 and S_2 could be achieved without any tropological device being brought into the picture, and so rhetoric would be relegated to its traditional role as adornment of language. But it is here that my remarks concerning the impossibility of achieving any closure of a signifying system without representing the unrepresentable become relevant. Once the centrality of catachresis is fully accepted, rhetoricity becomes a condition of signification and, as a result, of objectivity.

Thirdly, once the status of rhetoric has been recognized in its true ontological generality, relations that in this essay I have approached in a strictly tropological terminology are likely to be reproduced at different levels of analysis of human reality, even when the rhetorical nature of the distinctions introduced is not perceived or recognized. In psychoanalysis, to give the most obvious example, the rhetorical character of the workings of the unconscious was explicitly recognized a long time ago. Condensation has been assimilated to metaphor and displacement to metonymy. The logic of the *objet a* involves precisely an investment by which an ordinary object becomes a substitute for the unreachable Thing. In Lacan's terms, sublimation consists in elevating an object to the dignity of the Thing. This operation of investment is catachrestical through and through. And Copjec, in her film studies, has shown how close-ups are not a part within the whole, but a part that functions as the very condition of the whole, as its name, leading to that contamination between particularity and totality that, as we have seen, is at the heart of all tropological movement.

In the rest of this essay, I will try to show the operation within the political field of those distinctions that I have been discussing. I will argue that the tensions that we have detected along the metaphor-metonymy continuum can be seen as fully operating in the structuration of political spaces. I will discuss two cases. In the first, we will see an almost complete unilateralization of the metaphorical operation; in the second, a systematic blockage of the transition from metonymy to metaphor – in other words, a strategy to prevent that contiguity shades into analogy. The first possibility I will illustrate with the logic of the general strike in Sorel; the second, with the political strategy of Leninism.

III

We have to give some precise theoretical status to the operation in which we engage when trying to see the way rhetorical categories are (implicitly) present in those logics governing the distinctions that structure areas different from those in which rhetoric was originally thought to be operative. We should basically avoid two temptations. The first is to make of rhetorical categories the locus of a hard transcendentality – that is, of a level in which all pertinent theoretical distinctions would be formulated, and which would reduce the terrains of their 'application' to the empiricity of 'case studies'. But we should also avoid the other extreme, consisting of seeing the two levels as fully enclosed universes whose mutual relations could only be conceived in terms of purely external homologies. The question of the comparison itself between regions and levels should be conceived in tropological terms: no level has a transcendental priority over the other, so that their very interaction should be seen as an area of displacements blurring the frontiers between the empirical and the transcendental. Each should theoretically enrich the understanding of the other in an intertextuality that has no ultimate anchoring point.

If we try to think those organizing categories of the political field that make possible a comparison with our rhetorical analysis, we could advance the following thesis: politics is articulation of heterogeneous elements, and such an articulation is essentially tropological, for it presupposes the duality between institution and subversion of differential positions that we found as defining a rhetorical intervention. But social organization is not exclusively political; to a large extent it consists of differential positions that are not challenged by any confrontation between groups. It is only through this confrontation that the specifically political moment emerges, for it shows the contingent nature of articulations. Using a Husserlian distinction, we could say that the social is equivalent to a *sedimented* order, while the political would involve the moment of *reactivation*. Contemporary forms of technocratism would express this dissolution of the political and the reduction of the management of the community to a mere question of expertise. It is the replacement of politics by knowledge, whose earliest formulation we find in Plato.

We have here the basis for a comparison between the duality politics/administration and the two axes of signification – that of combinations and that of substitutions. The more social order is stable and unchallenged, the more institutional forms will prevail and organize themselves in a syntagmatic system of differential positions. The more the confrontations between groups define the social scene, the more society will be divided into two camps: at the limit, there will be a total dichotomization of the social space around only two syntagmatic positions: 'us' and 'them'. All social elements would have to locate their identities around one of these two poles, whose internal components would be in a mere relation of equivalence. While, in an institutionalist political discourse, there is a multiplication of differential positions in a relation of combination with each other, in an antagonistic discourse of rupture the number of syntagmatic differential positions is radically restricted, and all identities establish paradigmatic relations of substitution with all the others at each of the two poles. In my work, I have called these two opposed political logics the logic of difference and the logic of equivalence, respectively. Given that the equivalential chain establishes a paratactic succession between its component links, none of them can have a position of centrality founded in a combinatorial logic of a hypotactic nature. So, if the unity of the equivalential chain is going to be organized around a privileged signifier, such a privilege cannot be derived from a differential structural position, but only from a cathectic investment of a radical kind. The symbols of Solidarność in Poland derived their success not from any structural centrality of the Lenin shipyards in the country, but from the fact that they expressed radical anti–status quo feelings at the moment in which many other social demands were frustrated by not finding institutional channels of expression within the existing political system. This process by which identities cease to be purely immanent to a system and require an identification with a point transcendent to that system – which is the same as saying: when a particularity becomes the name of an absent universality – is what we call *hegemony*. Its logic is identical with the logic of the *objet a*, which I have already referred to, and, for the reasons that I have given, it is essentially catachrestical (= rhetorical).

One last point requires our consideration. A hegemonic operation is essentially tropological, but requires very particular strategic moves to be performed within the metaphoric–metonymic continuum. Other moves, however, are equally possible, given that the continuum does not prescribe a priori either the direction that interventions in it should take or the different forms of articulation between its two extreme poles. Genette presents the decision by Proust that made possible the existence of a narrative as precisely that: a decision. But he himself points out that other decisions would have been equally possible, in which case we would not have had a novel but, for instance, a succession of lyrical moments. In the same way, the emergence of a hegemonic logic in Gramsci's political thought takes place against the background of various different ways of conceiving politics in the Marxist tradition which, while still being describable in terms of the possibilities opened by the metaphoric/metonymic distinction, are different from the hegemonic turn. It is to that history that we have now to address our attention.

IV

I have spoken about a zero-degree of the rhetorical, whose attainment would ideally require that the syntagmatic differential logic is able to dominate the whole field of signification (in the expanded sense that I have given to this last term). The prerequisite for attaining such a zero-degree would be, of course, the ability of the syntagmatic logic to fully control paradigmatic substitutions (an ability that we have good reasons to be rather sceptical about). However, we have so far limited the question of the zero-degree to its structuralist version – in other words, to a purely *synchronic* system – while identifying the notion of diachrony with a retroactive fixation/transgression that would operate from 'outside' the structural 'inside'. Is this, however, the only true alternative? Is it necessary that a purely syntagmatic/combinatorial space is organized in a synchronic way? I think it is not. Insofar as diachrony is not conceived as a contingent, external intervention, but as structured by a teleology, a diachronic succession is perfectly compatible with a zero-degree of the tropological. Pure differentiality (our zero–degree) is not necessarily linked to either simultaneity or succession.

It is from this point that we have to commence our consideration of the Marxist tradition. For at the root of this tradition there is a discourse anchored in Hegelian teleology. We know the defining features of the latter: the essential determinations of any entity are to be found in its *conceptual* specificity; the *conceptual* contradictions inherent in this specificity force us to move to a new entity embodying a new conceptual stage – and so on. Marx did not change things in the least with his 'inversion' of Hegelian dialectics: if the ground is 'matter' rather than the 'Idea', but matter has inner laws of movement that are *conceptually* specifiable, Marx's materialism is as idealistic as Hegel's.

The important point for our subject is that, in the vision of History that emerges from this diachrony, the various stages in the succession are not conceived as *interruptions* of what preceded them but as *teleological fulfilments*. We are dealing with a pure combination in which each actor and task has an assigned place in a secular eschatology grounded in the 'necessary laws' of History. It comes as no surprise that the main political consequence of this approach is to privilege 'strategy' over 'tactics'. Long-term strategic calculations were considered to be possible because the teleologism of the premises opened the way to historical predictions, even if they were only 'morphological predictions', to use the words of Antonio Labriola. And any non-fulfilment of those predictions could be dismissed as a temporary aberration to be superseded once the 'necessary laws' reasserted their long-term validity.

The most extreme versions of this teleologism are to be found, of course, in the orthodox currents of the Second International, but it is enough to read the 'Preface' to the *Critique of Political Economy* to realize that, although in less crude ways, it impregnates the whole of the Marxist tradition. That is why we can speak of a rhetorical zero-degree: in this syntagmatic succession there is no place for either metonymic displacements or metaphoric reaggregations.

Marxist literalism required the reduction of the process of historical development to a mechanism that had to be conceptually apprehensible as far as its laws of movement are concerned. But that conceptual apprehensibility also required that anything escaping what is specifiable by those laws be discarded as historically irrelevant. Now, it is precisely this sharp distinction between what is relevant and what is not that is blurred during the first 'crisis of Marxism' at the end of the nineteenth century. Capitalism recovered after a long period of depression, and the transition began to the monopolistic phase and to imperialism. In such a situation, the socialist faith in the collapse of the system as a result of its internal contradictions was shaken. Historical development had revealed itself to be far more complex than had been assumed, and such a complexity took the form of a contamination between social levels which, according to the classical theory, should have remained distinct. ('Organized capitalism' ceased to be explainable by pure market laws, and an element of conscious regulation intervened at the very level of the infrastructure; imperialism led to the emergence of a 'labour aristocracy', and consequently to an attenuation of class conflicts, and so on.) The consequence for our analysis is that the very terrain that had made accessible the zero-degree of the tropological was shattered, and rhetorical movements became highly important in both metaphoric and metonymic directions.

But this tropological turn took a variety of forms and directions. As I anticipated, the first example I will refer to is the later work of Georges Sorel. Like many other socialist thinkers of his time, Sorel, at the time of writing the *Reflections on Violence*, had lost faith in the expectation that capitalism would bring about its own collapse as a result of purely economic laws. So, in order to keep alive the revolutionary vocation of the working class, it was necessary to appeal to something other than economic determinism. The principle capable of maintaining the purity of proletarian identity was *violence*. For this purpose, it was essential that the working class should not intervene in politics, for that would co-opt it into the mechanisms of the bourgeois state. He opposed 'proletarian violence' to 'political violence' – the latter being epitomized by Jacobinism.

Proletarian violence had to be organized around a myth: '[M]en participating in great social movements represent to themselves their immediate action under the form of images of battles ensuring the triumph of their cause. I propose to call *myths* these constructions whose knowledge is so important for the historian: the syndicalists' general strike and Marx's catastrophic revolution are myths'.[25] He counterposes 'myth' and 'utopia'. While the latter is a pure intellectual construction, the blueprint of a future or ideal society, myth is just a set of images capable of galvanizing the masses' imagination and galvanizing them into historical action.

The myth around which proletarian identity should be organized is that of the *general strike*:

> I understand that this myth of the general strike horrifies [*froisse*] many *wise people* because of its character of infinitude; the present world is very much inclined to return to the opinion of the ancients and to subordinate morals to the good management of public affairs, which leads to locate virtue in a just middle. Insofar as socialism remains a *doctrine entirely presented through words*, it is easy to make it deviate towards a just middle; but this transformation is clearly impossible once one introduces the myth of the general strike, which involves an absolute revolution.[26]

And, again: 'Today revolutionary myths are almost pure; they make it possible to understand the activities, feelings and ideas of the popular masses preparing themselves to enter into a decisive struggle; they are not descriptions of things, but expressions of wills.'[27]

In a myth, the infinitude of the task goes together with the paucity of its contents. Its function is, precisely, to separate the militant from the concrete aim of his particular action. Let us suppose that a group of workers participate in a strike for higher wages. If the strike is successful, and its only aim was that particular demand, success leads to demobilization and to the integration of the workers into the status quo. But if participation in that concrete action is seen as a mere episode, educating the proletariat for the final aim, the meaning of the particular struggle changes altogether. But, for this, the myth of the general strike has to be operating from the very beginning. This explains the *infinitude* of the task to which Sorel refers: it cannot be identified with any

25   Georges Sorel, *Réflexions sur la violence* (Paris: Seuil, 1990), p. 21.
26   Ibid., p. 25.
27   Ibid., pp. 29–30.

particular aim. And it explains also the poverty of its contents – which is actually more than poverty, for, as the name of an infinite task, it negates the very possibility of any content (which would necessarily have to be finite). The Sorelian myth is one of the purest examples of what I have called an 'empty signifier'. It does not matter whether or not the general strike is an event that could happen. Although Sorel is not entirely explicit in this respect, I think that the very logic of his argument leads towards a negative response, for any finite fulfilment would compromise the infinitude of the task. Its status approaches that of Kant's regulative idea.

But how should we read this set of displacements that Sorel brings about against the sequence of categories of classical Marxism? Where and how does the tropological turn take place, exactly? To start with, in Sorel there is not any syntagmatic plurality of places of enunciation, because they all converge to reinforce a unique proletarian identity. Whether we are dealing with a strike, a demonstration, or a factory occupation, they are simply occasions for the rehearsal of a unique 'future' event: the general strike. These occasions are certainly plural, but their plurality is present only to eclipse itself as a mere support for the single event that speaks through all of them. That is, we are faced with a pure metaphorical reaggregation which is not interrupted by any metonymical plurality. There is nothing to displace, because the sites of the metaphorical event are there only in order to be negated by the latter. To put it in clear terms: the revolutionary break does not proceed through equivalence but through absolute identity. So, in some way Sorel is the symmetrical reverse side of the 'rhetorical zero-degree' of the Second International. For the latter, there was no room for any tropological movement in the determination of the emancipatory subject. For Sorel, such a determination could only proceed through an extreme form of that tropological movement – namely, a pure metaphor that has eliminated all traces of its metonymical grounding. Analogy reveals an essence that has broken all links with contiguity. Equivalence is replaced by pure identity. (As this identity, however, is constructed around an empty place – the general strike – whose discursive effects depend on its lack of content, its assertion is close to nihilism. Not surprisingly, Sorelianism fed very divergent currents of thought, from radical communism and ultra-leftism to fascism.) We can return here to Genette's analysis of Proust. According to him, as we have seen, there is narrative in Proust only because metaphors are inscribed in a metonymic movement; otherwise we would only have a succession of lyrical moments. Well, this last possibility is what Sorel's text enacts. Each revolutionary act does not find its meaning in a succession endowing it with its *raison d'être* within the series; rather, each of them is the expression of some sort of repetition drive constantly reinstating, in a Sisyphean way, a single identity. That is why Genette's notion of a succession of lyrical moments as an alternative to Proust's narrative – in other words, pure metaphorical flashes not inscribed in any metonymical succession – applies so well to Sorel's vision of politics; and, also, why there can be no Sorelian strategy based in a long-term calculation. While, for a Kautsky or a Plekhanov, such calculation was based in supposedly known laws of history, for Sorel the mere idea of a long-term prediction makes no sense. The assertion of a revolutionary subjectivity largely escapes strategic considerations.

v

If Sorel's discourse is structured in a terrain in which political subjectivity can only operate through a total metaphor that conceals even the traces of its metonymic ground, the experience of Leninism is different: the metonymic subversion of the differential space of Marxist teleology has to remain visible, to the point of making impossible the movement towards its metaphorical *telos*. Leninism emerges as a *political* answer to an anomaly in historical development. Russia was supposed to follow the pattern of the classical bourgeois-democratic revolutions of the West. The task ahead was the overthrowing of Tsarism and the opening of a long period of capitalist democracy, so that socialism was only a long-term prospect, to be achieved as a result of the contradictions of a fully-fledged capitalist society. In that democratic revolution, the bourgeoisie was supposed to be the 'natural' leading force. Tasks and forces were assigned roles according to a pre-ordained succession. The anomaly was that the autochthonous Russian bourgeoisie had arrived too late to the historical scene, when a world capitalist market was already well established, and as a result it was too weak to carry out its own democratic revolution. But capitalism was rapidly developing in Russia as a result of foreign investment, so that there was the paradoxical situation – 'anomalous' according to the canonical pattern

– of a country that was mature for a democratic revolution but in which the 'natural' agent of that historical transformation was incapable of carrying out its task.

As a result of capitalist development, however, a robust working class was emerging, which had none of the limitations of the indigenous bourgeoisie, and so – this was the thesis of the Russian social-democrats – it had to take up the historical task of leading the democratic revolution (in alliance with the peasantry, in the Leninist account) that its natural agent, the bourgeoisie, had left unfulfilled. This anomalous taking up of a task by a force that was not its natural agent is what the Russian social-democrats called 'hegemony'. So we have a fracture in historical development, a discontinuity in the sequence of its categories. The taking up of the democratic tasks by the working class was an event politically explainable by a set of historical circumstances, but not insertable as one of the necessary links of the canonical paradigm. It was an 'exceptionality', to use the terminology of the time.

Now, if we study the structure of this exceptionality, we immediately see that it was the *presence* of the working class at the centre of historical events at a moment in which the country was mature for a democratic revolution that assigned it to that role. It was a relation of *contiguity*. So we are dealing with the construction of a new link between task and agent which can only be conceived as a metonymic displacement.

We know, however, that any metonymy has a natural tendency to shade into a metaphor – the relation of contiguity to become, through continuous association, one of analogy. So we could normally expect that the nature of the democratic task changed when taken up by the proletariat, and that the class nature of the latter was also altered as a result of its taking up a democratic task. But nothing of the kind happened. The whole Leninist strategy was designed to prevent the exceptional task from becoming the site of the construction of a new political subjectivity. The class nature of the proletariat had to remain unchanged. The Leninist motto was: 'to strike together and to march separately.' Why so? Various reasons combined, but the main one was, that for Russian revolutionaries – the Bolsheviks included – Russian exceptionality was exactly that: an exception and, on top of that, one that was going to be short-lived. Neither Trotsky nor Lenin – even after the 'April Theses' – thought that a proletarian power in Russia, given its backwardness, would have any prospect unless it found its natural continuity in a revolution in Germany, and the other major and highly developed capitalist countries in the West. If that had been the case, the Russian 'exceptionality' would have been quickly integrated into a 'normal' process of historical development.

If we consider the matter retrospectively, we find here the root of the double discourse that will be inscribed in the Communist experience of the years to come. The canonical sequence of categories had to be maintained as an ultimate unsurpassable horizon – the Marxist syntagm was never formally questioned; but, as a counterpart, actual politics was going to be dominated increasingly by an empiricism of exceptionalities that eluded any theorisation. Stalin's *Realpolitik* was the extreme expression of this divorce between theory and practice, but in more attenuated forms it would dominate the whole of Communist experience.

The way in which both levels were combined can perhaps be seen at its best in the case of Trotsky. The whole logic of 'permanent revolution' is only thinkable if the empiricism of exceptionalities is articulated with the discourse of 'normal' syntagmatic development. The argument runs as follows. Russia was mature for a democratic-bourgeois revolution in which the bourgeoisie – Trotsky accepted the point – was incapable of playing the leading role. This would result in a democratic revolution led by the proletariat. But, Trotsky added, the bourgeoisie would not tolerate proletarian power – even if confined within democratic limits – and would respond with a massive lock-out. The result would be that the workers' movement, in order to consolidate its power, would have to advance in a socialist direction. Revolutions always start with democratic banners, but their stabilization and consolidation require their transition to the socialist stage. This model would be repeated ad nauseam by Trotskyists in all imaginable historical contexts. The classic 'stageism', although interrupted by an 'exceptionality', was in full operation: the class nature of social agents was unquestioned, as well as that of the tasks and of the succession of phases.

So the metonymic moment had to be frozen, preventing the construction of new identities through metaphoric reaggregations. Here we see the difference with Sorel. For him there is no narrative, only the sequence of metaphorical moments through which proletarian identity is constantly reinforced. For Leninism, the interaction between the two discursive levels forces it to engage in a permanent narrative, so that the metonymic moment is never abandoned. It is for that reason that Leninism is an eminently strategic type of discourse, whose difference with the strategy of the Second International is nevertheless visible: for the latter, strategic reflection was based on an historical prediction grounded in the necessary laws of history, while for Leninism, given the operation of exceptionalities, strategies have more the character of conjunctural movements.

This notion of conjunctural analysis forces us, however, to move beyond Leninism's frozen metonymies and, indeed, beyond the historical horizon of Marxism. For the question is: How exceptional are the exceptions? According to Lenin, the world capitalist market is not only an economic but also a political reality: it is structured as an imperialist chain. Crises can take place at one point of it that result – given that the chain is broken by its weakest link – in dislocations of the relations of forces at other points. This makes possible a seizure of power even if the 'objective' material conditions have not been met. In such situations there is no longer any question of either a pure combination of stages – like the one postulated by the theory of combined and uneven development – nor of a necessary class belonging of social agents; for what is at stake is the constitution of complex social identities constructed on the basis of practices homogenizing the heterogeneous. That is, we are dealing with metaphorical reaggregations. Frozen Leninist metonymies no longer do the trick. I think that Gramsci's notion of 'collective wills' should be read in this light. But this incorporation of the metaphorical dimension does not lead us back to Sorel's camp, either. For Sorel there is a unilateralization of metaphor, because the proletarian identity that he tries to consolidate is given in advance. There is no question, for Sorel, of incorporating heterogeneous elements into a wider social identity. That could only lead, in his view, to an undermining of the class consciousness of the proletariat. But once the political process is seen not only as a reassertion of an identity but as its construction – as in Gramsci's 'war of position' – the metonymic dimension cannot be ignored. Hegemony means the passage from metonymy to metaphor, from a 'contiguous' starting point to its consolidation in 'analogy'. But here we are very close to the metaphor/metonymy relationship that Genette finds in Proust's text. Translating it into political language, we could say that, because there is narrative (*récit*), there is strategy. But as the identity of the agents of that strategy is not given beforehand, we will always have short-term strategic movements that are not anchored in any eschatology. They will operate exactly at the point at which metaphor and metonymy cross each other and limit each other's effects.

CHAPTER 4

The Politics of Rhetoric[*]

Why would a political theorist like me, working mainly on the role of hegemonic logics in the structuration of political spaces, be interested in the work of a prominent literary critic such as Paul de Man? I could suggest at least two main reasons. The first is that one of the leitmotifs of Paul de Man's work has been the subversion of the frontiers separating theoretical from literary disciplines, so that those dimensions that had traditionally been conceived as privative of literary or aesthetic language became, for him, defining features of language *tout court*. Against all attempts to differentiate between 'appearance' and 'saying' – between a primary text whose message would have been mediated by the materiality of the signs, of the figural, and a language of inquiry governed by reason – de Man always insisted that any language, whether aesthetic or theoretical, is governed by the materiality of the signifier, by a rhetorical milieu that ultimately dissolves the illusion of any unmediated reference. In this sense a generalized rhetoric – which necessarily includes within itself the performative dimension – transcends all regional boundaries and becomes coterminous with the structuration of social life itself. Conceived at such a broad level of generality, the literariness of the literary text breaks the limits of any specialized discipline, and its analysis involves something like the study of the distorting effects that representation exercises over any reference – effects that thus become constitutive of any experience.

Moreover, de Man himself was perfectly aware of the political and ideological implications of his approach to texts. In a famous interview with Stefano Rosso, where he is asked about the increasing recurrence in his works of the terms 'political' and 'ideological', he answered as follows:

---

* A preliminary version of this chapter was presented at the conference on 'Culture and Materiality' that took place at the University of California, Davis, on 23–25 April 1998. It was also discussed in the seminar on Ideology and Discourse Analysis at the University of Essex, a month later. I want to thank those whose commentaries led me to introduce precisions in my text and, in some cases, partial reformulations of the argument – at Davis, Jacques Derrida, Fred Jameson, J. Hillis Miller and Andrzej Warminski; at Essex, David Howarth and Aletta Norval.

I don't think I ever was away from these problems, they were always uppermost in my mind. I have always maintained that one could approach the problems of ideology and by extension the problems of politics only on the basis of critical-linguistic analysis, which had to be done on its own terms, in the medium of language, and I felt that I could approach those problems only after having achieved a certain control over those questions. It seems pretentious to say so, but it is not the case. I have the feeling I have achieved a certain control over technical problems of language, specifically problems of rhetoric, of the relation between tropes and performatives, of saturation of tropology as a field that in certain forms of language goes beyond that field . . . I feel now some control of a vocabulary and of a conceptual apparatus that can handle that.[1]

As for the second reason for a political theorist to be interested in de Man's work, it has to do with something related to the political field itself. Gone are the times when the transparency of social actors, of processes of representation, even of the presumed underlying logics of the social fabric, could be accepted unproblematically. On the contrary, each political institution, each category of political analysis, shows itself today as the locus of undecidable language games. The overdetermined nature of all political difference or identity opens the space for a generalized tropological movement, and thus reveals the fruitfulness of de Man's intellectual project for ideological and political analysis. In my work, this generalized politico-tropological movement has been called 'hegemony'. What I intend to do in this chapter is to stress some decisive points in the work of de Man, especially in his late work, where the direction of his thought might be helpful in developing a hegemonic approach to politics.

I

The requirements of 'hegemony' as a central category of political analysis are essentially three. The first is that something constitutively heterogeneous to the social system or structure has to be present in the latter from the very beginning, preventing it from constituting itself as

---

1   Stefano Rosso, 'An Interview with Paul de Man', in Paul de Man, *The Resistance to Theory* (Minneapolis/London: University of Minnesota Press, 1993), p. 121.

a closed or representable totality. If such a closure were achievable, no hegemonic event would be possible, and the political, far from being an ontological dimension of the social – an 'existential' of the social – would be just an ontic dimension of the latter. Secondly, however, the hegemonic suture has to produce a re-totalizing effect, without which no hegemonic articulation would be possible either. But, thirdly, this re-totalization must not have the character of a dialectical reintegration. It has, on the contrary, to maintain alive and visible the original and constitutive heterogeneity from which the hegemonic articulation started. How is a logic possible that can maintain these two contradictory requirements at the same time? Let us approach this question through the exploration of its possible presence in de Man's texts. We will start with the analysis of Pascal's *Réflexions sur la géometrie en général; de l'esprit géometrique et de l'Art de persuader*, which de Man carries out in 'Pascal's Allegory of Persuasion'.[2]

Pascal begins his study of the *esprit géometrique* with the distinction between nominal and real definitions – the first resulting from convention, and thus being exempt from contradiction, and the second being axioms or propositions to be proved – and asserts that the confusion between the two is the main cause of philosophical difficulties. Maintaining the separation between the two – as the geometrician does – is the first rule of philosophical clarity. But the argument runs quickly into difficulties, as geometrical discourse includes not only nominal definitions but also 'primitive terms' – such as motion, number and extension – that are indefinable but nonetheless fully intelligible. According to Pascal, these indefinable words find a universal reference not in the (impossible) fact that all men have the same idea concerning their essence, but instead in the fact that there is a relation of reference between name and thing, 'so that on hearing the expression *time*, all turn or direct the mind to the same entity'.[3] But, as de Man shows, this brings the real definition back into the geometrical camp itself, because

> the word does not function as a sign or a name, as was the case for
> the nominal definition, but as a vector, as a directional motion, that

2   'Pascal's Allegory of Persuasion', in Paul de Man *Aesthetic Ideology*, ed. Andrzej Warminski (Minneapolis/London: University of Minnesota Press, 1996), pp. 51–69.

3   Ibid., p. 56.

is manifest only as a turn, since the target towards which it turns remains unknown. In other words, the sign has become a trope, a substitutive relationship that has to posit a meaning whose existence cannot be verified, but that confers upon the sign an unavoidable signifying function.[4]

As the semantic function of the primitive terms has the structure of a trope, 'it acquires a signifying function that it controls neither in its existence nor in its direction'. Ergo, '[s]ince definition is now itself a primitive term, it follows that the definition of the nominal definition is itself a real, and not a nominal definition'.[5]

This contamination of the nominal by the real definition is still more visible when we move to the question of double infinitude, which is decisive in establishing the coherence and intelligibility of the relationship between mind and cosmos. Here, Pascal deals with the objections put to him by the Chevalier de Méré, according to whom – given the Pascalean principle of homogeneity between space and number – it is possible to conceive of an extension formed by parts that are not themselves extended, since it is possible to have numbers made up of units devoid of number. The principle of infinite smallness would thereby be put into question. Pascal's answer has two steps. He asserts, in the first place, that what applies to the order of number does not apply to the order of space. *One* is not a number – there is no plurality in it; but, at the same time, it is a number for it is part of the infinity postulated by the Euclidean principle of homogeneity ('magnitudes are said to be of the same kind or species when one magnitude can be made to exceed another by reiterated multiplication'). On that basis Pascal can distinguish between number and extension, but only at the expense of grounding the distinction in real and not nominal definitions. As de Man asserts,

> The synecdochal totalization of infinitude is possible because the unit of number, the *one*, functions as a nominal definition. But, for the argument to be valid, the nominally indivisible number must be distinguished from the *really* indivisible space, a demonstration that Pascal can accomplish easily, but only because the key words of the

---

4   Ibid.
5   Ibid., p. 57.

demonstration – indivisible, spatial extension (*étendue*), species (*genre*), and definition – function as real, and not as nominal definitions.[6]

But – second step – if the order of number and the order of extension had to be separated to answer Méré's objection, the rift between the two had also to be healed if the principle of homogeneity between both was to be maintained. This homology is restored by appealing, as far as number is concerned, to the zero – which, unlike *one*, is radically heterogeneous with the order of number – and by finding equivalences in the order of time and motion, such as 'instant' and 'stasis'. This appeal to the zero, however, has dramatic consequences for the coherence of the system, which de Man describes in a passage worth quoting in full:

> [T]he coherence of the system is now seen to be entirely dependent on the introduction of an element – the zero and its equivalences in time and motion – that is itself entirely heterogeneous with regard to the system and nowhere a part of it . . . Moreover this rupture of the infinitesimal and the homogeneous does not occur on the transcendental level, but on the level of language, in the inability of a theory of language as sign or as name (nominal definition) to ground this homogeneity without having recourse to the signifying function, the real definition, that makes the zero of signification the necessary condition for grounded knowledge . . . It is as sign that language is capable of engendering the principles of infinity, of genus, species, and homogeneity, which allow for synecdochal totalizations, but none of these tropes could come about without the systematic effacement of the zero and its reconversion into a name. There can be no *one* without zero, but the zero always appears in the guise of a *one*, of a (some)thing. The name is the trope of the zero. The zero is *always* called a one, when the zero is actually nameless, 'innommable'. In the French language, as used by Pascal and its interpreters, this happens concretely in the confusedly alternate use of the two terms *zéro* and *néant*. The verbal, predicative form *néant*, with its gerundive ending, indicates not the zero, but rather the one, as the limit of the infinitely small, the almost zero that is the one.[7]

---

6   Ibid., pp. 58–9.
7   Ibid., p. 59.

It is important to give serious consideration to this remarkable passage – remarkable among other things because de Man does not pursue later in his essay all the implications of his own *démarche* – for it contains, *in nuce*, all the relevant dimensions of the problem we are exploring. Everything turns around the role of the zero. The zero is, we are told, something radically heterogeneous with the order of number. The order of number, however, cannot constitute itself without reference to the zero. It is, in this sense, a supplement to the system which, nonetheless, is necessary for constituting it. With respect to the system, the zero is in an undecidable tension between internality and externality – but an internality that does not exclude heterogeneity. The zero, in the second place, is 'innommable', unnameable; but at the same time it produces effects, it closes the system, even at the price of making it hopelessly heterogeneous. It *re-totalizes* the system, though incurring an inconsistency which cannot be overcome. The zero is nothing – but it is the nothing of the system itself, the impossibility of its consistent closure, that is signified by the zero; and in that sense, paradoxically, the zero as empty place becomes the signifier of fullness, of systematicity as such, of that which is lacking. The semantic oscillation between *zéro* and *néant* that de Man observes is the result of this dual condition of the moment of closure – which makes reference to an object that is necessary but also impossible. Finally, if the zero as moment of closure is impossible as an object but also necessary, it will have to have access to the field of representation. But the means of representation will be constitutively inadequate. They will give to the 'innommable' a body, a name; but this can be done only at the expense of betraying its true 'non-being'. Hence the tropological movement which prolongs *sine die* the non-resolvable dialectics of the zero and the one. In the words of de Man that I have just quoted, 'There can be no *one* without zero, but the zero always appears in the guise of a *one*, of a (some)thing. The name is the trope of the zero. The zero is *always* called a one, when the zero is actually nameless, "innommable"'.

Now, this succession of structural moments coincides, almost step by step, with the logic of hegemony that I have tried to describe in my work, and which I see operating in the texts of Gramsci – to whom I will return below. To start with, the condition of any hegemonic suture is the constitutive non-closure of a system of political signification. The systematicity of a system, its closure – which is the

condition of signification in a system, such as Saussure's, whose identities are merely differential – coincides with the determination of its
limits. These limits, however, can only be dictated by something
beyond them. But, as the system is a system of differences – of all
actual differences – that 'beyond', which should be heterogeneous
with the system in order to fulfil its function of truly closing it, lacks
the condition of a true heterogeneity if it consists in one more difference. The latter would be, in some way, undecided, suspended between
being internal and external to the system. This jeopardizes the role of
the 'beyond' as limit and, as a result, the possibility of constituting the
differences as truly intra-systematic differences. It is only if what is
beyond the limit has the character of an exclusion that its role as limit
is restored, and with it the possibility of the emergence of a full system
of differences.[8]

But this fullness of the system (obtained, it is true, at the expense
of a dialectical retrieval of its negation) has a shortcoming. For, with
respect to the excluded element, all differences within the system
establish relations of equivalence between themselves. And equivalence is precisely that which subverts difference. So the 'beyond' that
is the condition of possibility of the system is also its condition of
impossibility. All identity is constituted within the unsolvable tension
between equivalence and difference.

So, as with the Pascalean zero, we arrive at an object that is at the
same time impossible and necessary. As impossible, it is an empty
place within the structure; but, as necessary, it is a 'nothing' that will
produce structural effects, and this requires that it has access to the
field of representation. And, as in the dialectics of the zero and the
one, this double condition of necessity and impossibility will be
constitutively inadequate. The fullness of the system, its point of
imaginary saturation, will be, as in the example of de Man, a nothing
that becomes a something. What are the possible means of this
distorted representation? Only the particular differences internal to
the system. Now, this relationship by which a particular difference
takes up the representation of an impossible totality entirely incommensurable with it is what I call a hegemonic relation.

8   For the full development of this argument, see my *Emancipation(s)* (London:
Verso, 1996) – especially the essay 'Why Do Empty Signifiers Matter to Politics?',
pp. 36–46.

There are only two differences between the hegemonic logic and the Pascalean dialectics of the zero and the one, as described by de Man. The first is that – given the numerical nature of Pascal's case – the zero can only be embodied by the one, while in the case of the hegemonic logic *any* element within the system can be a bearer of a hegemonic function.[9] The second difference is that, given de Man's interests, the determination of the heterogeneous character of the tropological displacement from the zero to the one is the point of arrival of his analysis, while for a student of hegemonic logics the analysis of the exact nature of this tropological movement becomes imperative. In de Man's detotalizing discourse, what matters is to show the heterogeneity out of which the tropological movement operates. This is also a vital part of a hegemonic analysis. But what is decisive for the latter is the determination of the partial re-totalizations that the tropological movement makes possible.[10] This is the dimension that we now have to take into account. I will do so by reference to the metaphor/metonymy opposition, as presented in de Man's essay on Proust in *Allegories of Reading*.[11]

II

The text on Proust deals, as is well known, with the discourse of young Marcel on the pleasure of reading, and with the way in which such pleasure is constructed through a set of metaphoric substitutions that

---

9 Compare the disagreement between de Man and Louis Marin, as presented by de Man in 'Pascal's Allegory', p. 60.

10 What is important is to realize that these re-totalizations do not operate through a simple and retrievable negation. As de Man asserts, 'What is here called, for lack of a better term, a rupture or a disjunction is not to be thought of as a negation, however tragic it may be. Negation, in a mind as resilient as Pascal's, is always susceptible of being reinscribed in a system of intelligibility . . . It is possible to find, in the terminology of rhetoric, terms that come close to designating such disruptions (e.g. *parabasis* or *anacoluthon*), which designate the interruption of a semantic continuum in a manner that lies beyond the power of reintegration' (de Man, 'Pascal's Allegory', p. 61). But the very fact that there are tropoi that make describable that which is beyond the power of reintegration clearly shows that we are not dealing with a simple collapse of the system, but rather with an orderly drifting away from what would otherwise have been the conditions of its full closure. It is in the field of this drifting away that the hegemonic logics operate.

11 Paul de Man, 'Reading (Proust)', in his *Allegories of Reading Figural Language in Rousseau, Nietzsche, Rilke and Proust* (New Haven/London: Yale University Press, 1979), pp. 57–8.

are, nevertheless, persuasive only through the operation of a series of contingent metonymic movements:

> The crossing of sensory attributes in synaesthesia is only a special case of a more general pattern of substitution that all tropes have in common. It is the result of an exchange of properties made possible by a proximity or an analogy so close and intimate that it allows the one to substitute for the other without revealing the difference necessarily introduced by the substitution. The relational link between the two entities involved in the exchange then becomes so strong that it can be called necessary: there could be no summer without flies; no flies without summer . . . The synecdoche that substitutes part for whole and whole for part is in fact a metaphor, powerful enough to transform a temporal contiguity into an infinite duration . . . Compared with this compelling coherence, the contingency of a metonymy based only on a casual encounter of two entities that could very well exist in each other's absence would be entirely devoid of poetic power . . . If metonymy is distinguished from metaphor in terms of necessity and contingency . . . then metonymy is per definition unable to create genuine links, whereas no one can doubt, thanks to the butterflies, the resonances of the crates, and especially the 'chamber music' of the flies, of the presence of light and of warmth in the room. On the level of sensation, metaphor can reconcile night and day in a *chiaroscuro* that is entirely convincing.[12]

We see that this passage establishes the distinction between metaphor and metonymy on the basis of the two oppositions contiguity/analogy – the dominant opposition in classical rhetoric – and contingency/ necessity. As far as the first opposition is concerned, the difficulty is that the distinction between analogy and contiguity is rather slippery. Contiguity, in rhetorical terms, cannot be equivalent to mere physical contiguity, for the latter can be the basis of a metaphoric relation. And analogy can depend on such a variety of criteria that we are in fact faced with a continuum in which analogy fades into mere contiguity. De Man himself points out, for instance, that '[s]ynecdoche is one of the borderline figures that creates an ambivalent zone between metaphor and metonymy and that, by its spatial nature creates the illusion

---

12 Ibid., pp. 62–3.

of a synthesis by totalization'.[13] And in one of the essays included in *Blindness and Insight*, he asserts that

> it is notoriously difficult, logically as well as historically, to keep the various tropes and figures rigorously apart, to establish precisely when catachresis becomes metaphor and when metaphor turns into metonymy; to quote an apt water-metaphor to which an expert of the field (Lansberg) has to resort precisely in his discussion of metaphor: 'the transition (of one figure to another, in this case, from metaphor to metonymy) is fluid'.[14]

We could say that the frontiers between figures and tropes in classical rhetoric is ancillary to the main objective distinctions of ancient ontology. This is evident from Aristotle to Cicero and Quintilian. It is precisely the close character of this system of distinctions that is put into question by the deconstructive turn. Both de Man and Gérard Genette, for example, have shown how Proust, great defender of the creative role of metaphor, had to ground his own metaphors in a generalized system of metonymic transitions.[15]

The distinction between necessity and contingency is more promising. In this case, without being entirely able to avoid the continuum by which one figure fades into the other, we have at least a less ambiguous criterion of classification: a discourse will be more or less metaphoric depending on the degree of fixation that it establishes between its constitutive components. De Man attempts to show how all metaphorical totalization is based on a metonymic textual infrastructure that resists this totalizing movement. In *Hegemony and Socialist Strategy*,[16] we asserted that hegemony is always metonymic. In the light of our previous analysis, we see why this has to be the case. What is constitutive of a hegemonic relation is

---

13   Ibid., p. 63.

14   Paul de Man, *Blindness and Insight: Essays in the Rhetoric of Contemporary Criticism* (Minneapolis: Minnesota University Press, 1983), p. 284.

15   Gérard Genette, 'Métonymie chez Proust', in his *Figures III* (Paris: Éditions du Seuil, 1972), pp. 41–3. Paul de Man finds the use by Genette of the category of diegetic metaphor limited as far as Proust is concerned. Both, however, agree in privileging the metonymic transitions in Proust's text.

16   Ernesto Laclau and Chantal Mouffe, *Hegemony and Socialist Strategy. Towards a Radical Democratic Politics* (London: Verso, 1985).

that its component elements and dimensions are articulated by
contingent links. A trade union or a peasant organization, for
instance, can take up political tasks that are not related by necessary
links to their own corporative specificity. The hegemonic links by
which those political tasks become workers' or peasants' tasks are
metonymic displacements based on relations of contiguity. In that
sense, if there is going to be hegemony, the traces of the contingency
of the articulation cannot be entirely effaced.

The type of relationship involved in a hegemonic link can be
further clarified if we return for a moment to the Pascalean zero. As
in the case of the hegemonic relation, the heterogeneous character
of the element that brings about whatever totalization can exist –
the zero – is a contingent remainder that cannot be eradicated. But
there is a crucial difference between the latter and that inhabiting
the tropological movement at the root of hegemony. Where in
hegemony there is free variation as far as the element that occupies
the hegemonic position is concerned, in the case of the zero we do
not have such a latitude of manoeuvre: the zero can only be a *one*.
In that case we are not dealing, properly speaking, with a metonymy but with a catachresis.[17] Now, in the field of rhetoric, catachresis
occupies a very special position. At the time of the last codification
of classical rhetoric in the early nineteenth century, it was even
denied the status of a figure. Thus, Fontanier defined it in the
following way:

> *Catachresis, generally, consists in assigning a sign already assigned to
> a first idea to a new idea, that had either no sign corresponding to it, or
> no more left in that particular language.* It corresponds, consequently,
> to the use of a forced and necessary change in meaning (*Trope*), to
> every word for which *meaning* is purely *extensive*, being a literal
> meaning but coming from a second origin, being the intermediary
> between *primitive literal meaning* and *figurative meaning*. But in its
> nature it comes closer to the former than to the latter, although it
> could have been itself *figured* in the principle.[18]

---

17   I thank J. Hillis Miller for having called my attention to the need for further
elaborating the distinction between catachresis and metonymy – a distinction that, as
will be seen, is crucial for my analysis.

18   Pierre Fontanier, *Les figures du discours* (Paris: Flammarion, 1968), p. 213.

For instance, if I speak of the 'wings of an aeroplane' or the 'wings of the building', the expression was metaphorical at the beginning, but the difference with a proper metaphor that fully operates as a figure is that there is no proper designation of the referent. I am not free to call the 'wing' in any literal way.

So if the only defining feature of a catachresis is its being based in a figural name that has no counterpart in a proper one, it is clear that there is no specificity in the kind of figuration introduced by catachresis, and that it will repeat the figures of language *sensu stricto* with the only *differentia specifica* of there being no tropological movement from the proper to the figural. Thus Fontanier can speak of a catachresis of metonymy, of synecdoche and of metaphor. The difficulty is that the distinction between a catachresis of metonymy and a proper metonymy depends on the possibility of establishing an uncontaminated frontier between the proper and the figural. As soon as some *flexibility* is introduced, the exchanges between these polar extremes become more complicated: the proper becomes the extreme, the *reductio ad absurdum* of a continuum that is figural through and through. The possibility of a *radical* heterogeneity on which the sharp distinction between catachresis and metonymy is grounded is thereby considerably eroded. The only thing we can say is that the very possibility of a hegemonic relationship depends on this erosion, on keeping an unstable equilibrium between heterogeneity and contiguity, between catachresis and metonymy – an equilibrium whose conditions of extinction would be either a heterogeneity without common measure between the elements, or a contiguity that becomes total, and thus absorbs within an implicitly assumed space the contiguous positions as internal differences.[19] (These two conditions of extinction of the hegemonic link are, in fact, only one and the same: in order to be *radically* heterogeneous, two elements require a common ground out of which their heterogeneity can be thought.)

On the other hand, however, all hegemony tries to re-totalize and to make as necessary as possible the contingent links on which its articulating power is based. In this sense, it tends to metaphorical totalization. This is what gives it its dimension of power. It is a power, however, which maintains the traces of its contingency and is, in that sense, essentially metonymic. Hegemony is always suspended between

---

19   With this, of course, the tropological movement would come to an end.

two impossible poles: the first, that there is no displacement, that contiguity becomes mere contiguity and that all tropological move- ment ceases – this would be the case of what Gramsci called the 'corporative class'; the second, that the metaphorical totalization becomes complete, and that purely analogical relations fully saturate the social space – in which case we would have the 'universal class' of the classical emancipatory discourse. Both poles are excluded by the hegemonic relation. It is only on the traces of (contingent) contiguity contaminating all analogy that a hegemonic relation can emerge.

III

Let us now translate these reflections on Sorel into our tropological argument.[20] Any attempt by the proletariat to constitute its subjectiv- ity through a variety of loosely related subject positions can only lead, according to Sorel, to corporative integration and to decadence; so all metonymic variation had to be eliminated. In that case, how to aggre- gate working-class struggles in such a way that the proletarian identity is maintained and reinforced? Through an education of the will grounded in the myth of the general strike. Each action of the workers – whether a strike, a demonstration or a factory occupation – should be seen, not in its own specificity and particular objectives, but as one more event in the formation of the revolutionary will. That is, they are all analogous from the point of view of their ultimate deep aims and are, as a result, in a relation of metaphorical substitution with each other. Their mutual relations – like that between flies and summer in Proust's text – are necessary ones. The drawback of this vision is that, in that case, the myth unifying the struggles beyond all specificity cannot be specific either. The reduction of all specificity to the repeti- tion of something analogous can only be the metaphor of metaphoricity as such. We know what this involves: the interruption of any hegem- onic operation. The metaphor of metaphoricity can only be a zero that is in no tropological relation with a one, or – at most – a zero that is in a catechretical relation with *only one* position. Only at that price

---

20   In the original publication of this piece, this section is preceded by a presentation of the main lines of Sorel's theoretical-political approach. As these aspects have already been discussed in Chapters 1 and 3, I omit the first part and go straight to the conclusions relevant to de Man's distinctions that concern the argument presented in this chapter.

can revolutionary closure be achieved. And this is precisely what Sorel attempts to achieve by making the general strike totally heterogeneous with the empirical world of limited and partial struggles. The general strike is presented as a myth and not a utopia – it has lost all the detailed descriptive features of the latter; it has no particular objectives; it is merely an empty image galvanizing the consciousness of the masses; it is exhausted in this last function without possibly corresponding to any actual historical event. It is a radical non-event that is, paradoxically, the condition of all events if there is going to be grandeur in society.

In that case, why revolutionary general strike rather than anything else? Is there any ground to think that the general strike is the (necessary) catachresis of that radical non-event that brings about grandeur? Sorel cannot answer this question, and the oscillations of his political career are a clear indication that the question is unanswerable. The relationship between grandeur and general strike is a hegemonic incarnation, which entails all metaphoric aggregation being ultimately grounded in (reversible) metonymic displacements. The attempt to ground the revolutionary will in a metaphoric totalization that would avoid the particularism of hegemonic variations ends in failure. As Plato knew, perhaps better than Sorel, only protracted metonymic displacements between Athens and Syracuse can give any hope that the king will agree to become a philosopher.

Perhaps this point could be made in a slightly different way: it is only through the pure, irreducible event that consists in a contingent displacement not retrievable by any metaphorical reaggregation that we can have a history, both in the sense of *Geschichte* and of *Historie*. It is because there is hegemony (and metonymy) that there is history. Could not some deconstructive strategies, such as iteration, be seen as attempts at introducing metonymy at the heart of metaphor, displacement at the heart of analogy?

Perhaps this is, exactly, the intellectual displacement leading from Sorel to Gramsci. While in the first the analogizing movement of the metaphor of metaphoricity led to a repetition that tried to eliminate the possibility of any *proper* event, Gramsci's notion of war of position, of a narrative–political displacement governed by a logic of pure events that always transcend any preconstituted identity, announces the beginning of a new vision of historicity – one governed by the ineradicable tension between metonymy (or synecdoche) and metaphor.

IV

We now arrive at a decisive point in my argument on hegemony. If hegemony means the representation by a particular social sector of an impossible totality with which it is incommensurable, then it is enough that we make the space of tropological substitutions fully visible, to enable the hegemonic logic to operate freely. If the fullness of society is unachievable, the attempts at reaching it will necessarily fail – although they will be able, in the search for that impossible object, to solve a variety of partial problems. That is, the particularism of the struggles, which was systematically demoted in Sorel's analysis, now becomes central. The metonymic game thus occupies centre stage, and politics, which was for Sorel the nemesis of proletarian action, takes the upper hand.

All this becomes more visible if we compare Sorel's discursive *démarche* with other socialist discourses of the time, which faced in the opposite direction. But let us clarify an important point before engaging in that comparison. Both metaphor and metonymy are tropological movements – that is, forms of condensation and displacement whose effects are achieved on the basis of going beyond literal meaning. Now, from this point of view, classical Marxian discourse presented itself as the zero-degree of tropology – as a scientific discourse describing the necessary laws of history, which did not need to go beyond the literality of their formulation in order to achieve the totalizing effects that they postulated. That this ideal of scientificity points to an impossible task, and that whatever totalizing effects Marxian discourse could have can only be achieved by putting into operation a whole arsenal of tropological movements, is well known; but the important point is that, as an ideal governing its own discursivity, literality is fully present in it and produces a whole set of concealing effects. Sorel had ceased to believe in objective, necessary laws of history, and wanted to substitute them with an *artificial* necessity grounded in the power of the will; so he had, as we have seen, to have full recourse to the principle of analogy – which in a literal discourse of necessary, objective laws would have no incidence – and to install himself, fully conscious of the fact, in the terrain of metaphor. But, as we have also seen, metaphorical necessity was decisively contaminated by metonymic contingency. What were, in that case, the politico-discursive and strategic effects of accepting the metonymic terrain as inevitable?

Let us consider the discussions in Russian social-democracy at the turn of the century. The general view was that Russia was ripe for a bourgeois-democratic revolution in which the bourgeoisie, as in all major revolutions of the West, would carry on the tasks of sweeping away the remainders of feudalism and creating a new state along liberal-democratic lines. The drawback was that the Russian bourgeoisie arrived in the historical arena too late, and was weak and incapable of carrying out its political tasks. But the need for a democratic revolution remained. This led to the conclusion – drawn at least by some sections of the social-democrats – that, in that case, those tasks had to be taken up by some other social sector *that was not its natural bearer* – in this case, the working class. This relationship by which a sector takes up tasks that are not its own is what the Russian social-democrats called *hegemony*. So we see how the political steps that this analysis took led in the opposite direction to Sorel's. While Sorel tried to close the working class around its own *natural* tasks through metaphoric totalizations, here we find the opening of a field of metonymic displacements in the relations between tasks and agents – an undecided terrain of contingent articulations in which the principle of contiguity prevails over that of analogy. It was only the contingent peculiarity of the Russian situation – the presence of a weak bourgeoisie and a strong working class – that gave rise to the working-class leadership in the democratic revolution.

This complicated dialectics between analogy and contiguity can be seen to expand in a plurality of directions. Firstly, as the non-tropological succession of programmed stages is interrupted, a space of logical indeterminacy arises: 'Tsarism, having entered into complete contradiction with the demands of Russia's social development, continued to exist thanks to the power of its organisation, the political nullity of the Russian bourgeoisie and its growing fear of the proletariat'.[21] Secondly, this indeterminacy is the source of pure relations of contiguity that break the possibility of totalizations either in terms of syntagmatically retrievable differences or metaphorically 'necessary' aggregations:

Russian capitalism did not develop from artisanal trade via the manufacturing workshop to the factory for the reason that European capital,

---

21   Leon Trotsky, *1905* (London: Allen Lane, 1971), p. 328.

first in the form of trade capital and later in the form of financial and industrial capital, flooded the country at a time when most Russian artisanal trade had not yet separated itself from agriculture. Hence the appearance in Russia of modern capitalist industry in a completely primitive economic environment: for instance, a huge Belgian or American industrial plant surrounded by dirty roads and villages built of straw and wood, which burn down every year, etc. The most primitive beginnings and the most modern European endings.[22]

This gap interrupting any non-tropological succession of *necessary stages*, but also any metaphoric aggregation of events around a pre-given *necessary point*, gives proletarian identity in Russia an open character in which contingent displacements, *pure events*, assume a constitutive role which no aprioristic logic can govern:

I remember an old friend, Korotkov, a cabinetmaker from Nikolayev, who wrote a song back in 1897. It was called *The Proletarians March* and it began with the words: 'We are the alpha and the omega, we are the beginning and the end . . .' And that's the plain truth. The first letter is there and so is the last, but all the middle of the alphabet is missing. Hence the absence of conservative traditions, the absence of casts within the proletariat, hence its revolutionary freshness, hence, as well as for other reasons, the October Revolution and the first workers' government in the world. But hence also the illiteracy, the absence of organisational know-how, the lack of system, of cultural and technical education . . .[23]

And then the inevitable consequence:

From the viewpoint of that spurious Marxism which nourishes itself on historical clichés and formal analogies . . . the slogan of the seizure of power by the Russian working class was bound to appear as a monstrous denial of Marxism . . . What then is the real substance of the problem? Russia's incontestably and incontrovertibly backward development, under the pressure of the higher culture of the West, leads not to a simple repetition of the Western European

22   Ibid., p. 339.
23   Ibid., p. 340.

historical process but to a set of fundamentally new features which
requires independent study . . . Where there are not 'special features',
there is no history, but only a sort of pseudo-materialistic geometry.
Instead of studying the living and changing matter of economic
development it is enough to notice a few outward symptoms and
adapt them to a few ready-made clichés.[24]

Could it be clearer? Historicity is identified with 'special features'
unassimilable to any form of repetition. History is a field of contingent displacements that are not retrievable by any of its (analogical)
figures.

Of course, this field of contingent variations can be more or less
extended, depending on the width of the area in which the literal still
prevails and arrests the tropological movement. Now, what happened
in socialist discourses like those we are considering was that what I
have described as a tropological movement expanded ever more, and
covered wider and wider sections of political life. Let us consider a
concept such as 'combined and uneven development'. It was introduced to refer to the experience of social struggles in Third World
countries, in which – even more than in the case of Russia – a non-
orthodox combination of developments that should have corresponded
to successive stages makes more contingent and risky hegemonic
interventions possible. In the 1930s, Trotsky drew the inevitable
conclusion: combined and uneven development is the terrain of all
social and political struggles in our time. The only thing we have is an
unlimited tropological movement that is the very terrain on which
society constitutes itself. And we see why metonymy is, in some sense,
more 'primordial' than metaphor (or, as in other of de Man's analysis,
why allegory takes precedence over the symbol): because in a situation of radical contingency no criterion of analogy is stable; it is
always governed by changing relations of contiguity that no metaphorical totalization can control. Metaphor – with analogy – is at
most a 'superstructural' effect of a partial stabilization in relations of
contiguity that are not submitted to any literal principle of a priori
determination.

This process of general rhetorization takes place only insofar as
none of the conditions in which each of the tropoi would become what

24   Ibid., p. 339.

it literally claims to be can be met. If metonymy was *just* a metonymy, its ground should be a contiguity uncontaminated by analogy, and in that case the literal separations within a given discursive space would be fully in control of the limits of the metonymic movement. If analogy dominated unchallenged, a full totalization would have taken place that would make analogy collapse into identity – and the tropological movement would cease. If synecdoche was actually able to substitute the whole with the part, this would mean that the whole could have been apprehended independently of the part. If catechresis could be grounded in a tropological movement that started from total heterogeneity, it could only take place insofar as the distinction between the homogeneous and the heterogeneous would be established with entire precision. It is as if, in some way, the conditions for a rhetoric whose tropological movements are going to occupy the terrain of a ground which is not itself grounded are to be found in the impossibility of taking the definitions of each of the tropoi at face value, and in the need to stress the logics by which each tends to fade into the other. The same goes for hegemony: the conditions of its full success are the same as the conditions of its extinction.

This can be shown by a couple of historical examples. The first concerns Italy. At the end of the Second World War there was a confrontation of tendencies within the Italian Communist Party about the right strategy to be followed in the new democratic environment. There were two positions: one that asserted that the Communist Party, being the party of the working class – and the latter being an enclave in the industrial north – had to limit its efforts mainly to creating forms of representation for that enclave; the second, more Gramscian tendency maintained that the party had to build up its hegemony, spreading its activities to a variety of areas, the agrarian Mezzogiorno included. How was this possible, given the particularistic social and geographical location of the working class? Simply by making the party and the unions the rallying point of a variety of democratic initiatives in a country moving away from fascist dictatorship. The democratic initiatives postulated by this approach were entirely contingent – their success was not guaranteed by any logic of history – and thus depended on the construction of a collective will; but, unlike Sorelian will, they were not aiming for the reinforcement of a purely proletarian identity. They tended, instead, to the creation of a multifarious democratic identity, always spreading beyond itself in directions only graspable through a contingent narration. Togliatti wrote in 1957:

> A class may lead society insofar as it imposes its own rule, and to this end the force of arms can also be used. It becomes a national class, however, only insofar as it solves the problems of the whole of society . . . The proletariat becomes a national class insofar as it takes on these problems as its own and thence comes to know, by the process of changing it, the whole reality of national life. In this way it produces the conditions of its own political rule, and the road to becoming an effective ruling class is opened . . .
>
> We have to spread the activity of an organised vanguard over the whole area of society, into all aspects of national life. This activity must not be reduced to preaching propaganda, to phrase-making or clever tactics, but must stick closely to the conditions of collective life and give, therefore, a foundation, real possibilities and prospects to the movement of the popular masses . . . Our struggle for the unity of popular, democratic forces is, therefore, not imposed by tactical skills, but is an historical requirement, both to maintain conquests already achieved, to defend and safeguard democracy, and to develop it.[25]

Here we have a tropological space in which each of the figures tends to fade into the other. The various struggles and democratic initiatives are not united to each other by necessary links – so we have metonymical relations of contiguity. But the hegemonic operation tries, nonetheless, to make the condensation of these struggles as strong as possible – so the metonymies fade into metaphoric totalization. The hegemonic relation is synecdochal, insofar as a particular section in society – the working-class party, in this case – tends to represent a whole exceeding it. But since this whole lacks any precisely defined limits, we are dealing with an impure synecdoche: it consists in the undecidable movement between a part attempting to incarnate an indefinable whole and a whole that can only be named through its alienation in one of its parts. Finally, the heterogeneity can only be a relative one – with the result that the line separating catachresis from

---

25   Palmiro Togliatti, *On Gramsci and Other Writings* (London: Lawrence & Wishart, 1982), pp. 157–9.

metonymy becomes also undecidable. I think that all the main categories of Gramscian theory – war of position, collective will, organic intellectuals, integral state, historical bloc, hegemony – could be read rhetorically, as circumscribing the space of tropological movements that bring about a new strategic flexibility in political analysis.

CHAPTER 5

Antagonism, Subjectivity and Politics

The inaugural manifesto of modern socialism begins with the assertion that the history of humanity is the history of class struggle. This postulate of Marx and Engels, which is halfway between a merely factual acknowledgement and a programmatic motto, involves three theses whose reciprocal coherence is not obvious at first sight: first, that the 'history of humanity' would be a unified object, which would have a coherent and comprehensive structure; second, that it would be possible to determine with precision the agents of this history – namely, social classes; third, that the type of relation defining the existing interaction between those agents – and determining the nature of the totality (the history of humanity) – would be one of *struggle*. If we want to give any meaning to the initial postulate of the *Manifesto of the Communist Party*, we should ask ourselves about the relations operating between these three dimensions. Could they converge into a harmonious whole? From the very beginning we have reasons to doubt it: what is being proposed to us under the form of an unproblematic entity (the history of humanity) would be the presence of an object that could be rationally grasped, but whose diverse instances, simultaneous or successive, would be the result of conflict. If this were the case, however, what guarantees would we have that the conflictual moment is not so deep that it is not possible to domesticate it and lead it back, in each case, to the place designed for it in a 'history of humanity' conceived as a rational totality? I will try to make the point clearer. Antagonism *presupposes* the incompatibility between opposed elements, while the coherence within a structure involves the *complementarity* between its internal moments. So if the structure is constituted by antagonistic opposites, it can only retain its internal coherence if the antagonistic dimension is a purely fictitious one – that is, a surface phenomenon behind which, and through which, a substantial structural unity operates. This means that, whenever the totalizing dimension prevails, the antagonistic moment will be subordinated to a deeper history – while if, on the contrary, antagonism goes beyond a certain threshold, 'history' will break into pieces and will be deprived of all internal coherence. As far as 'social classes' – the presumed subjects of history – are concerned, they are also captured in the tension of this alternative: if the unity of history, conceived by Marxism as a history of production, prevails over the antagonistic moment, subjects, conceived as classes, will have a precise structural location within this process; if, on the other hand, the unity of this process is put into question by antagonism, so also – and radically – is the identity of social agents.

To analyze this system of alternatives, it is necessary to define an absolutely crucial variable: What do we understand by *antagonism*? I am not asking myself what are the actually existing antagonisms in society, but something more fundamental: What is an antagonism? What type of relation between social forces does it presuppose? This is a question usually overlooked in the sociological literature, which usually concentrates on actual 'conflicts', 'confrontations' and 'struggles', but which does not pose the question about the ontological nature of these categories. It is, however, on this nature that we must focus if we want to advance on the theoretical front.

REAL OPPOSITION AND DIALECTICAL CONTRADICTION

I will begin with the analysis of one of the few philosophical debates explicitly dedicated to the examination of this problem: the debate, in the school of Della Volpe, around the Kantian distinction between real opposition and logical contradiction. The distinction can be found in some of the pre-critical writings of Kant – such as the 'Attempt to Introduce the Concept of Negative Magnitudes into Philosophy' and 'The Only Possible Argument in Support of a Demonstration of the Existence of God' – but also in the *Critique of Pure Reason*, in the section on the 'Amphiboly of the Concepts of Reflection'. According to Kant, there are two types of opposition, not only one, as Leibniz and Wolff had assumed. The first type of opposition, the only one accepted by Leibniz, is logical opposition, and it is expressed by the formula A–not A. If I assert in a proposition what a second proposition negates, I incur a contradiction. The result is null (*nihil negativum irrepresentabile*). If I assert of a certain body that it is in movement and, at the same time, that it is not in movement, I am not asserting anything about that body. Ergo, I can only incur a contradiction at the conceptual level. The proposition is the only terrain in which a contradiction can emerge.

But there is a second type of opposition, linked to real objects: it is a type of opposition without contradiction. If a body is moved by a force in one direction and by an identical force in the opposite direction, the result is the absence of movement, which is something positive and representable. We are still faced with an opposition, but one that does not involve contradiction. The two opposite forces operate at the same time and are, as a result, positive and real predicates of the same object (*negativum representabile*). While the formula of the logical contradiction is A–not A (each of the two poles is only the symmetrical negative of the other), in a real opposition the formula is A–B: each pole is something determinate, independent of the other. The positivity of being is not interrupted at any point. Kant concludes that contradictions can only take place between concepts (or, rather, between propositions), while between actually existing objects there can only be real oppositions (*Realrepugnanz*).

The conclusion that Della Volpe, and especially his disciple, Lucio Colletti, derived from this Kantian distinction, was that social antagonisms can only be real oppositions. An idealist philosophy like Hegel's, which reduced reality to the concept, could somehow speak about contradictions in the real world; but a materialist philosophy like Marxism, which asserts the extra-logical character of the real, cannot follow this route. So when Marxists speak of social contradictions, they incur a regrettable confusion: a truly materialist programme should involve the reconceptualization of social antagonisms as real oppositions. Colletti, in particular, shows that both Lenin (*Materialism and Empiriocriticism*) and Mao Zedong (*On Contradiction*) have been victims of this quid pro quo: all the examples of contradictions that they offer – and Mao just repeats Lenin's list – are in fact real oppositions.

But we have to ask ourselves: To what type of relation, logical contradiction, or real opposition, do we have to appeal in order to clarify the specificity of social antagonisms? We have to agree, firstly, with Della Volpe and his school in accepting that the category of 'contradiction' is inappropriate for explaining social antagonisms. Contradiction is not a type of opposition taking place between *real* objects (or subjects). Once this has been accepted, however, the question is more complex, because the Marxist (and Hegelian) contradiction is not only a *logical* but also a *dialectical* contradiction; as a result, the relation between its two poles is not exhausted at the level of a *nihil privativum irrepresentabile*, but adds something else: the dialectical contradiction, as distinct from the merely logical one, tries to add to the logical contradiction an element that is fully representable – namely, a third term that goes beyond the contradiction and thus 'resolves' it.

However, is it the logical derivation of this third component legitimate? Colletti's answer is inspired by Trendelenburg's critique of Hegelian dialectics. Its central steps are the following:

1. For Kant, *existence* is located outside the concept and outside logic. 'All this leads back to what – using a very Della Volpian expression – we could call the *positive conception* of the empirical and sensuous entity.'[1] Colletti quotes a series of passages in which Kant criticizes Leibniz for his reduction of sensibility to a simple lack – lack of clarity – which leads to a hypostatization of the abstract, of the conceptual, which turns the idea into the only substantial reality.

2. This is the starting point of Trendelenburg's critique. The argument begins, once more, with the Kantian distinction between real opposition and logical contradiction. The question posed to dialectical logic is: To what type of opposition does dialectical contradiction belong? Apparently it should be to logical opposition. But, following this route, we find countless difficulties. The main one is that, from a logical contradiction it is impossible to derive, as dialectics require, a third term. Hegel himself, in the *Encyclopaedia*, had shown the vacuity of the idea of deriving something from a purely logical contradiction.

3. As a result, for Trendelenburg – and for Colletti – the only alternative is the conclusion that dialectical contradiction is not a logical contradiction but a real opposition. But once this point has been reached we are confronted with a new problem, which is the main objection of Trendelenburg to Hegel. *Real opposition* in fact has several credentials for being recognized as the true content of *dialectical opposition*. The *negative* appearing in it is always something positive and real in itself, and, as it is well known, Hegel asserts that the dialectical negation is a 'determinate negation'. Moreover, as Aristotle observed (and as Trendelenburg reminds us), the real opposition or relation between contraries 'always takes place within the same genre, the same field'. This means

---

1   Lucio Colletti, *Tramonto dell'ideologia* (Roma-Bari: Laterza, 1986), p. 99.

that, unlike contradictory terms, which do not have a middle term, contraries do have a third term. However – and this is where Trendelenburg poses his decisive objection – can we obtain the third term of the real opposition through a purely logical method? As Colletti points out, the answer is unnecessary. In the real opposition something new and diverse emerges from the first term from which the opposition proceeds. But this third term can only be introduced into the argument by smuggling into it empirical presuppositions; the negative term is itself positive, and it is evident that it is not possible to arrive at it by a purely logical method. As Trendelenbug asserts, 'it is never possible logically to find a feature that "makes it possible to know a contrary concept", given that this concept corresponds to a *real* entity. To reach it, it will be necessary to appeal "to sensible intuition, that is, to experience". But this invalidates, at root, the ambition of dialectics to be "the self-movement of a pure and presuppositionless thought" '.[2]

4. The conclusion of Trendelenburg is that the so-called dialectical logic is a hybrid. The *third term* can only be introduced into the argument by smuggling into it empirical assumptions not provided by the logical structure of the argument. So, in spite of the deduction claiming to be strictly logical (and this brings Hegel closer to Leibniz), it is impossible to derive the third term logically. Hegel will establish the apparent coherence of his discourse by illegitimately mixing logical contradiction (what Marx called his uncritical idealism) and real opposition (what Marx called his uncritical positivism). For Colletti, this confusion is present not only within Hegelianism, but within a great deal of the debates in the Marxist tradition.

5. Most of the objections posed by Della Volpe and Colletti to dialectic logic are irrefutable. Certainly, the fusion of the two types of opposition does not produce a coalescence into a coherent logical assemblage. If the argument ended at this point, it would be irrefutable. But, unfortunately, it does not end at this point. In relation to other questions, Della Volpe and Colletti's analysis is far less satisfying. Some questions emerge in connection with this point. For instance: Is the positivity of the empirical and sensible the only possible alternative to an opposition understood as logical contradiction? Is the category of real opposition

2 Colletti, 1986, log-109

sufficiently wide to include any kind of opposition, in both the
natural and the social world? Is dialectical negativity the only
kind of negativity to which we have access?

In light of all this, it does not seem adequate to assert that dialectical
contradiction is a valid tool for articulating the specificity of an antagonistic relation. To this I would like to add a last consideration. If the
third term led the first two to an effective resolution, and if such a
'resolution' were only the logical consequence of the terms of the initial
contradiction, the negativity inherent to antagonisms would be purely
apparent, fictitious: it would be a mere passage to a higher identity. The
logic of identity would not have been broken at any point.

Once this conclusion has been reached, let us move to the other
pole of the alternative posed by Della Volpe and Colletti, and ask
ourselves whether we could conceive of social antagonisms as real
oppositions. There are several reasons to doubt it. One of them, the
most important, is the following: there is nothing antagonistic in a real
opposition. Colletti waxes indignant at Marxist theoreticians because,
according to him, they have completely ignored the category of 'real
opposition'. I do not think that this has been the case. Lukács was a
professional philosopher and, to ignore such a category, he would have
to have neglected to read the *Critique of Pure Reason*, which is unthink-
able. I think that Marxist theoreticians were not tempted to conceive of
social antagonisms as real oppositions for a different reason: because
there is no antagonism without negativity, and there is no negativity
whatsoever in a real opposition. Antagonism is a relation between
inimical forces, so that negativity becomes an internal component of
such a relationship. Each force negates the identity of the other. But in a
real opposition we do not have this type of negation, this mutual interruption of identities. In the clash between two stones, in which one of
the two is broken, the fact of getting broken expresses the identity of
that stone as much as that of not getting broken in other circumstances.
The two stones are in *pari materia* – they both belong to the same space
of representation. But in the case of antagonisms, things are different.
The presence of the enemy prevents me from constituting my own
identity. In contrast to what takes place in a real opposition, there is
here a negation of identity. The gap between opposite forces is more
radical in the case of an antagonistic relation – in particular, it is structurally different from the one taking place in a real opposition. It is

certainly possible to define real opposition in such a way that its only distinctive character is, finally, its alterity with respect to logical contradiction. In that case the concept would embrace very different types of relations. But if we did so, the notion of real opposition would lose all specificity. *Opposition* is either a category belonging to the social world, subsequently extended metaphorically to the physical world, or vice versa. But the risk is always that the metaphor loses its figural dimension and is transformed into an identity of nature between utterly diverse phenomena. Marxist theoreticians wanted to preserve the negativity inherent in antagonistic relations, and, given that the only negativity they had access to was the dialectical one, they continued speaking of antagonisms as contradictions. In this, no doubt, they were mistaken, but for different reasons from those suggested by Della Volpe and his disciples.

But one has to accept that the reading of Kant offered by Colletti is not entirely arbitrary, as it is based in theoretical results reached by Kant himself. Kant begins his argument with an acute analysis of the status of negative quantities in mathematics. He clearly shows that negative quantities do not involve absolute negations – as in the case of logical contradiction – but that they are, in fact, positive:

> Suppose that a ship sails from Portugal to Brazil. Let all the distances that it covers with the east wind be designated by '+' while those which it covers with the west wind are designated by '-'. The numbers themselves signify miles. The week's journey is $+12+7-3-5+8 = 19$ miles; this is the distance the ship has sailed westwards. The magnitudes preceded by '-' have this sign in front of them to signify opposition, for they are to be combined with those magnitudes that are preceded by '+'. But if they are combined with magnitudes which are preceded by '-', then there is no longer any opposition, for opposition is a reciprocal relation which only holds between '+' and '-'. And since subtraction is a cancelling which occurs when opposed magnitudes are taken together, it is evident that the '-' cannot really be a sign of subtraction, as is commonly supposed; it is only the combination of '+' and '-' together which signifies subtraction. Hence the proposition '$-4-5 = -9$' is not a subtraction at all, but a genuine increase and addition of magnitudes of the same kind.[3]

---

3   Immanuel Kant, 'Attempt to Introduce the Concept of Negative Magnitudes

The argument is irrefutable. Kant is maintaining that the opposition is not of a logical nature (as in A–not A), and that its two poles are positive: the wind proceeding from the west is something in itself, independently from its encounter with the wind blowing from the east. His attempt is to refute the assimilation (sustained by Leibniz and Wolff) of all opposition to a contradiction. Starting from there, Kant shows how the positive character of the two poles of an opposition can be found in other types of relation, whether natural or social, beyond the strictly mathematical field. Both poles of the opposition being positive, the negation of which they are bearers is mutual and always interchangeable. Thus 'descent' can be conceived as a negative 'ascent'; 'fall' a negative 'rise'; 'retrogression' as a negative 'advance'. Once the argument has been posed at this level of generality, we might imperceptibly go on to assimilate relations of a very different type, whose only common feature is their not being logical oppositions:

> Suppose that the news is brought to a Spartan mother that her son has fought heroically for his native country in battle. An agreeable feeling of pleasure takes possession of her soul. She is thereupon told that her son has died a glorious death in battle. This news diminishes her pleasure a great deal, and reduces it to a lower degree.[4]

This example shows how the assimilation between various forms of human relations operates. Kant is simply trying to show that the opposite to pleasure is something in itself positive, which cannot be identified with 'absence of pleasure', and that, as a result, the opposition 'pleasure/opposite to pleasure', is different from 'pleasure/absence of pleasure' – which would be a merely logical opposition. From this viewpoint, the relation 'pleasure/opposite to pleasure' is not different from that existing between the eastern and the western wind, but the analogy ceases at that point. Pleasure, as a subjective feeling, involves *identification* of the agent with that feeling, as far as the opposite to pleasure puts into question the identity of the agent, while the clash between the two winds is a purely meteorological phenomenon, in which the identity of the two intervening forces is not perturbed.

---

into Philosophy', in Kant, *Theoretical Philosophy 1755–1770* (Cambridge: CUP, 2007 [1763]), pp. 212–13.

    4   Ibid., p. 219.

For the problem that Kant is posing – connected to his dispute with the Leibnizians – the distinction I am pointing out is not relevant; but for a consideration of social antagonisms it is crucial. Kant himself does not speak of social antagonisms, but that Rubicon was crossed rather blithely by those who attempted to apply his category of real opposition to the social field – the Della Volpian school, in this case. Some of the texts quoted by Colletti to support his argument are very revealing. Thus, he quotes a passage from Irving Copi:

> That there are situations in which opposite forces are active, is something which has to be admitted; this is so both in the mechanical and in the social and economic fields. But to call those conflicting forces 'contradictory' is to use a clumsy and inapposite language. A gas submitted to heat, which tends to make it explode, and a barrier preventing the expansion of the gas can be described as forces in conflict, but none of them is the negation, or refutation, or contradiction of the other. The owner of a big factory, whose functioning requires the work of thousands of labourers, can oppose the union of the workers and to suffer (reciprocally) their opposition . . . but neither the owner nor the union is in reciprocal negation, or in refutation, or in contradiction.[5]

As can be seen, the compression of a gas and a union mobilization are equated, by the simple reason that none of them is contradictory – which is doubtless true – but what is completely overlooked is the fact that the term 'opposition' means something entirely different in each case.

This chapter is not the right place to develop an in-depth analysis of the epistemology of Della Volpe and his disciples. It is enough to point out that their approach is grounded in a realist–empiricist perspective which, while using some Kantian categories, develops them within an intellectual context that is explicitly non-Kantian. I will just mention their critique of what is called – not only by them – Kantian 'phenomenalism'. 'Now, all this leads back [in Kant, but Hume is also quoted] to what we could call – to return to an expression loved by Della Volpe – *the positive conception* of the empirical and sensible being. We are obviously dealing, in this case, with a conception which,

---

5 Irving Copi, *Introduzione alla logica* (Bologna: Il Mulino, 1964), quoted in Colletti, *Tramonto dell'ideologia*, p. 95.

in Kant, has a partial and reduced development – undermined by Kant's 'phenomenalism', which we have already referred to'.[6] This interpretation was already in question at the time of Kant. As Henry Allison points out,

> The first and most basic point to be made here is that phenomenalism, as Bennett describes it, is transcendentally realistic in the same sense and for the same reasons as Berkeleian idealism: in spite of its conception of objects as 'logical constructs', it treats (implicitly, of course) the sensible data out of which 'objects' are supposedly constructed as things in themselves. Consequently, it is no more suitable for explicating transcendental idealism than is Berkeleian idealism. In short, transcendental idealism is neither a theory about the translatability of object language statements into some more precise or primitive sense datum language nor a theory about the ontological type (material object or collection of sense data) of the objects of human experience.[7]

I cannot enter into this discussion here, except to stress that accepting the positive character of the two poles of a real opposition does not necessarily involve accepting an empiricist–realist perspective; only – and this is a very different assertion – recognizing that those poles are not internally interlinked in a logically contradictory way. There are alternatives other than the one I have just mentioned. For instance, it is possible to assert a discursive construction of the opposition in which each pole is semantically differentiated from the other without this differentiation being established in logical terms. It is here that a reading of Kant in terms of phenomenalism starts to disintegrate. It is on these alternatives that I will now focus.

ANTAGONISMS AND SOCIAL OBJECTIVITY

Where does our discussion, up to this point, leave us in relation to the notion of social antagonism? Neither of the two categories that we have explored so far as possible means capturing the specificity of

---

6   Colletti, *Tramonto dell'ideologia*, p. 99.
7   Henry E. Allison, *Kant's Transcendental Idealism: An Interpretation and Defence* (New Haven, CT: Yale University Press, 1983), pp. 30–1.

antagonism is sufficiently radical to avoid reducing the antagonistic relation to something different from itself. Both the category of 'contradiction' and that of 'real opposition' inscribe the strictly antagonistic dimension in a wider space of representation, in which antagonisms are a transitory moment, an evanescent component irrupting on the horizon of the visible only to be immediately transcended. Or, in other words, negativity is never *constitutive* (in the transcendental sense of the term). As I indicated earlier, a dialectical contradiction gives us only a fictitious negativity. It is present as a moment in the dialectical chain, but it has already, within itself, the seeds of its own supersession. In the ultimate unity of the Absolute Spirit, all contradictions find the point of their final supersession. Any contingency is present as the phenomenal surface through which an underlying unity asserts itself. And, of course, a negativity that is only the bridge towards a higher positivity cannot be radical and constitutive.

But if we move now to consider 'real opposition', we immediately notice that, for reasons that I have already mentioned, negativity cannot be radical either. The cornerstone of Kant's argument is the assertion of the *positive* nature of the two poles of the opposition. In that case, the negativity internal to antagonism cannot be constitutive either. In a *real* opposition, the opposition fully expresses the identity of its two poles. This is the part of Kant's argument that Colletti stresses, giving to it an empiricist turn that eliminates the transcendental dimension clearly present in Kant.

Having reached this point, we might ask ourselves whether, after all, dialectical contradiction and real opposition do not in fact share something – and whether this shared dimension is not, precisely, the one that does not capture the centrality of the negativity inherent to antagonism. The two types of relation do in fact share something, which is the fact that both are *objective* relations – between conceptual objects in one case and between real objects in the other. This already shows us the necessary step that we have to take if we are going to attribute to negativity a grounding role in the structuration of antagonisms. To be more precise: society does not succeed in constituting itself as an entirely objective order as a result of the presence, within itself, of antagonistic relations.

What would involve the constitution of a fully realized objective order? That all its internal components belong to the same space of representation. This would mean that the ontic content of each element would exhaust its ontological signification. In the case of the interaction between the easterly and the westerly winds – which in the most exactly balanced case could lead to the perfect rest of the boat – this interaction does not lead in the least to an interruption of the identity of either of the two winds. The *positive* character of each wind is not modified by its encounter with the other wind. The ontic identity of each wind expresses itself both when its natural course is impeded by the presence of the other wind and when it can operate without any kind of obstacle. And the same happens in a dialectical contradiction: both the contradiction as such and its resolution are only the unfolding of something that was fully preannounced – included – in the logical structure of each of the two contradictory terms. In a philosophy like Hegel's there is a perfect overlapping of the ontic and ontological orders. Each ontic difference, in its naked objectivity, has an ontological signification. And, conversely, there is no ontological dimension that is not constructed through an ontic differentiation.

But, to return to a previous example, in the case of the negative pleasure of the Spartan mother to whom the death of her son is announced, things happen in a very different way. Here the identity of the mother is indeed interrupted by the death. As she identifies her being, at least partially, with the survival of her son, his death prevents the full constitution of that identity. This means that the opposition between the two winds and the opposition between pleasure and the negation of pleasure are ontologically structured in different ways: with interruption of identity in one case, and without such interruption in the other. Neither of the two oppositions is logical; neither of them is the expression of a logical contradiction; but the principles of their internal structuration are different.

This means that, while Kant's aim was just to show that there are oppositions that are different from logical contradiction, our task is to advance in the analysis of the differentiations that emerge in the field of those oppositions. Let us return to the example of the Spartan mother. As I said, the painful episode blocks the full constitution of the mother's identity. The survival of her son becomes the symbol of an unreachable full identity. There is only one more step to take: to transform the enemy army into a symbol of her non-being. When this happens, we are fully in the field of social antagonisms. For the emergence of an antagonism, the first condition is to have an inter-ruption (or a preventing of the constitution) of a full identity. So the discursive construction of an antagonism is different both from a real opposition and from a dialectical contradiction, given that these two presuppose full identities. This explains my earlier assertion that antagonisms are not objective relations, but relations that show the limits that society encounters in constituting itself as an objective order. The corollary of this thesis is that the *social*, as distinct from *society*, is always going to be a *failed objectivity*.

Let us extract some further consequences from this thesis. There are several, and we can explore them summarily. In the first place, what happens with the positive nature of the two poles of the opposi-tion once we have moved away from Colletti's empiricist–realist reading? A first consequence is that the 'positive' content is always there, but it is no longer a positive, ontic content. If I *identify* with a certain content, the latter ceases to be mere content; it is invested in such a way that it becomes a symbol of my own being. That is, it comes to fulfil a different ontological role. But this new role is only possible insofar as another 'positive' content becomes a threat to my own iden-tity. And this threatening content is also invested with a new ontological function: that of symbolizing the very possibility of my not being. As nothing is *only* what it is, for the possibility itself of this being is threatened by this excess of investment (positive or negative), the exact overlapping between the ontic and the ontological orders is impossible. Certain particular objects will be invested with a new dimension transcending their ontic reality. Thus, an *ontological differ-ence* emerges splitting the field of objectivity. This difference is, at the same time, a condition of possibility of that field and also a putting-into-question of its merely objective character (I will return to this point). For the Spartan mother, the bravery of her son is a source of pleasure and his death a source of sadness, but it is only as a result of her identification with motherhood that the 'glorious death' can become a threat. (A reader with psychoanalytic leanings might of course find, in this episode, more complex sources of pleasure and its opposite.)

The whole vision of a positivity of being that would operate as a ground of a real opposition is, in this way, brought into question, at least in relation to the social world. The more we move from examples like that of the two winds cancelling each other's effects, to cases like that of the Spartan mother, and from the latter to social antagonisms, it becomes increasingly less possible to absorb the ontological dimension in the field of ontic objectivity. But, as a result, the attempt to subsume those oppositions – different from the logical one – under the unified category of 'real opposition' becomes increasingly more problematic.

But where do these considerations leave us? The notion of two opposite poles in a real opposition had been the basis for distinguishing the latter from the logical contradiction. But now, does the putting into question of that full positivity through the split between the ontic and the ontological not also threaten the very terrain on which the Kantian distinction between the two types of opposition takes place? Even worse: If we are now asserting that a positive, purely ontic content would be a substitute for a failed identity, would we not be smuggling the formula A–not A, on which logical contradiction is grounded, back into the discussion? The answer is in the negative.

But understanding why this is the case requires the introduction of some further preliminary considerations. In the case of a dialectical contradiction, as we have seen, the contradiction is present only in order to be later superseded by a higher positivity. This means that the contradictory moment has, within itself, everything needed to advance towards its later supersession. That is, the negative dimension is essentially transitory (in a logical and not a temporal sense, of course). This is the point at which the legitimacy of a strictly dialectical transition was questioned by Trendelenburg, Della Volpe, Colletti and others. (Schelling's critique of Hegel's idea of a presuppositionless philosophy goes, partially, in the same direction.) The central point is that it is not possible to derive a *real* extreme through a purely logical method. I have already stressed the correctness of this critique. As far as Hegel's formulations of his own method are concerned, there is no doubt that he was himself embarking on an impossible task. But we cannot avoid the feeling that there is something in this critique that is not entirely grasped. I think it is this: that the critique is formulated from an ontological perspective from which there is only room for two types of entities: concepts and real objects. Colletti's unnuanced defence of the adequation theory of truth illustrates the point. Once this point is reached, it is evidently easy to show that Hegel's pseudo-coherence can only be maintained by smuggling real oppositions into a discourse that is supposed to be entirely conceptual. This is something we can accept only with one proviso: that perhaps the apparent eclecticism of Hegel's text – which we should accept – partially results from the narrow ontological dualism of the reading of his critics. If this was the case, perhaps a new possibility should be explored: that Hegel's hybrid eclecticism was an attempt *avant la lettre* of going beyond the rigid dualism of concept/real object.

In order to explore this point, let us return to our discussion of social antagonisms.

ANTAGONISMS AND REPRESENTATION

Let us explore the various dimensions of this structural gap that renders an exact overlap between the ontic and the ontological impossible – that is, what I have called the 'interruption' of an identity. In the first place, the being of an entity is never merely *given*; it is the result of the investment of an ontic content with an ontological signification that does not logically emerge from that content. (Or, in other words, the articulation between the ontic and the ontological will be always discursively mediated). This applies to both sides of the equation. There is no ontic content that, by itself, has a precise ontological signification. But, conversely, there is no ontological signification constructed other than through an investment of an ontic content. Everything turns, as a result, around the precise theoretical status of this notion of 'investment'. Is it categorically representable? If it was, we could pass from the ontic to the ontological through resources internal to both levels. But, in that case, there would be a total eclipse of the notion of 'investment'. That is, the transition would be entirely objective – there would be no interruption of identity. But if, on the contrary, there is such interruption, the investment would become foundational and constitutive and, for that very reason, it would become ontologically *unrepresentable*. If this were the case, as I think it is, the interruption could not be inscribed in anything different from itself. I can *name* that interrupting gap, but I cannot conceptually apprehend the content of that name. This gap, nameable but not conceptually apprehensible, is, exactly, *the place of the subject*.

At this point, we can attempt to detect the consequences of these categorical distinctions for an understanding of social antagonisms. If antagonisms were objective relations, the notional resources of their two poles would make possible an easy transition between those poles, without abandoning a common space of representation (as in the case of the eastern and western winds). But, in that case, the strictly antagonistic moment of the *clash*, the moment in which identities do not *coalesce* between themselves but *interrupt* each other, would be merely apparent. If, conversely, the moment of interruption is radical and constitutive, the idea of an objective ground embracing both poles of the antagonistic relation would dissolve. A social antagonism, unlike the opposition between natural forces, requires a type of negativity that is absent from a purely physical world.

So the key question concerns the confluence or interruption of identities. Let us explore, in turn, what is involved in each of these alternatives – in the first place, coalescence. As I have suggested, it involves a level of representation embracing everything that each pole positively asserts. There is no ontological difference in a purely physical universe. What happens if we move to the other alternative, where a true interruption takes place? It then becomes clear that the only possibility of maintaining full representation as an operating principle is to introduce one form or other of *reduction*. That is, the idea of a spurious interruption that would make us return, finally, to an underlying coalescence. And it is here that we find 'real opposition' is entirely inadequate to carry out this reduction. Real oppositions are only operative within relations whose identitary terms show themselves *à ciel ouvert*. To conceive of something in terms of reduction would entail flirting with categories such as 'alienation', which are necessarily absent from a world in which 'contradiction' has ceased to be ontologically productive.

So the only alternative is to move to a notion of coalescence from which the dimension of interruption is not totally excluded. This dimension has to be maintained as part of a logical movement through which coalescence asserts itself. This new articulation between coalescence and interruption corresponds to dialectical logic. Its theoretical meaning could be approached from two different perspectives. In one sense, it is the highest moment of rationalism, the moment in which the whole world of antagonistic interruptions has been led back to a radically representable ensemble. The category of 'alienation' operates this transubstantiation (scarcely more than a sleight-of-hand). But dialectical logic can also be seen from another perspective: as the irruption, within philosophical discourse, of ruptural points shattering the ultimate possibility of any smooth coalescence. As I suggested earlier, this second alternative undermines and exceeds the Hegelian text at several points.

The terrain of dialectical retrievals is that of an *immanence* without fissures. Any type of interruption in the chain of being is conceived as the phenomenal expression of a deeper reaffirmation of the chain as such. As I said, 'alienation' is the category through which this pseudo-negativity operates. In some sense, the root of the difficulties surrounding any immanentist conception is the problem of *korismos*, which Plato was confronted with in his attempt to explain the relationship between the world of ideas and the phenomenal and empirical reality. The Aristotelian distinction between form and matter does not supersede but reproduces this dilemma. Immanentism – the only terrain on which a dialectical logic can operate – represents the most radical attempt to colonize negativity, to lead it back to the *fundamentum inconcussum* of a determination in the last instance. Let us mention just a couple of examples. The transition from the moment of an absolute transcendence, conceived as complete in itself, and as a result self-sufficient, to an imperfect and limited world, already posed problems that were strictly insoluble. In neo-Platonism: Why would a self-sufficient One be the root of a less perfect world? Categories such as 'emanation' defer the problem without solving it. Or, in the Christian version: Why did God need to create a world?

But a more radical immanentism is confronted by deeper challenges. Let us consider one of the most serious obstacles to the idea of an uninterrupted chain of being: the question of evil. John Scotus Eriugena maintained that evil is a distorted representation elaborated by us, finite beings, but that, from the infinite perspective of the Divinity, evil is only the expression of one of the stages through which He has to pass in order to reach His absolute perfection. This means that evil is purely apparent. Once evil has been assimilated in this way to the world of being, of full representability, no negativity can enter the picture. The history of this process of assimilation/representation is well known.

A similar vision is to be found in Northern mysticism, in Nicholas of Cusa, in Spinoza, in Hegel, and in Marx. Its most mature expression is to be found in Hegel's cunning of Reason. From the viewpoint of a finite mind, History is an irrational process governed by violence, evil and irrationality. But from the viewpoint of Absolute Spirit this irrationality is the expression of a deeper rationality that realizes itself through the opacity of its phenomenal manifestations. And in Marx we find what is essentially the same argument. At the beginning of History, in primitive communism, we find a non-antagonistic society. History, however, is governed by a strictly immanent logic: it is a history of production. So, in order to develop the productive forces of humanity, it was necessary to pass through the whole hell of class-divided societies in order to reach, finally, in a fully developed communism, a reconciled society. As we can see, in all these formulations the strictly antagonistic moment is present, but only to be dissolved through its supersession/reabsorption in a higher positivity.

There is no lack of attempts, in contemporary thought, to apprehend the structural dimensions and the forms of operation of this ontological difference. Let us mention three of them. The first reference is, of course, to Heidegger, from whom the notion of 'ontological difference' proceeds.[8] The central category here is *Abgrund* – a ground that is, at the same time, an abyss. In the place of the ground there is an abyss; or, to be more precise, the abyss itself is the ground. To say that the abyss itself is the ground does not purely and simply mean the *absence* of a ground, which would be just an absence, but is rather to assert *the presence of an absence*. And this absence, being present, needs to be represented. A simple absence does not require any type of representation, but if the absence as such is present *within* the structure, it requires access to the field of representation. This representation, however, cannot be a direct one, because what is represented is an absence; so it can only be represented as *a process of de-grounding*. It is here that the ontological difference makes its appearance: the ontic content does not disappear, but it is distorted through this activity of *de-grounding*, if we are allowed the neologism, which is, at the same time, an investment. And this de-grounding operation is not merely negative, for it has a positive side: given that there is no ultimate ground, neither is there ultimate fixation of meaning; but because this moment of non-fixation has to be represented, it opens the way to partial fixations – that is, to fixations showing the traces of the contingency penetrating them. They are the only means of discursively showing the abyss present in place of the ground. In other words, the distortion – partial fixation – is the only means of

---

8   A clear analysis of the Heidehherian categories, in this respect, with an acute perception of their relevance for politics can be found in Oliver Marchart, *Post-Foundational Political Thought: Political Difference in Nancy, Lefort, Badiou and Laclau*, Edinburgh University Press, 2007.

representing that which is constitutively non-representable. This – in words of Marchart – is the location of the distinction between 'anti-foundationalism' and 'post-foundationalism'. 'Anti-foundationalism' would be the pure and simple absence of a ground, which could only be expressed through a proliferation of ontic identities. 'Post-foundationalism' means something different: the ground does not disappear, but is penetrated by a dimension of absence or contingency that renders impossible any reduction of the ontological to the ontic.

Something similar to what, in a different theoretical register, I have presented as the logic of empty signifiers happens with the Heideggerian *Abgrund*.[9] An empty signifier cannot simply be a signifier without a signified – that would turn it into mere noise, and would put it outside the field of signification. An empty signifier, to remain significative, must mean something: a gap that has emerged within signification, which, as a result, does not have a signification of its own, but which nevertheless has to be named, because it is the condition of any signifying process. For this very reason, this gap only shows itself as distortion of any structural moment – of any sutured space of differences. In structural language: it only makes itself visible through the subversion of the signifier–signified relationship; in the phenomenological language of Heidegger: through the impossibility of an overlap between the ontic and the ontological.

The second example is that of the Lacanian *objet a*. In this case we find an object which, although partial, assumes the role of the totality.[10] The Freudian Thing (*Das Ding*) is the object that sutures a totality but is, nevertheless, an impossible object – a retrospective illusion deprived, as a result, of access to a direct representation. So it is both an impossible and a necessary object. Its representation is thus only possible if a partial object, without ceasing to be partial, is invested with the role of representing that impossible totality. In the words of Lacan: sublimation consists in raising an object to the dignity of the Thing. We find here, again, the ontological difference. If sublimation was merely a change *of* object, we would be confronted with a simple displacement within the ontic terrain. But what we are confronted

9   Ernesto Laclau, 'Why do Empty Signifiers Matter to Politics?', in Laclau, *Emancipation(s)* (London: Verso, 1996).

10   Ernesto Laclau, *On Populist Reason* (London: Verso, 2005), pp. 142–57; and Joan Copjec, *Imagine There's No Woman: Ethics and Sublimation* (Cambridge, MA: MIT Press, 2002).

with is not a change *of* object but a change *in the* object. The ontological function of the *objet a* is to transcend its ontic particularity and become the incarnation of the Thing, of the impossible totality.

The third example is that of the 'hegemonic class' in Gramsci. What does Gramsci mean by it? To the 'hegemonic class' he opposes the 'corporative class', representing sectoral interests within a sutured totality. The hegemonic class, on the contrary, *universalizes* in some way its own objectives, which thus become those of much wider social forces. For the question we are addressing – the emergence of an irreducible ontological difference – what is decisive is the way in which this universalization operates. Classical Marxism had its own theory about the universalization of interests, which was the notion of the proletariat as 'universal class'. But there was no question of universalization in the strict sense of the term – rather, of a sector that had the universal, from the beginning, inscribed in its own being: the proletariat, having no particular interests to defend, liberated the ensemble of Humanity in the process of liberating itself. And the process leading to this ontological centrality of the proletariat was linked to its increasing ontic centrality: there was, presumably, an increasing simplification of the social structure under capitalism, leading to a disappearance of the middle classes and the peasantry, so that the last antagonistic confrontation of history would take place between the capitalist bourgeoisie and a homogeneous proletarian mass. As we can see, there is, in this vision, an exact overlap between the ontic and the ontological levels: the proletariat did not need to universalize anything given that it is, in and for itself, the universal. (In this way Hegel's universal class reappears within Marxism, which operates according to the same parameters. In the case of Hegel the universal class is not the proletariat but the bureaucracy – understood as the ensemble of the state apparatuses; but it is, in any case, a determinate instance not needing to construct its own universality, because it has it inscribed, from the very beginning, in its own being.) No investment is thus required.

This is the point at which we perceive the originality of the Gramscian intervention. For Gramsci, universality is not a datum but a contingent construction: it is *a process of hegemonic universalization*. To understand this notion, we should start from the terrain on which it was originally formulated, which was signed by the increasing complexity of the relationship between tasks and agents. The paradigmatic case was, of course, the Russian Revolution. The demo-cratic revolution against Tsarism should have been headed, according to the canonical conception of social-democracy, by the bourgeoisie – it would, in that case, have been a classical bourgeois-democratic revolution. But the Russian bourgeoisie was too weak to assume what would have been its 'normal' task, which therefore had to be taken up by a different force: the working class in alliance with the peasantry. And here a new problem emerges: Does the working class, in assum-ing the democratic tasks, not modify its class identity? And do the democratic tasks, through being assumed by an agent different from the bourgeoisie, not find that their nature is internally modified? This ambiguity of the link between tasks and agents was already pointing towards a different social logic – one that puts into question the very idea of a solid ground of history in which agents, tasks and stages were chained by a strict internal necessity. In the 1920s and 1930s this non-orthodox articulation of stages was raised to the status of a principle articulating the terrain in which political interventions took place: it is what was called combined and uneven development, which Trotsky was to postulate as the primary terrain of all revolutionary action.

It was Gramsci who would understand the conclusions to be derived from this new heterogeneity, not assimilable to the sequences of the classical paradigms: social heterogeneity requires a moment of radical and constitutive construction not depending on any aprioris-tic sequence. This is what he called 'hegemony'. Certain contents are *invested* with the function of representing the absent fullness of the community. This fullness is realized in what we have called 'empty signifiers' – which are also, as a result, hegemonic. But this ontological function of expressing the presence of an absence can only take place through an investment in an ontic content. Like the Heideggerian *Abgrund* and the Lacanian *objet a*, the hegemonic operation consists in a radical investment which, at the same time as it attempts to estab-lish a bridge between the ontic and the ontological, reproduces their impossible convergence.

If we wish to think in a comparative example that even more clearly shows the specificity of the Gramscian intervention, let us note what Lukács was writing in those years. He also perceived a moment of maladjustment between the project of a radical change in the exist-ing social order and the empirical materiality of the agents who could embody it. But while, in Gramsci, this non-adjustment was superseded in the direction of a radical constructivism – social agents are not 'classes' in the traditional sense but 'collective wills'; historical action depends on the discursive articulation of partial aims – in Lukács, everything is resolved into a question of 'alienation'. Proletarian consciousness, in the conditions of capitalist society, was a reified consciousness – 'false consciousness' – and the true proletarian consciousness appears embodied in an instance external to the materiality of the class – the Party. What in Gramsci was radical constructivism becomes, in Lukács, mere teleology.

PRELIMINARY CONCLUSIONS

The Heideggerian *Abgrund*, the Lacanian *objet a*, and the Gramscian 'hegemonic class' show a similar ontological structure. In all three cases we have the ontological investment in an ontic object, and in all three cases the contingent character of this investment shows itself through its radical putting-itself-into-question: there is no 'manifest destiny' requiring that the ontological investment take place in that particular object. It is in that sense that the moment of the investment is constitutive: it cannot be explained by any underlying logic different from itself. It is for that reason that the abyss is also ground.

Thus, antagonism has a revelatory function. On the one hand, the moment of identitary institution transforms an ontic object into symbol of my possibility of *being*; but, on the other, the presence of the antagonistic force shows the contingent character of that identitary investment. Paradoxically, the internal structuration of the investment shows itself through that which interrupts and limits it. This interruption is decisive, and it is what makes the antagonistic relation non-assimilable to the other two logics that have tried to apprehend it – real opposition and dialectical contradiction – which, as we have seen, are entirely identitary logics that have no need to abandon a unified level of representation.

It is here that we can see all of the theoretical productivity of the old Husserlian distinction between *sedimentation* and *reactivation* – although giving to it a turn of which, no doubt, Husserl would not have approved. Sedimentation would be the strictly ontic moment of objects, when the contingent instance of their originary institution has been entirely concealed; reactivation would be the moment of return to that originary instance, to that contingent institution (not, as in Husserl, to a transcendental subject who would be a source of meaning). This means that the instituting act only shows itself in full through that which puts it into question. But this act of contingent institution, taking place in a field criss-crossed by the presence of antagonistic forces, is exactly what we understand by the *political* (in the ontological sense of the term, which has little to do with political organizations and structures, in their narrow meaning, which can perfectly well correspond to entirely sedimented practices). But, in that case, the field of a political ontology would also be the field of a general ontology.

There is a second aspect of this ontology that should be stressed. The three examples I have mentioned show a common feature: what is invested in an ontic particularity is a necessary dimension, but also an impossible one – an object lacking any direct form of representation. Investment consists precisely in transforming the ontic dimensions of the object in the expression or representation of something different from the object – that is, in an absent fullness. This means that that *representation will always be figural or rhetorical*. Rhetorical figures are thus endowed with an ontological value. Cicero asserted that we are forced to use rhetorical figures because there are more objects in the world to be named that the words our language provides. For him this was, of course, an empirical limitation, but we know that what is at stake is something more fundamental: a constitutive impasse in the process of signification by which something radically incapable of being signified is nevertheless the condition to trigger the signifying process. Starting from here, this process can only consist in an infinite series of figural successions that finds no point of anchorage in any ultimate literality. And a central place in this rhetorical ordering is occupied by *catachresis* – that is, by *figural* terms that cannot be substituted by *literal* ones. This means that the representation of the presence of an absence which, as we have seen, is a requirement for the apprehension of social antagonisms, will be essentially catachrestical.

Let us return, in conclusion, to the initial assertion of the *Communist Manifesto* with which I opened this chapter, according to which human history should be understood as class struggle. This assertion, we can now say, is essentially ambiguous. On the one hand, it asserts the ontological centrality of struggle, of antagonism. Our whole analysis leads us to subscribe to it. But – and here comes the second thesis of Marx and Engels – what is for them in question is not just any antagonism, but a very precise one: the antagonism of classes. And this second assertion is impossible without changing the onto-logical perspective on which the first was based. For, while the assertion of the primary ontological character of antagonism breaks with the overlap between the ontic and the ontological and gives way to a plurality of contingent investments not predetermining the nature of the social agents resulting from them – the 'collective wills' of Gramsci – and, especially, not allowing a unification of all struggles in global entities such as the 'history of Humanity', the aprioristic asser-tion that those agents are, necessarily, 'social classes' can only be made from a teleological–objectivist perspective.

Let us be clear about the meaning of what I am asserting: I am not arguing that the latter is the only perspective present in Marxist discourse, but rather that this discourse is ambiguous, and that we can find in it discursive sequences allowing us to advance in different directions. If this was not the case, a discourse such as Gramsci's, which clearly breaks with the objectivist overlapping between the ontic and the ontological, could not have emerged from the historical matrix of Marxism. But, although the ambiguity cannot be denied, there is no doubt that, historically, the objectivist route is the prevail-ing one within the Marxist tradition. And this is not because of mere economistic deviations in the discourse of the Second International, for this orientation was already formulated unambiguously by Marx. Let us think only of the 'Preface' to the *Critique of Political Economy*, where it is openly asserted that the movement of history can be detected with the precision of a natural process, while the way in which men live their conflicts is relegated to a merely epiphenomenal role. Strictly speaking, the option here is not between an 'infrastruc-turalist economism' and a vision asserting a more autonomous role for the superstructure. This was attempted by Lukács, but if the advent of the 'class for itself' is only the culmination of a process strictly dominated by objective historical necessity, one has not advanced a single step in the rupture with fundamentalist objectivism. For this rupture to take place, something else is needed: that the abyss come to inhabit the terrain of the ground, and that contingent investments become the very logic of hegemonic articulations. Detecting in the texts coming from the socialist tradition those points in which the two routes were possible, and the discursive operations through which one or the other was chosen, represents a project of reading that might illuminate many decisive kernels of emancipatory struggle. This represents something similar to what, according to Derrida, happens with the ethico-theoretical decisions structuring Husserl's discourse. Husserl had made possible a fundamental advance in breaking the link uniting meaning and knowledge: it is possible that an expression or concept has meaning even when it does not give us the intuition of any object. But, a moment later, he closes the door that he has opened: even if I am still speaking when my sense does not give access to any intuition, I am only speaking well when an intuition follows sense. But, as Derrida points out, this sequence sense–knowledge does not follow from the internal logic of Husserlian reasoning: it is the result of an interruption of the text by an ethico-theoretical decision external to it. Other decisions were possible at this point – Joyce, for instance, took a route opposite to Husserl's. I hope that the reader of this chapter will have no doubt that we are following the route of Joyce, not of Husserl – especially if we replace 'ethico-theoretical' with 'ethico-political', and Joyce with Gramsci.

CHAPTER 6

Ethics, Normativity and the Heteronomy of the Law

The question I will address in this chapter could be formulated in the following terms: What is the relationship between the ethical (a term that I will try to define below) and the plurality of actually existing normative orders? Can the latter be derived consistently from the former? And, if not, what kind of link might be established between the two? The answer to these questions is highly relevant to a further type of interrogation concerning the grounding of law: if the relationship between the ethical and the normative order were a transparent one, so that the grasping of the nature of the first would give us all we needed to choose between the various alternatives at the level of the second, there would be an exact overlap between ethical subjects and subject positions within the normative order of the law. This transparency would, in that sense, be compatible with an autonomy conceived as self-determination. If, on the contrary, the transition between ethics and the normative order presupposes less than a strict overlap between the two, the institution of law would require a grounding at least partially different from an ethical one; a dimension of heteronomy would necessarily inhabit the legal order, and a gap would consequently emerge between the ethical and the normative subject.

But there is a previous distinction concerning the normative that needs to be deconstructed before we begin our exploration: the one grounding the opposition between the normative and the descriptive, between *being* and *ought*. The classical distinction between fact and norm comes from Kant's attempt to draw a strict separation between theoretical and practical reason. We do not find any such stark division in the previous philosophical tradition. The distinction cannot be strictly maintained, because there are no facts that are not grounded in the elaboration of our practical relationship with the world. If I try to move to a door at the end of the room, the table opposite me is an obstacle; but if I try to protect myself from an attack, it can become a means of defence. It is only in practical life – in a life governed by

norms – that the facts *as facts* can emerge. Even a purely contempla-
tive attitude sees what it sees because it relies on systems of signification
that are nothing other than the sedimentation of previous practical
experiences. There are no facts without signification, and there is no
signification without practical engagements that require norms
governing our behaviour. So there are not two orders – the normative
and the descriptive – but normative/descriptive complexes in which
facts and values interpenetrate each other in an inextricable way.
What we usually call morality belongs to those complexes.

But if morality belongs to those complexes, what I want to suggest
is that the ethical does not. We have to proceed here to a second
deconstruction, of an opposite sign to the first one. In the case of the
descriptive/normative distinction, we had to demonstrate the mutual
contamination of two dimensions that are usually presented as separated. Our second deconstruction has to show the distance between
two types of social experience that are usually presented as necessarily
linked with each other. What is inherent in an ethical experience? It
is, at first, difficult to answer the question, because our first reaction is
to look for a norm more fundamental than the plurality of norms to
be found in the various codes of morality. But this type of answer
cannot escape the *petitio principii* that inhabits it: that of a ground that
is not itself grounded, of a beginning by irrational *fiat*, by a *fact* at the
root of a normative order that is supposed to be essentially different
from the factual one. There is no way of finding the experience constitutive of the ethical if we try to locate it within the positivity of the
normative order.

How to go beyond this blind alley? If the *positive* character of the
norm is the source of our difficulties in grasping the specificity of the
ethical experience, perhaps the way to proceed is to go beyond that
positivity, to detect the points at which it fails to constitute itself. Let
us concentrate for a moment on the opposition between 'being' and
'ought to be'. If my previous assertion that the normative/descriptive
complexes contaminate and subvert the distinctiveness of their two
intervening terms stands, then we cannot refer 'ought' to the normative order and 'being' to the descriptive – that would simply reproduce
the distinction that we are putting into question. There is no advance
in opposing the fact of actual behaviour to the fact of the norm. There
is, however, something that remains if we put aside these two positivities – namely, the distance between the two. How to conceive of this

distance? It is important to realize that it can only be approached if content (positivity) is resolutely ignored. The distance between two positivities can only be conceived as *difference*, and, all identity being differential, the identity of one side of the opposition would become the prerequisite of the identity of the other. In that case, distance and proximity would be strictly synonymous. But there is another way of approaching the matter. It is not the *content* of the ought which is opposed to the content of actual behaviour, but the fact that the ought expresses a fullness that actual behaviour lacks. The ought expresses fullness of being, while actual behaviour shows *deficient* being. We are not far away from characterizing actual behaviour in terms of contingency and finitude. It is this distance between full and deficient being that is, in my view, at the root of the ethical experience.

But this still leaves us with the problem of the relation between the fullness of the ought and its own content. For if the experience of the fullness as an ethical command were necessarily attached to a particular content, we would still be prisoners of the positivity of the norm and would have made little progress in our argument. But let us consider the experience of the distance between being and ought in more detail. If the distance between being and ought is not the differential content between two positivities but the one between deficiency and fullness of being, then there is a *lack* in actual being that is the source of the distance. But, in such a case, the content of the ought appears as essentially split: it is on the one hand a particular normative content while, on the other, this content functions as the representative or incarnation of the absent fullness. It is not the particularity of the content that is, per se, ethical, but that content in so far as it assumes the representation of a fullness that is incommensurable with it. This is why the ethical experience tends to express itself through terms such as 'truth', 'justice', 'duty', and so on – nobody will deny their ethical character, but their actual realization can be referred to the most diverse normative contents. I will discuss presently the meaning of such a description. But what we have to emphasize from the start is that, if ethical experience is the experience of the unconditioned in a fully conditioned universe, it has to be necessarily empty and devoid of all normative content.

Let us address some examples of what I have in mind in making this distinction. The mystical experience is the experience of the absolutely transcendent. God, being absolutely ineffable, can be approached only by an experience that is beyond any worldly determination, which can only be expressed along the lines of a negative theology. Being God, the locus of a fullness incommensurable with any determination of the *ens creatum*, it has also to be, by necessity, absolutely empty – fullness and emptiness in fact become synonymous. It is important to stress that this emptiness, this absence of any concrete content, has nothing to do with any formalism. A formal determination is still a determination, and as such has a content. Kant's ethical formalism, for instance, is grounded in the normative content of the categorical imperative. Moreover, abstraction and generality are inherent to any formalism, while the mystical experience is absolutely individual and concrete. The emptiness with which we are dealing is not simply the absence of content, but is itself a content – it is a fullness that *shows* itself through its very absence. Now, the important point is that the mystical experience leads those who have passed through it not to live the recluse life of an anchorite, but to engage themselves in the world in a more militant way, and with an ethical density that other people lack. Eckhart compares the mystic to somebody who is in love: he will continue to immerse himself in daily activity, but the feeling of being in love will accompany all his actions. It is, paradoxically, the withdrawal of the mystic from the world that is the source of the ethical seriousness of his engagement in it.

Something similar could be said of the revolutionary militant. If I participate in a strike, in a factory occupation, in a demonstration, just for the concrete objectives of these actions – a rise in wages, a change of the system of authority in the factory, the demand for some budgetary reform, and so on – my militant engagement comes to an end once these objectives have been achieved. If, on the contrary, my participation in all these activities is conceived as episodes in a more universal struggle for revolutionary aims, my identification with the particular aims of those activities will be less complete but, paradoxically, for that reason, my militant engagement in them will be more intense. The revolutionary objective operates as a transcendent 'beyond' of all particular experience and is, in that sense, the point of identification allowing me to withdraw from the particularism of all concrete experience. This withdrawal, however, is only the prelude to the militant engagement in those very particularistic struggles, which cease to be merely particularistic as soon as they are seen as episodes in the prosecution of more universalistic aims.

Let us take the motto of the 'general strike' in revolutionary syndicalism. All particular actions of the working class are seen as steps towards that ultimate event that is the general strike. Thus, the particular actions are not exhausted in their particularism: all of them are equivalent as far as the *Endziel*, the final objective, is concerned. The final objective splits the aims of the particular struggles and demands: their particularism is simply the bearer of a universalistic aim traversing all of them. It is in this dialectic of withdrawal/engagement that the distinctive feature of an ethical life lies. The experience of the ethical is the experience of that moment of transcendence that takes us beyond any particular aim, norm or action. What, in the mystical experience, we see in an extreme form is in fact something belonging to the structure of all experience.

Before moving to our next problem, which is the relationship between the ethical and the normative, I have to say something more about the nature of the former. It is crucially important to stress that the equation fullness = emptiness, which we have found to be inherent to the mystical experience, is not exclusive to the latter, but is the trademark of the ethical as such. Let us return for a moment to the example of the general strike. What is the general strike? According to Sorel, it is not an actual event but a social myth. Social myths, for him, do not have all the precise details of a blueprint of society, such as a utopia, but are restricted to a few simple images capable of galvanizing the imagination of the masses. What is the source of this simplification? The answer is to be found in the fact that a myth such as that of the general strike is no actual event, but the name of a fullness that is merely the positive reverse of a situation experienced in which such fullness is denied. It is because we live a situation as unjust that we have the experience of 'justice' as an actual fullness; but there is no logical transition from injustice-as-lack to justice-as-fullness that would remedy such a deprivation. Many concrete contents can present themselves as the positivization of 'justice'. In the example that I have been using, 'general strike' is not the description of an actual event: its meaning is exhausted in symbolizing – naming – the series of particular struggles and demands that thereby acquire their ethical dimension. It is through this equivalential function that the symbol weakens its particularistic meaning and develops the emptiness (= fullness) that transforms it into the name of the ethical experience.

We have now all the necessary elements to address the question of the relationship between the ethical and the normative order (the second deconstructive move that I alluded to at the beginning of this chapter). There is here a clear alternative: either we can *deduce* from the emptiness of the ethical moment a normative content that would necessarily correspond to it, or – given the emptiness inherent in the ethical experience – such a deduction is impossible and, in that case, the transition from the ethical to the normative can only take place through something that can only be described as a *radical investment* of the ethical into the normative. Needless to say, the latter is the path that I am prepared to take. If the ethical experience is really the experience of the unconditioned in an entirely conditioned world, of a fullness – as the ground of the ought – that is beyond all determination, there is no way of moving in a straight line from that experience to a norm or injunction. It is only if the latter becomes the symbol of something essentially heterogeneous to itself that a relation between the ethical and the normative can be established at all. This confronts us, however, with a set of theoretical difficulties that we have to address if the nature of this relation is really going to be brought to light.

A first dimension of the relation can be grasped by answering a possible objection. The objection is the following: If the ethical can only exist invested in the normative, how can we really distinguish between the two? Would it not be simpler to speak about ethico-normative complexes in which the distinction between the two sides would become purely analytical? The answer to this objection can be given at two levels: first, by pointing out that the investment of the ethical into the normative does not simply consist in a confluence of the two orders, but also in a structural mutation that the former introduces into the latter. I have already mentioned what this structural mutation consists of: the establishment of an equivalential chain between the components of the normative order and the isolation of a set of key terms as signifiers of the emptiness (= fullness = ethical). In that sense, it is not true that a normative structure is indifferent to the presence or absence of ethical investment, or that the latter is not altered at all by the former. The ethical/normative duality is shown in the distinction, within a discourse, between those elements that the ethical investment 'universalizes' through an equivalential relation, and those that function as grounds of such universalization – in other words, as names of the ethical. In my previous example, 'general strike' would be a name of the ethical, while the aims of the particular struggles are components of an ethically invested normative order, as far as an equivalential relation can be established between them. The second answer to the objection mentioned above is that the quality of the ethical life existing in a given society is far from indifferent either to the distinction between the ethical and the normative or to their differential positivization in the discursive field. If the ethical were *entirely* absorbed into the normative, there would not be distinction between – for instance – justice and what a certain society considers as just at some point in time. This is the best prescription for totalitarianism. It is only if justice functions as an empty term, whose links with particular signifieds are precarious and contingent, that something such as a democratic society becomes possible. There is no democracy without an equation between fullness and emptiness. That is why the reduction of politics to the *contents* of a certain normative order and the identification of the ethical with the normative are inimical to democracy – and why the distinction of the ethical and the normative frees both the ethical and the political from their totalitarian fixation to any aprioristic and all-embracing normativity. I have sometimes been confronted with the objection that conceiving of the ethical as empty leaves social normativity without a ground. My answer is that it is precisely that absence of ground and the possibility of signifying the resulting emptiness that makes life in society worth living.

But another version of the same objection is frequently presented in the following terms: If there is no logical transition between the ethical and a certain normative order, if the presence of the ethical in the normative is the result of a radical investment, why prefer one normative order rather than other? Do we not end up in that case with a normative deficit? Are we not risking the worst consequences of a pure decisionism? Let us consider the matter carefully. A pure decisionism would involve the existence of an omnipotent subject. Only somebody who is not subjected to any limitation could choose without any restriction – except that, as the existentialists would have it, such an omnipotent chooser does not have any reason for his choice. But, most importantly, such a chooser is a pure fiction. We are always *already* within a certain normative order, and all we can do is to displace through our decisions the areas of that order that are going to be the object of the ethical investment. I have written elsewhere that the subject is the distance between the undecidability of the structure and the decision. This means that an omnipotent chooser would also be an absolute subject – and, conversely, a chooser who is less than omnipotent would also be less than a subject. We live in a world of sedimented social practices that limit the range of what is thinkable and decidable.

This sedimentation of social practices is an *existential* in the Heideggerian sense: it is constitutive of all possible experience. So, to the questions, Why prefer a certain normative order to others? Why invest ethically in certain practices rather than in different ones? the answer can only be a contextual one: Because I live in a world in which people believe in A, B and C, I can argue that the course of action D is better than E; but in a totally presuppositionless situation in which no system of beliefs exists, the question is obviously unanswerable. In the case of the mystic, as we have seen, the contact with divinity as an absolute beyond all positive determination is followed by a normative investment that is the source of a militant engagement; but it is clear that the particular normative order that is the object of such an invest-ment is not dictated by the content of the mystical experience – which has no content – but by the positive system of religious beliefs – the sedimented practices – within which the mystic lives. Many times I have been asked if there is not a normative deficit in the theory of hegemony that I have elaborated with Chantal Mouffe in *Hegemony and Socialist Strategy* – the argument being that the theorization of hegemony is an objective, neutral description of what is going on in the world, while the book also makes a normative choice (radical democracy) that does not necessarily follow from such theorization. My answer is twofold: first, as I argued above, there is no such thing as a neutral factual description: the system of supposedly descriptive categories that we have used corresponds to 'facts' that are only such for somebody who is living within the socialist tradition and has experienced the set of defeats, social transformation and renaissance of hopes to which we allude; second, within that normative/descrip-tive complex it makes perfect sense to advocate the normative displacement involved in the notion of 'radical democracy'. The latter is the result of a pluralization of social struggles anchored in the new structures of contemporary capitalism. These displacements are both factual and normative, but it is clear that, on both counts, the story that we are telling only makes sense to particular interlocutors who have been part of a certain history, not to an unencumbered spectator.

To ask for an absolute grounding of a system of norms would be tantamount to requiring, first, a radical separation between fact and value, and, second, legislation for humanity in general, independently of all communitarian frameworks.

Once we have characterized the relation between the ethical and the normative in terms of radical investment, we still have to address two closely related questions: What is the structure of a radical investment? And what determines the terrain of the investment? Our answer that such a terrain is determined by the ensemble of the sedimented social practices is clearly insufficient. Even if the ethical investment does not operate in a vacuum – it is not the source of the norm – it changes the norm to some extent, and it is possible at all because of the constitutive dislocations of the normative order. Let us give a couple of examples. A set of social dislocations generates a series of situations that people live as unjust. Between them a relation of equivalence is established in the way I described above, and as a result a widespread sense of injustice starts to prevail in that society. As we have seen, justice – as one of the names of social fullness – does not have a content of its own, and needs to borrow it from some of the normative proposals that present themselves as incarnations of justice. Let us suppose that a content such as 'socialization of the means of production' begins to play such a role. In order to do so, and to become the signifier of social fullness (an absent fullness, as we have seen), it has to be absolutely empty, and this is only achieved because of the plethora of signifieds resulting from the operation of the equivalential chain. 'Socialization of the means of production' not only signifies what it directly designates, but also the end of all injustices present in society: the unfair distribution of income, the unevenness of access to the means of consumption, unequal opportunities of access to employment, all kinds of social discrimination, and so on. It is in this way that 'socialization of the means of production' becomes the signifier of the lack (= fullness). This is the moment of the ethical investment in the normative. A certain *order* fulfils the *ordering* function. Because the ordering function fills a lack that is not associated with any actual content, this duality between order and ordering, between the ontic and the ontological, can only reproduce itself *sine die*.

Why is it that one order rather than another fulfils the ordering function? A first answer is *availability*. It is the order that presents itself as fulfilling the ordering function that will be the object of the ethical investment. This is possible because the gap between order and ordering can never be ultimately filled. In a situation of generalized disorder, people need *some* order, and the concrete order that fulfils this ordering function is only a secondary consideration. It is for this reason that the order best located to fulfil the ordering function will be the object of the ethical investment. This cannot, however, be the whole answer, for, as we have seen, there is in all society a normative order governing institutional arrangements, contacts between groups, circulation of goods, and so on. This is what we have called the 'realm of the sedimented social practices'. It is clear that, although many aspects of it can be threatened by antagonisms and dislocations, many social practices subsist that are not affected by these traumatic events. Even in periods of deep social dissolution – what Gramsci called 'organic crisis' – vast areas of society remain unshaken. Thus, if a certain normative proposal clashes with central aspects of social organization that are not put into question, it will not be recognized as an order able to fulfil the ordering function, and will not be the object of a hegemonic ethical investment. This constant renegotiation of the relationship between the ethical and the normative in fact constitutes the very fabric of social life.

There is one last point to address. I have said that the relation between the ethical and the normative is one of investment (for there is nothing that could be called an ethical normativity), and that this investment is radical (for there is no way of logically moving from ethical experience to norm). In that case, however, there is a heteronomy of the law that is inherent to social life. For Hegel, for instance, true infinitude, self-determination and freedom were synonymous. If, in passing into the other, I only pass into myself, I am entirely self-determined, and the distinction between freedom and necessity collapses. This means that there is going to be a full transparency of the social order to the subject ('the truth of the individual is the state'), and that the gap between 'order' and 'ordering' will ultimately be closed. But if that gap is, as I have asserted, permanent, then there is a heteronomous dimension of social life that cannot be eliminated. This does not mean that the category of autonomy (as self-determination) becomes obsolete, but it *does* mean that autonomy and heteronomy are in a more complex relation than it is usually supposed. If the gap between order and ordering could be rationally closed because there was an order that is (as in Plato) the good society, then order and ordering would exactly overlap, and there would be no need for any ethical radical investment. The world of ethics would simply be the world of specifiable social norms. But there is no possibility of such a rational closure – not because one advocates any irrationality, but because the gap that we have detected is inherent to rationality itself. In that case there is no order that can claim a monopoly of the ordering function, emptiness is at the heart of the structure, and the distinction between the ethical and the normative, and with it the notion of investment, becomes crucial. There is an extent to which one reveres the law because it is law, and not because it is rational. But this opacity of the law, and the necessary heteronomy that it involves, is perhaps at the origin of another type of freedom – one that no longer conceives itself as unchallenged self-determination. For the subject that is free because it is entirely autonomous can only be a universal subject for whom there is no constitutive exterior, while the subject emerging from the undecidable game between autonomy and heteronomy is one inhabiting a more humble but more human environment – one for whom there is no universality but universalization, no identity but identification, no rationality but partial rationalization of a collective experience.

CHAPTER 7

Why Constructing a 'People' Is the Main Task of Radical Politics[*]

I have been rather surprised by Slavoj Žižek's critique[1] of my book *On Populist Reason*.[2] Given that the book includes a strong critical reference to Žižek's approach, I was of course expecting some reaction on his part. He has chosen for his reply, however, a rather indirect and oblique road: he does not answer a single one of my criticisms of his work, but instead formulates a series of objections to my book that only make sense if one fully accepts his theoretical perspective – which is precisely what I had questioned. To avoid continuing with this dialogue of the deaf, I will take the bull by the horns, reasserting what I see as fundamentally wrong in Žižek's approach; in the course of this argument, I will also refute his criticisms.

POPULISM AND CLASS STRUGGLE

I will leave aside the sections of Žižek's essay dealing with the French and Dutch referenda – a matter on which my own views are not far from his[3] – and concentrate instead on the theoretical parts, where he states our divergences. Žižek starts by saying that I 'prefer' populism to class struggle.[4] This is a rather nonsensical way of presenting the argument. It suggests that 'populism' and 'class struggle' are two entities actually existing in the world, between which one would have to choose, such as when one chooses to belong to a political party or to a football club. The reality is that my notion of the 'people' and the

---

[*] I want to thank the editors of *Critical Inquiry* for having invited me to answer Slavoj Žižek's criticisms of my work.

1 Slavoj Žižek, 'Against the Populist Temptation', *Critical Inquiry* 32 (Spring 2006).

2 Ernesto Laclau, *On Populist Reason* (London: Verso, 2005).

3 Except, of course, when he identifies the particular feature of the 'No' campaigns with defining characteristics of all possible populism.

4 Žižek, 'Against the Populist Temptation', p. 4.

classical Marxist conception of 'class struggle' are two different ways of conceiving the construction of social identities, so that if one is correct the other has to be dismissed – or, rather, reabsorbed and redefined in terms of the alternative view. But Žižek gives an accurate description of the points where the two outlooks differ:

> 'class struggle' presupposes a particular social group (the working class) as a privileged political agent; this privilege is not itself the outcome of hegemonic struggle, but is grounded in the objective social position of this group: the ideologico-political struggle is thus ultimately reduced to an epiphenomenon of 'objective' social processes, powers and their conflicts. For Laclau, on the contrary, the fact that some particular struggle is elevated into the 'universal equivalent' of all struggles is not a pre-determined fact, but itself the result of the contingent political struggle for hegemony – in one constellation, this struggle can be the workers' struggle, in another constellation, the patriotic anti-colonialist struggle, in yet another constellation, the anti-racist struggle for social tolerance . . . *there is nothing in the inherent positive qualities of some particular struggle that predetermines it for such a hegemonic role* of the 'general equivalent' of all struggles.[5]

Although this description of the contrast is obviously incomplete, I do not object to the general picture of the basic distinction between the two approaches that it provides. In addition, however, Žižek proposes a further feature of populism that I have supposedly not taken into account: while I have rightly pointed out the empty character of the Master-Signifier embodying the enemy, I have not mentioned the pseudo-concreteness of the figure incarnating such an enemy. I must say that I do not find any substance in this charge: my whole analysis is precisely based in asserting that any politico-discursive field is always structured through a reciprocal process by which 'emptiness' weakens the particularity of a concrete signifier – but, conversely, that particularity reacts, giving to universality a necessary incarnating body. I have defined hegemony as a relationship by which a certain particularity becomes the name of an utterly incommensurable universality. So the universal, lacking any means of direct

---

5   Ibid. My emphasis.

representation, obtains only a borrowed presence through the distorted means of its investment in a certain particularity.

But let us leave this issue aside for the time being, for Žižek has a far more fundamental addition to propose to my theoretical notion of populism. According to him, 'a thing to be added is the way the populist discourse displaces the antagonism and constructs the enemy: in populism, the enemy is externalised/reified into a positive ontological entity (even if this entity is spectral), whose annihilation would restore balance and justice; symmetrically, our own – the populist political agent's – identity is also perceived as pre-existing the enemy's onslaught'.[6] Of course, I never said that populist identity pre-exists the enemy's onslaught, but exactly the opposite: that such an 'onslaught' is the precondition of any popular identity. To describe the relation I had in mind, I have even quoted Saint-Just as saying that the unity of the Republic is only the destruction of what is opposed to it. But let us see how Žižek's argument unfolds. He asserts that reifying antagonism into a positive entity involves an elementary form of ideological mystification, and that although populism can move in a variety of political directions (reactionary, nationalist, progressive nationalist, and so on), 'insofar as, in its very notion, it displaces the immanent social antagonism into the antagonism between the unified "people" and its external enemy, it harbors "in the last instance" a long-term proto-Fascist tendency'.[7] To this he adds his reasons for thinking that Communist movements can never be populist: that while in Fascism all idea is subordinated to the will of the leader, in Communism Stalin is a *secondary* leader – in the Freudian sense – because he is subordinated to the Idea. A beautiful compliment to Stalin! As everybody knows, he *was not* subordinated to *any* ideology, but manipulated ideology in the most grotesque way to make it serve his pragmatic political agenda – for example, the principle of national self-determination had pride of place in the Stalinist ideological universe; there was, however, the proviso that it had to be applied 'dialectically', which meant that it could be violated as many times as was considered politically convenient. Stalin was not a particularity subsumable under a conceptual universality; it was rather conceptual universality that was subsumed under the name 'Stalin'. From this point of view, Hitler was

6 Ibid., p. 5.
7 Ibid., p. 7.

not lacking in political 'ideas' either – the 'Fatherland', the 'race', and so on – which he equally manipulated for reasons of political expediency. With this, of course, I am not saying that the Nazi and Stalinist regimes were indistinguishable, but instead that, whatever differences one can find between them, they are not grounded in a different ontological relationship between the 'Leader' and the 'Idea'.[8] (As for the actual relationship between populism and communism, I will come back to that presently.)

But let us return to the logical steps through which Žižek's analysis is structured – to how he conceives of his 'supplement' to my theoretical construct. His argument is hardly anything more than a succession of non sequitur conclusions. The sequence is as follows: first, he quotes a passage from my book in which, referring to the way popular identities were constituted in British Chartism, I show that the evils of society were not presented as deriving from the economic system, but from the abuse of power by parasitic and speculative groups;[9] second, he finds that something similar happens in fascist discourse, where the figure of the Jew becomes the concrete incarnation of everything that is wrong with society (this concretization is presented by him as an operation of reification); third, he concludes that this shows that in all populism (why? how?) there is 'a long-term proto-fascist tendency'; fourth, communism, however, is supposedly immune to populism because, in its discourse, 'reification' does not

---

8 A cheap trick to be found at several points in Žižek's work consists in identifying the assertion by some authors of a certain degree of comparability between features of the Nazi and the Stalinist regimes, with the impossibility of distinguishing between them postulated by conservative authors such as Nolte. The relationship between a political leader and his 'ideology' is in fact a very complicated business, involving multiple nuances. There is never a situation in which the leader would be *totally* exterior to his ideology, having a purely instrumental relation to it. Many strategic mistakes made by Hitler in the course of the war, especially during the Russian campaign, can only be explained by the fact that he actually identified with basic tenets of his own ideological discourse – that he was, in that sense, a 'secondary' leader in relation to it. But if it is wrong to make of the manipulative relation between leader and ideology the essence of some kind of undifferentiated 'totalitarian' regime, it is equally wrong to assert, as Žižek does, a mechanical differentiation between a (communist) regime in which the leader would be purely secondary and a (fascist) regime in which he would have an unrestricted primacy.

9 In the passage quoted by Žižek I am simply summarizing, approvingly, the analysis of Chartism in Gareth Stedman Jones, *Languages of Class: Studies in Working Class History 1832–1902* (Cambridge: CUP, 1983).

take place, and the leader safely remains as a secondary one. It is not difficult to perceive the fallacy of this whole argument: first, Chartism and fascism are presented as two species of the genus 'populism'; second, one of the species' (fascism's) *modi operandi* is conceived as 'reification'; third, for no stated reasons (at this point the Chartist example is silently forgotten), that makes *modi operandi* of the species become the defining feature of the whole genus; fourth, as a result, one of the species becomes the teleological destiny of all the other species belonging to that genus. To this we should add, as a further unwarranted conclusion, that if 'communism' cannot be a species of the genus 'populism', it is *presumably* (the point is nowhere explicitly made) because reification does not take place in it. In the case of communism we have an unmediated universality – this would be the reason why that supreme incarnation of the concrete, the leader, has to be entirely subordinated to the Idea. Needless to say, this last conclusion is not grounded on any historical evidence, but on a purely aprioristic argument.

More important, however, than insisting on the obvious circularity of Žižek's whole reasoning, is to explore the two unargued assumptions on which it is based. They are as follows: first, any incarnation of the universal in the particular should be conceived as 'reification'; second, such an incarnation is inherently 'fascistic'. To these postulates we will oppose two theses: first, that the notion of 'reification' is entirely inadequate to understand the kind of incarnation of the universal in the particular that is inherent in the construction of a popular identity; and, second, that such an incarnation – rightly understood – far from being a characteristic of fascism or of any other political movement, is inherent to any kind of hegemonic relation – in other words, to the kind of relation inherent to the political as such.

Let us start with reification. This is not a common language term but has a very specific philosophical content. It was first introduced by Lukács, although most of its dimensions were already operating *avant la lettre* in several of Marx's texts – especially in the section of *Capital* concerning commodity fetishism. The omnipotence of exchange-value in capitalist society renders impossible access to the viewpoint of totality; relations between men take an objective character and, while individuals are be turned into things, things appear as the true social agents. Now, if we take a careful look at the

structure of reification, one salient feature becomes visible immediately: it essentially consists in an operation of *inversion*. What is
derivative appears as originary; what is only apparent is presented as
essential. The inversion of the subject–predicate relationship is the
kernel of any reification. It is, in that sense, a process of ideological
mystification through and through, and its subjective correlate is the
notion of 'false consciousness'. The categorical ensemble reification–
false consciousness only makes sense, however, if the ideological
distortion can be reversed; if it was constitutive of consciousness, we
could not speak of distortion. This is the reason why Žižek, in order
to stick to his dinosaurian notion of false consciousness, has to
conceive social antagonisms as grounded in some kind of immanent
mechanism that has to conceive the consciousness of social agents as
merely derivative – or, rather, a mechanism in which the latter, if it is
admitted at all, is seen as a transparent expression of the former. The
universal speaks in a direct way, without needing any mediating role
from the concrete. In his words, populism 'displaces the immanent
social antagonism in to the antagonism between the unified "people"
and its external enemy'. That is, the discursive construction of the
enemy is presented as an operation of distortion. And indeed, if the
universal inhabiting antagonism had the possibility of an unmediated expression, the mediation through the concrete could only be
conceived as reification.

Unfortunately for Žižek, the kind of articulation between the
universal and the particular that my approach to the question of
popular identities presupposes is radically incompatible with notions
such as 'reification' and 'ideological distortion'. We are not dealing
with a false consciousness opposed to a true one – which would be
waiting for us as a teleologically programmed destiny – but with the
contingent construction of a consciousness *tout court*. So, what Žižek
presents as his 'supplement' to my approach is not a supplement at all,
but the questioning of its basic premises. These premises result from
an understanding of the relation between the universal and the
particular, the abstract and the concrete, which I have discussed in my
work from three perspectives – psychoanalytical, linguistic and political – and which I want briefly to summarize here, to show its
incompatibility with Žižek's crude 'false consciousness' model.

Let us start with psychoanalysis. I attempted to show in *On
Populist Reason* how the logic of hegemony and that of the Lacanian

objet a largely overlap, and refer to a fundamental ontological relation in which 'fullness' can only be touched through a radical investment in a partial object – which is not a partiality *within* the totality but a partiality which *is* the totality. On this point my work has drawn a great deal from the analysis of Joan Copjec, who has made a serious exploration of the logical implications of Lacanian categories, without distorting them *à la* Žižek with superficial Hegelian analogies. The most relevant point for our subject is that fullness – the Freudian Thing – is unachievable; it is only a retrospective illusion that is substituted by partial objects embodying that impossible totality. In Lacan's terms, sublimation consists in elevating an object to the dignity of the Thing. As I have tried to show, the hegemonic relation reproduces all these structural moments: a certain particularity assumes the representation of an always-receding universality. As we can see, the reification/distortion/false consciousness model is radically incompatible with the hegemony/*objet a* one: while the former presupposes the achievement of fullness through the reversion of the process of reification, the latter conceives of fullness (the Thing) as unachievable because it is devoid of any content; and while the former sees incarnation in the concrete as a distorted reification, the latter sees radical investment in an object as the only way in which a certain fullness is achievable. Žižek can maintain his reification/false consciousness approach only at the cost of radically eradicating the logic of the *objet a* from the field of political relations.

Next step: signification. (What I have called before the 'linguistic perspective' refers not only to the linguistic in the strict sense, but to all systems of signification. As the latter are coterminous with social life, the categories and relations explored by linguistic analysis do not belong to regional areas but to the field of a general ontology.) Here we have the same imbrication between particularity and universality that we have found in the psychoanalytic perspective. I have shown elsewhere[10] that the totalization of a system of differences is impossible without a *constitutive* exclusion. But the latter has as a primary logical effect the split of any signifying element between an equivalential and a differential side. As these two sides cannot be logically sutured, the result is that any suture will be rhetorical: a certain

10   See Ernesto Laclau, 'Why Do Empty Signifiers Matter to Politics?', in Laclau, *Emancipation(s)* (London: Verso, 1996).

particularity, without ceasing to be particular, will assume a certain role of 'universal' signification. Ergo, unevenness within signification is the only terrain upon which a signifying process can unfold. Catachresis = rhetoricity = the very possibility of meaning. The same logic that we found in psychoanalysis between the (impossible) Thing and the *objet a* we find now, again, as the very condition of significa-tion. Žižek's analysis does not directly engage with signification, but it is not difficult to draw the conclusions that would derive, in this field, from his 'reification' approach: any kind of rhetorical substitution that stops short of a fully-fledged 'signifying' reconciliation would amount to false consciousness.

Finally, politics. Let us take an example I used at several points in *On Populist Reason*: Solidarność in Poland. We had there a society in which the frustration of a plurality of demands by an oppressive regime had created a spontaneous equivalence between them – an equivalence which, however, needed to be expressed by some form of symbolic unity. We are faced here with a clear alternative: either there is an ultimately *conceptually* specifiable content that is negated by the oppressive regime – in which case that content can be directly expressed, in its *positive* differential identity – or the demands are radically heterogeneous, and the only thing they share is a *negative* feature: their common opposition to the oppressive regime. In that case, it is not a question of a *direct* expression of a positive feature underlying the different demands: since what has to be expressed is an irreducible negativity, its representation will necessarily have a symbolic character.[11] The demands of Solidarność will become the symbol of a wider chain of demands whose unstable equivalence around that symbol will constitute a wider popular identity. This constitution of the symbolic unity of the popular camp – and its correlate, the symbolic unification of the oppressive regime through similar discursive/equivalential means – is what Žižek suggests that we should conceive as reification. But he is utterly wrong: in reifica-tion, we have, as we have seen, an inversion in the relation between true and distorted expression, while here the opposition true/distorted

---

11   Here I am using the term 'symbolic' not in the Lacanian sense, but in the one to be frequently found in discussions concerning representation. See, for instance, Hanna Fenichel Pitkin, *The Concept of Representation* (Berkeley, CA: University of California Press, 1967), Chapter 5.

does not make any sense – the equivalential link being established between radically heterogeneous demands, their 'homogeneization' through an empty signifier is a pure *passage à l'acte*, the construction of something essentially new and not the revelation of any underlying 'true' identity. This is the reason why, in my book, I insisted that the empty signifier is a pure name, which does not belong to the conceptual order. So there is no question of 'true' or 'false' consciousness. As in the case of the psychoanalytical perspective, the elevation of an object to the dignity of the Thing – and in the case of signification, the presence of a figural term that is catachrestical because it names, and thus gives discursive presence to, an essential void within the signifying structure; we have in politics also a constitution of new agents – 'peoples', in our sense – through the articulation between equivalential and differential logics. These logics involve figural embodiments resulting from a *creatio ex nihilo* that it is not possible to reduce to any preceding or ultimate literality. So let us leave 'reification' behind.

What I have said so far already signals that, in my view, the second thesis of Žižek, according to which symbolic representation – which he conceives as reification – would be essentially, or at least tendentially, fascist, does not fare any better. Here Žižek uses a demagogic device: the example he chooses is the role of the Jew in Nazi discourse, which immediately evokes all the horrors of the Holocaust and provokes an instinctive negative reaction. Now, it is true that fascist discourse employed forms of symbolic representation, but there is nothing specifically fascist in doing so, for there is no political discourse that does not construct its own symbols in that way. I would even say that this construction is the very definition of what politics is about. The arsenal of possible ideological examples different from the one Žižek has chosen is inexhaustible. What else but a symbolic embodiment is involved in a political discourse that presents Wall Street as the source of all economic evils? Or in the burning of the American flag by Third World demonstrators? Or in the rural, anti-modernist emblems of Gandhi's agitation? Or in the burning of Buenos Aires's cathedral by the Peronist masses? We identify with some symbols while rejecting others, but that is no reason to assert that the matrix of a symbolic structure varies according to the material content of the symbols. That assertion is not possible without some notion of reification *à la* Žižek, which would make it possible to ascribe certain contents to true consciousness and others to false consciousness. But even this naive operation would not succeed without the further postulate that any form of symbolic incarnation will be an expression of false consciousness, while true consciousness would be totally exempt from symbolic mediation. (This is the point at which Lacanian theory becomes Žižek's nemesis: to do away entirely with symbolic mediation and have a pure expression of true consciousness is the same as to claim that there is a direct access to the Thing as such, while *objets a* will only be granted the status of distorted representations.)

DEMANDS: BETWEEN 'REQUESTS' AND 'CLAIMS'

The minimal unit in our social analysis is the category of 'demand'. It presupposes that the social group is not an ultimately homogeneous referent, but that its unity should rather be conceived as an articulation of heterogeneous demands. Žižek has formulated two main objections to this approach. The first is that the notion of demand does not grasp the true confrontational nature of the revolutionary act. ('Does the proper revolutionary/emancipatory act not move beyond this horizon of demands? The revolutionary subject no longer operates at the level of demanding something from those in power – he wants to destroy them . . .').[12] The second objection is that there is no correlation between the plurality implicit in the notion of an equivalential chain of demands and the actual aims of a populist mobilization because many populist movements are structured around single-issue objectives:

> A more general remark should be made about one-issue popular movements. Take, for example, the 'tax revolts' in the US. Although they function in a populist way, mobilising the people around a demand that is not met by the democratic institutions, it [sic] does not seem to rely on a complex chain of equivalences, but remains focused on one singular demand.[13]

Žižek's two objections have utterly missed the point. Let us start with the first. Although Žižek refers to the tension between *request* and

---

12   Žižek, 'Against the Populist Temptation', p. 8.
13   Ibid., pp. 10–11.

claim around which my notion of demand is explicitly constructed, he is entirely unaware of its theoretical consequences. In my view, any demand starts as a *request*: institutions of local power, for instance, are asked to meet the grievances of people in a particular area – housing, for example. This is the only situation Žižek envisages: those in power are asked to acquiesce graciously to the request of a group of people. From this perspective, the situation would be utterly uneven: granting the demand would be a *concession* from those in power. But to reduce the issue to that case is to ignore the second dimension of my analysis – the social process through which a request is transformed into a *claim*. How does this mutation take place? As I have argued, through the operation of the equivalential logic. People whose demands concerning housing are frustrated see that other demands concerning transport, health, security, schooling, and so on, are not met either. This triggers a process that I have described at length in my book. It boils down to the following: the frustration of an *individual* demand transforms the request into a claim insofar as people see themselves as bearers of rights that are not recognized. But these claims are limited, for the referential entity to which they are addressed is perfectly iden- tifiable – in my example of housing, the town hall. But if the equivalence between claims is extended – in my example: housing, transport, health, schooling, and so on –then determining which is the instance to which the claims are addressed becomes far more difficult. One has to construct the enemy discursively – the oligarchy, the establishment, big money, capitalism, globalization, and so forth – and, for the same reason, the identity of the claimers is transformed in this process of 'universalization' of both the aims and the enemy. The whole process of the Russian Revolution began with three demands: 'peace, bread and land'. To whom were these demands addressed? The more the equivalence expanded, the clearer it became that it was not just to the Tsarist regime. Once we move beyond a certain point, what were requested *within* institutions became claims addressed *to* institutions, and at some stage they became claims *against* the institutional order. When this process has overflown the institutional apparatuses beyond a certain limit, we start having the 'people' of populism.

We could ask ourselves: Why should social actions always be conceived as demands? The reason, as we have explained in our book, is that the subject is always the subject of lack – it always emerges out of an asymmetry between the (impossible) fullness of the community and the particularism of a place of enunciation. This also explains why the 'names' of fullness will always result from a radical investment of 'universal' value in a certain particularity – again: the elevation of a particular object to the dignity of the Thing. But it is important to realize that this investment does not leave the particular object unchanged; it 'universalizes' that object through its inscription within an infrastructure of equivalential relations. That is why this can never be a pure matter of 'reification', as Žižek argues. (Reification involves, as I have said, an *inversion* by which particularity and universality exchange places without changing their identities, while the hegemonic relation presupposes contamination between the particular and the universal.)

This situation, whereby a certain particularity is never *mere* particularity because it is always criss-crossed by equivalential relations that 'universalize' its content, is enough to answer the second of Žižek's objections – namely, that single-issue mobilizations, having particularistic aims, cannot constitute wider political identities. This is a complete illusion. The ostensive issue might be particular, but it is only the tip of an iceberg. Behind the individual issue, a much wider world of associations and affects contaminate it and transform it into the expression of much more general trends. To take the 'single-issue' character of mobilization at face value would be the same as reducing the analysis of a dream to its manifest content. The French and Dutch referenda are good examples. The issue was a punctual one but, as Žižek himself shows, a whole world of frustrations, fears and prejudices found their expression in the 'No'. And everybody knows that what is at stake in the tax referenda in the US are deep political displacements of the communitarian common sense. The conclusion is that the latent meaning of a mobilization can never be read off its literal slogans and proclaimed aims; a political analysis worth the name only starts when one probes the overdetermination sustaining that literality.

So what general conclusions can be derived from this complex set of interconnections between popular identities and demands and, within demands themselves, between 'requests' and 'claims'? The most important one is that each of the possible articulations within this structural matrix leads to a different way of constituting social identities, and to different degrees in the universalization of their claims. At one extreme, when the demands do not go beyond the stage of mere requests, we have a highly institutionalized arrangement. Social actors have an 'immanent' existence within the objective locations delineating the institutional order of society. (Of course this is a purely ideal extreme: society is never so structured that social agents are entirely absorbed within institutions.) The second scenario is one in which there is a more permanent tension between demands and what the institutional order can absorb. Here, 'requests' tend to become 'claims', and there is a critique of institutions rather than just a passive acceptance of their legitimacy. Finally, when relations of equivalence between a plurality of demands go beyond a certain point, we have broad mobilizations against the institutional order as a whole. We have here the emergence of the 'people' as a more universal historical actor, whose aims will necessarily crystallize around empty signifiers as objects of political identification. There is a radicalization of claims which can lead to a revolutionary reshaping of the entire institutional order. This is probably the kind of development that Žižek has in mind when he speaks of not demanding anything from those in power but wanting to destroy them instead. But the difference between his approach and mine is that, for me, the emergence of emancipatory actors has a logic of its own, which is anchored in the structure of the demand as a basic unit of social action, while, for Žižek, there is no such logic: emancipatory subjects are conceived as fully-fledged creatures, who emerge without any kind of genetic process, in the manner of Minerva from Jupiter's head. The section in my book that deals with Žižek's work has, as a title, 'Žižek: waiting for the Martians'. There is, indeed, something extraterrestrial about Žižek's emancipatory subjects: their conditions as revolutionary agents are specified within such a rigid geometry of social effects that no empirical actor can fit the bill. In his recent writings, however, Žižek deploys a new strategy in naming revolutionary agents, consisting in choosing some 'actually existing' social actors to whom he nevertheless attributes so many imaginary features that they become Martians in anything but name. I will return below to Žižek's strategy of 'Martianization'.

HETEROGENEITY AND SOCIAL PRACTICES

We should now move to a set of remarks that Žižek makes concerning the status of Marxist theory. The most important one refers to Marxian political economy. According to him, my basic reproach to the latter would be that it is 'a positive "ontic" science which delimits a part of

substantial social reality, so that any direct grounding of emancipatory politics in [a critique of political economy] (or, in other words,
any privilege given to class struggle) reduces the political to an epiphenomenon embedded in substantial reality'.[14] In order to refute the
claims that he attributes to me, Žižek then embarks on a long tirade in
which he tries to show that commodity fetishism is an internal effect
of the capital form as such, and that this form is not abstract because
it determines actual social processes: 'this abstraction . . . is real in the
precise sense of determining the structure of the very material social
processes. The fate of whole strata of population and sometimes of
whole countries can be decided by the solipsistic dance of capital,
which pursues its goal of profitability in a blessed indifference with
regard to how its movement will affect social reality'.[15] Having thus
detected the central systemic violence of capitalism, Žižek concludes:
'Here we encounter the Lacanian difference between reality and the
Real: "reality" is the social reality of the actual people involved in
interaction and in the productive process, while the Real is the inexorable "spectral" logic of the Capital that determines what goes on in
social reality'.[16]

The last remark is, purely and simply, a misrepresentation of the
Lacanian notion of the Real – a good example of how Žižek systematically distorts Lacanian theory to make it compatible with a Hegelianism
which is, in most respects, its very opposite. The Real cannot be an
inexorable spectral logic, and even less something that determines
what goes on in social reality, for the simple reason that the Real is not
a specifiable object endowed with laws of movement of its own but,
on the contrary, something that only exists and shows itself through
its disruptive effects within the Symbolic.[17] It is not an *object* but an
internal *limit* preventing the ultimate constitution of any objectivity.
To identify the Real with the logic of capital is a nice example of that
'reification' to which Žižek always returns. His mistake is similar to
that of Kant, who, after having said that categories apply only to
phenomena and not to things in themselves, asserted that the latter
are the external cause of appearances, thus applying a category – cause

---

14   Ibid., p. 16.
15   Ibid., p. 17.
16   Ibid.
17   We now move to the strictly Lacanian notion of the Symbolic.

– to something that cannot legitimately be subsumed under *any* category. The reason why Žižek has to distort the notion of the Real in this way is clear: only if the logic of capital is self-determined can it operate as an infrastructure determining what goes on in social 'reality'. But the Real, in the Lacanian sense, does exactly the opposite: it sets a limit preventing any self-determination by the Symbolic. All this cheap metaphorical use of the reality/Real duality to refer to something that is no more than the old base/superstructure distinction is entirely out of place: it is evident that the logic of capital is as symbolic as the social reality it is supposed to determine. The consequence is that, if the logic of capital and social reality are in *pari materia* – both of them are symbolic – the holes and disruptions created in social reality by the presence of the Real will also be present within the very logic of capital's self-development (which, as a result, will be contaminated by something heterogeneous with itself; it will not be pure *self*-development).

What I am saying is not that the Real is not relevant for the issues we are discussing, but that Žižek has looked for it in all the wrong places. To conceive the Real as an objective, conceptually specifiable logic does not make any sense. However, before attempting to give to the Real its precise ontological location – if we can use these terms in connection with something whose presence, precisely, subverts all locations – I want to refer to Žižek's assertion that I have 'reproached' Marxist political economy of being an ontic science delimiting a region of social reality and reducing the political to an epiphenomenal position. This 'reproach' attributed to me is a pure invention of Žižek's. I have never asserted that Marx's political economy is a regional science, for the simple reason that, whatever its merits or deficiencies, it is a discourse concerning the social totality ('the anatomy of civil society is political economy'). So the only two possible ways of criticizing it are either to prove that there are logical inconsistencies in the sequence of its categories, or to show that there is a heterogeneous 'outside' preventing political economy from closing itself around its internal categories, and thus constituting the *fundamentum inconcussum* of the social. Now, the first criticism is possible, and – although I have not myself engaged in formulating it – has been repeatedly made over the last century, to the point where little remains of the labour theory of value in the manner presented by Marx. It is enough to mention the names of Böhm-Bawerk, Bortkiewicz, Joan

Robison or Piero Sraffa.[18] The whole discussion about the transformation of values into prices at the beginning of the twentieth century was a first stage in this critical analysis. Žižek totally ignores this literature, and continues to assert Marx's version of the labour theory of value as an unchallengeable dogma.

But let us not waste time with this sterile dogmatism, but instead move on to the second possible criticism of Marxian economics, which is far more relevant for our subject. The alternative is as follows. A first possible scenario would be one in which there is no 'outside' to the process described by the succession of the economic categories: history would just be their endogenous unfolding, so that – to use Žižek's terms – the ontic story they depict would, at the same time, be ontological. Thus we would have a purely internal process not interrupted by any outside. The logical succession would also have a metaphysical value. But what about the forces *opposing* capitalism? In this model, they can only be an internal effect of capitalism itself. It is well known how 'class struggle' features in this objectivist perspective: capitalism creates its own gravediggers. The second scenario results from the opposite assumption: forces opposing capitalism are not just the result of a capitalist logic, but *interrupt* it from the outside, so that the story of capitalism cannot result from the unfolding of its internal categories. To give just one example: as several studies have shown, the transition from absolute to relative surplus value is not only the result of movements in the logic of profit in a conflict-free space, but also a response to workers' mobilizations. If this is so, there is no purely internal history of capitalism, such as the one described by the 'Preface' to the *Critique of Political Economy*, but only a conflict-riven history which cannot be apprehended by any kind of conceptually graspable development. I want to insist on this point because it will lead us straight onto the notion of 'people' as presented in *On Populist Reason*.

Needless to say, of the two options within this alternative, I definitely choose the second. In fact, *On Populist Reason* is, to a large extent, an attempt to unfold the theoretical consequences following from this choice. But Žižek thinks he knows better, and opts for denying that the alternative exists. Thus: 'Marx distinguishes between "working class" and "proletariat": "working class" effectively is a

---

18   See the excellent book by Ian Steedman, *Marx after Sraffa* (London: New Left Books, 1977).

particular social group, while "proletariat" designates a subjective position.'[19] Now, to start with, Marx *never* made such a distinction. Perhaps he should have done so, but he did not in fact do so. On the contrary, all his theoretical effort tended to show that the riddle of history could only be solved insofar as revolutionary subjectivity was firmly rooted in an objective position, resulting itself from a process governed by immanent and necessary laws. Has Žižek ever read the *Communist Manifesto*? If he had, he would have known that, for Marx and Engels, 'Not only has the bourgeoisie forged the weapons that bring death to itself; it has also called into existence the men who are to wield those weapons – the modern working class, the proletarians.' Has he read *The Holy Family*, where, against Bruno Bauer, they argue for the inevitability of communism based precisely in the dehumanization of the proletariat (working class) brought about by the logic of private property? Has he read *The German Ideology*, where they oppose 'true socialism', and present the division of labour – a structured ensemble of objective social positions – as the root and source of human alienation? And what are *Capital* and *Grundrisse* but a sustained attempt to root exploitation in an objective process whose necessary counterpart is working-class struggle? Enough. There is no point in continuing to refer to an argument that any undergraduate knows. Moreover, it is plainly clear what Marx would have thought about a taxonomic distinction between the 'subjective' and the 'objective': he would have said that, from the point of view of social totality, what matters is not the distinction as such but the logic and topography of the interconnections between its two terms – and the 'Preface' to the *Critique of Political Economy* makes perfectly clear what such interconnection was for him.

The alternative that I have presented is, actually, reflected in a contradictory way in Žižek's thought. The distinction between the 'subjective' and the 'objective', on the one hand, is vital for Žižek since, following Alain Badiou's duality of 'situation' and 'event',[20] he wants to establish a radical discontinuity between the revolutionary break and what had preceded it. The corollary is that the revolutionary act should have nothing in common with the situation within which it takes place. But Žižek has also insisted, ad nauseam, on the centrality

19 Žižek, 'Against the Populist Temptation', p. 15.
20 Alain Badiou, *L'être et l'événement* (Paris: Seuil, 1988).

of the anti-capitalist *economic* struggle, which means that something in the existing situation – the 'economic' as particular location within a social topography – has a transcendental structuring role of sorts, determining a priori the 'events' that can actually take place. So the situation has ontological primacy over the event, whose chasm with that situation could not, as a result, be radical. Žižek is thus confronted with an *exclusive* alternative, and it is rather comical that he does not realize it, and continues asserting both options in a perfectly contradictory way.

Let us leave Žižek to enjoy his contradiction, and move instead to the way in which the alternative is dealt with in Marx's work. There is no doubt that, for Marx, the objective side has the upper hand. History is a coherent story because the development of productive forces establishes its underlying meaning. Technological progress leads to increasing exploitation, so that workers' struggle helps to hasten the crisis of capitalism but is not its source. The final breakdown of the system, although it is not mechanical, does not have its ultimate source in the actions of the workers. But it would be a mistake to think that, for him, historical necessity reduced freedom of action to a mere epiphenomenon. The point is, rather, that historical necessity and free revolutionary action coincide in such a way that they become indistinguishable from each other. The Spinozan notion of freedom as being consciousness of necessity, which still had an essentially speculative dimension in Hegel, becomes in Marx an *active* principle identifying necessity and freedom. That is the reason why, for Marx, there is no possible distinction between the descriptive and the normative – and why, as a result, Marxism cannot have an ethics independently grounded. And this is also why Žižek's distinction between 'proletariat' and 'working class', 'subjective' and 'objective', would have been anathema for Marx.

The difficulties started later on, with the increasing realization that there was an essential opaqueness preventing the smooth transition from one economic category to the next, and from one social antagonism to another. Marxist views of the destiny of capitalist society were based on the following postulate: the simplification of the social structure under capitalism. The peasantry and the middle classes would disappear and, in the end, the bulk of the population would be a vast proletarian mass, so that the last antagonistic confrontation of history would be a showdown between the bourgeoisie and the working class. Very quickly, however, it was seen that this strategic model showed all kinds of inconsistencies, both at the theoretical level and as a reading of what was going on in society. The labour theory of value was shown to be plagued by theoretical inconsistencies; the internal differentiations between sectors of the economy could not be intellectually grasped by any kind of unified law of tendency; social structure, far from being more homogeneous, became more complex and diversified; even within the working class, the splits between economic and political struggle became increasingly less politically manageable. In this situation, the initial reaction was to try to maintain the basic lines of classical theory, but to multiply the system of mediations that, while becoming the guarantors of its ultimate validity, would assume the heroic task of homogenizing the heterogeneous. Lukács's notion of 'false consciousness' – whose correlate was the location of the 'true' consciousness of the proletariat in the Party – is a typical expression of this laborious but ultimately useless exercise. And, within structurally oriented Marxism, Poulantzas's distinction between 'determination in the last instance' and 'dominant role' did not fare any better. The only possible alternative was to accept heterogeneity at face value, without trying to reduce it to any kind of concealed or underlying homogeneity, and to address the question of how a certain totalization is possible, which is nevertheless compatible with an irreducible heterogeneity. Outlining the contours of an answer to this issue is our next task.

Before embarking upon it, however, I would like to comment on pages 15–18 of Žižek's essay, for they present what most approaches in his piece a sustained and coherent argument. The main points are the following:

1. There are two logics of universality that have to be strictly distinguished. The first would correspond to the state conceived by Hegel, as the universal class, 'the direct agent of the social order'. The second would be a 'supernumerary' universality, internal to the existing order but without a proper place within it – the 'part of no part' of Rancière. So we would not have a particular content which 'will hegemonise the empty form of universality, but a struggle between two exclusive *forms* of universality themselves'.
2. The proletariat embodies this second kind of universality. (This is the place where Žižek distinguishes between 'proletariat' and

'working class' in the manner discussed earlier). Here Žižek criticizes my book's approach to the question of the *lumpenproletariat*,
arguing that its difference from the proletariat *stricto sensu* is not
'the one between an objective social group and a nongroup, a
remainder-excess with no proper place within the social edifice,
but a distinction between two modes of this remainder-excess that
generates two different subjective positions.' While the *lumpenproletariat*, as a non-group, can be incorporated into the strategy of
any social group – in other words, it is infinitely manipulable – the
working class *as a group* is in the contradictory position of having
a precise location within capitalist accumulation while nevertheless being unable to find a place within the capitalist order.

3. The abstract logic of capital produces concrete effects. Here Žižek
proposes his distinction between 'reality' ('actual people involved
in interaction and in the productive process') and the 'Real' ('the
inexorable abstract spectral logic of capital that determines what
goes on in social reality'). I have already shown the inconsistence
of this distinction, and I will not go back to it. But he adds a
further point: 'the categories of political economy (say the value
of the commodity working force [*sic*], or the degree [*sic*] of profit)
are not objective socio-economic data, but data that always signal
the outcome of a 'political struggle.' So the political cannot be an
epiphenomenon.

4. Žižek then adds a critique of the way I conceptualize, in an opposition 'A–B' the B-ness of the B which resists symbolic transformation
into a pure relation 'A–not A'. As discussion of this point requires
reference to some premises of my argument that I will present later
in this chapter, I postpone discussion of this criticism.

5. 'Capitalism is thus not merely a category that delimits a positive
social sphere, but a formal–transcendental matrix that structures
the entire social space – literally, a mode of production.'

Which, among these various criticisms, has an at least tentative plau-
sibility? The answer is simple: none. Let us consider them one after
the other.

1. The two universalities described by Žižek cannot coexist in the
same space of representation, not even under the form of an
antagonistic presence. The mere presence of one of them makes

the other impossible. The universality inherent in Hegel's universal class *totalizes* a social space, so nothing *ultimately* antagonistic could exist within it – otherwise the state would not be the sphere of reconciliation of the particularities of civil society, and it would be unable to fulfil its universal role. What happens, however, if this role is threatened by a particularism that it cannot master? In that case there is, simply, no reconciliation; universality, *conceived as uncontaminated universality*, is a sham. As the relation between the state's universality and what escapes its reconciliatory role is a relation of pure exteriority, it is essentially contingent, which is the same as saying that it should be conceived as a system of *power*. Universality is not an *underlying* datum, but a power that, like all power, is exercised over something different from itself. Ergo, any kind of universality is nothing other than a particularity that has succeeded in contingently articulating around itself a large number of differences. But this is nothing other than the definition of a *hegemonic* relation. Let us now move to the second of Žižek's universalities – that of a sector which, although present within a social space, cannot be counted as a member of that space. The case of the *sans-papiers* in France is frequently quoted as a relevant example. Let us say, to start with, that the mere fact of being outside the system of locations defining a social framework does not endow a group of people with any kind of universality. The *sans-papiers* want to have *papiers*, and if the latter are conceded by the state, they could become one more difference within an expanded state. In order to become 'universal', something else is needed – namely, that their situation as 'outsiders' becomes a symbol to other outsiders or marginals within society: in other words, that a contingent aggregation of heterogeneous elements takes place. This aggregation is what I have called a 'people'. This type of universalization, again, is what we understand by 'hegemony'. We arrive at the same conclusion I reached when I referred to the universality of the state. This is why Gramsci spoke of the 'becoming State of the working class', which presupposes a reaggregation of elements by a certain nodal point at the expense of others. Gramsci called this movement a 'war of position' between antagonistic universalities. The fact that Žižek hypostasizes his two universalities and cannot explain what the struggle between them could consist of – and that, in addition, he conceives the hegemonic struggle as one particularity hegemonizing 'the empty form of universality' – shows that he has not understood even the ABC of the theory of hegemony.

2. Concerning the question of the *lumpenproletariat*, Žižek is, again, clouding the issue. He says that, in the case of the proletariat, there is a contradiction between its precise location within capitalist accumulation and its lack of place within the capitalist order; while, in the case of the *lumpenproletariat*, the first type of location would be absent, so that its sociopolitical identity would be infinitely malleable. The real question, however, is whether the lack of place of the proletariat is so anchored in its precise location within capitalist accumulation that an equivalence could not be established with other 'out of place' sectors, so that a broader identity of the excluded could be formed that overflows *any* particular location. If so, the marginality of the *lumpenproletariat* would be the symptom of a much wider phenomenon. I will return to this point.

3. The economic field is, for Žižek, intrinsically political, because it is the field where class struggle is structured. With an assertion of such a generality, I also, of course, agree. Gramsci wrote that the construction of hegemony starts at the factory level. But the disagreement starts when we try to define what we understand by the political. For me, the 'political' has a primary structuring role because social relations are ultimately contingent, and any prevailing articulation results from an antagonistic confrontation whose outcome is not decided beforehand. For Žižek, on the other hand, socioeconomic data always signal the outcome of a 'political' struggle – so, if there is a logical transition from the economic data to the political outcome, the political is simply an internal category of the economy. It is not, perhaps, an epiphenomenon, in the sense that its ontological status is not merely reflective of a substantial reality but part of it; but, precisely because of that, it lacks any autonomy. While my analysis leads to a 'politicization' of the economy, Žižek's ends in an 'economization' of politics.

As I have said, I will discuss point 4 later on. As for point 5, Žižek does not simply maintain that there is such a thing as a structured space called 'mode of production'; he also asserts, first, that such a space is a formal-transcendental matrix; and, second, that it directly structures the entire social space – in other words, that at no point does social reality overflow what that matrix can determine and control (except, presumably, in the transition from one mode of production to another; but since such a transition, if the model is coherent, would have to be governed by a logic internal to the mode of production itself, this would not make any difference). Žižek's whole account stands or falls depending on the validity of these two assumptions, to which I will now turn my attention.

HETEROGENEITY AND DIALECTICS

I will begin my discussion by trying to determine the status of the 'heterogeneous'. We understand by a heterogeneous relation one existing between elements that do not belong to the same space of representation.[21] This notion requires a set of specifications, for a space of representation can be constituted in a plurality of ways. The unity of such a space can, firstly, be the result of dialectical mediations – a type of connection between elements in which each contains everything needed to move logically to all the others. In the duality 'A–not A', the identity of each pole is exhausted in being the pure negation of the other. So dialectical transitions are not only compatible with contradiction, but have to rely on contradiction as the condition of their unity within a homogeneous space. There is nothing heterogeneous in a dialectical contradiction. For that reason, dialectical transitions can take place only in a saturated space. Any remnant of a contingent empiricity that is not dialectically mastered by the whole would jeopardize the latter for, in that case, the contingency of the unmastered element would make the whole equally contingent, and the very possibility of a dialectical mediation would be put into question (this is the 'Krug's pen' objection to dialectics, which Hegel answered with a brisk dismissal that hardly concealed the fact that he had no answer). Žižek's assertion that socioeconomic data 'signal the outcome of a "political" struggle' is a good example of a dialectical transition – one taking place in a homogeneous space which therefore entirely eliminates the possibility of radical negativity. But homogeneity does not necessarily require dialectical transitions between the

---

21 How a relation is possible between elements belonging to different spaces of representation is something I will discuss later on.

elements delimiting a space. A semiological relation between elements is also a possible alternative. Saussure's conception of language as a system of differences also presupposes homogeneity, insofar as the identity of each element requires its difference from all the others. Heterogeneity only enters the game if it can be shown that the very logic of totality – being dialectical or semiological – fails at some point as a result of an aporia that cannot be resolved within that totality's structuring principles.

Let us take as our starting point the Hegelian conception of History. The basic premise is that the movement of historical events is governed by an inner logic that is conceptually apprehensible and conceived as a succession of dialectical reversals and retrievals. The arrival of various peoples in the historical arena is the phenomenal manifestation of such logic. But there is a blind spot in this picture: what Hegel calls the 'peoples without history', who do not represent any differentiated moment in the dialectical series. I have compared them, in my book, with what Lacan calls the *caput mortuum* – the residue left in a tube after a chemical experiment. This non-historical presence is like the drop of petrol that spoils the bowl of honey, for the existence of a contingent excess overflowing the dialectic of history makes this dialectic equally contingent and, as a result, the whole vision of history as a coherent story is at the very least jeopardized. The same happens with Žižek's model of historicity: for capitalism to be 'a formal–transcendental matrix that structures the entire social space', what is necessary is that such a 'matrix' strictly functions as a ground – that is, that nothing in the 'social space' exceeds the mastering abilities of the matrix. Some sort of pragmatic version of the dialectical model is possible, however: although this new version would considerably water down the dialectical ambitions, it could still be asserted that the 'excess' is marginal in relation to the main lines of historical development, so that from the perspective of a 'universal history' it can be safely ignored. If the whole issue comes to that, it is clear that it is just a matter of appreciation to decide whether the facts vindicate the assumptions of this pragmatic new version.

At this point we should move from Hegel to Marx, from whose work most of Žižek's analyses can be considered as derivative. First, however, I will recapitulate my previous theoretical steps. First, as we have seen, any kind of dialectical transition is grounded in a saturated logical terrain where nothing can escape dialectical determination.

Second, however, this logical closure is unachievable, because something within that terrain escapes dialectical mastery – we have taken the example of 'peoples without history' but, obviously, many others could be brought forward. Third, referring now to the terrain of history, this excess with respect to dialectical development can only be conceptualized through its contingent relation with the *main line* of historical development. Fourth, the fact that this 'main line' has a contingent relation to something external to itself means that it, itself, becomes contingent. Fifth, the claims of that line to be the 'main one' cease, as a result, to be grounded in a necessary dialectical development, and may only be asserted as an historically *proved* contingent process. So the question is: Is there any entity in Marx's theory that, in its contingency, is homologous to Hegel's 'peoples without history'? In my view there is, and it is the *lumpenproletariat*. And the result of its presence will be to destroy the claims of the proletariat to having an a priori central role as a necessary agent of historical development.

History, for Marx, insofar as it is a coherent story, is a history of production (the development of productive forces and their compatibility or incompatibility with the relations of production). So occupying a precise location within the relations of production offers, for Marx, the only possible claim to being a historical actor. But this location is precisely what the *lumpenproletariat* does not have. Without hesitation, Marx draws what, starting from his premises, is the only possible conclusion: the *lumpenproletariat* should be denied any historicity; it is a parasitic sector inhabiting the interstices of all social formations. We see here the structural similitude with Hegel's 'peoples without history': in relation to the main line of historical development, its existence is marginal and contingent. If that was the whole matter, there would be no major problem: although the *lumpenproletariat* would have no place in a dialectically conceived historical narrative, its confinement as a category to the rabble of the city – which is clearly a marginal sector – would not put into question the pragmatic version of the dialectical story. But the difficulties persist. For Marx, the *lumpenproletariat* doubtless has the rabble of the city as an intuitive referent, but he also gives a conceptual definition of that referent, to be found in the *lumpenproletariat*'s distance from the productive process. Very soon, however, he realized that such a distance is not exclusive to the rabble of the city, but present in many other sectors – he speaks, for instance, of the financial aristocracy as the re-emergence of the *lumpenproletariat* at the heights of society. And with the unfolding of the whole discussion concerning produc- tive and unproductive labour – an issue that had already attracted the attention of classical political economists – the notion of history as the history of production came increasingly under fire, and its defence required the most unlikely contortions. Clearly, the pragmatic test had not been passed. This is why the question of the *lumpenproletar- iat* is important for me – because it is the royal road that makes visible a wider issue: the whole question of the logics structuring social total- ity. That is why I have said that the question of the *lumpenproletariat* is a symptom.

But there is something else that puts Žižek's approach even more radically into question. It is the whole issue concerning the theoretical status of social antagonisms. Let us return to his assertion that the working class 'is a group which is in itself, *as a group* within the social edifice, a non-group, i.e. whose position is in itself "contradictory": they are a productive force, society (and those in power) need them in order to reproduce themselves and their rule, but, nonetheless, they cannot find a proper place for them'.[22] This can only mean one of two things: either that the objective position of the worker within the rela- tions of production is the *source* of their contradictory position within capitalist society as a whole, or that the absence of that objective posi- tion within capitalist society as a whole derives from something that the worker is *beyond* their objective position within the relations of production. Given Žižek's general outlook, it is clear that he can only mean the first. But this is what is theoretically unsustainable. For the worker's position within the relations of production to be a purely objective one, the worker has to be reduced to the category of 'seller of labour-power', and the capitalist to that of 'buyer' of labour-power as a commodity. In that case, however, we are not defining any antago- nism, because the fact that the capitalist extracts surplus labour from the worker does not involve antagonism unless the worker *resists* such an extraction, but that resistance cannot be logically derived from the mere analysis of the category 'seller of labour-power'. That is why, in several places in my work,[23] I have argued that social antagonisms are

---

22   Žižek, 'Against the Populist Temptation', p. 16.
23   See Ernesto Laclau and Chantal Mouffe, *Hegemony and Socialist Strategy* (London: Verso, 1985), Chapter 3; Ernesto Laclau, *New Reflections on the Revolution of*

not objective relations but the limit of all objectivity, so that society is never a purely objective order but is constructed around an ultimate impossibility.

It is clear at this point that the only way out of this theoretical blind alley is to move to the second possible meaning of Žižek's assertion (which he systematically avoids) – namely, that the capitalist does not negate in the worker something inherent in the category 'seller of labour-power', but something the worker is, *beyond* that category (the fact that, below a certain wage level, he/she cannot have access to minimal consumption, to a decent life, and so on). So antagonism is not internal to the relations of production but takes place *between* the relations of production and something external to them. In other words, the two poles of the antagonism are linked by a non-relational relation: they are essentially heterogeneous with each other. As society is criss-crossed by antagonisms, heterogeneity is to be found at the very heart of social relations.

The consequences of this displacement from the notion of a homogeneous, saturated space to one in which heterogeneity is constitutive, rapidly follow. In the first place, asserting that a social antagonism emerges out of an insurmountable heterogeneity involves as a necessary corollary that the antagonistic relation is conceptually ungraspable. There is no Absolute Spirit that can assign to it an objectively determinable content. This means that its two poles do not belong to the same space of representation. We are here in a strictly homologous situation to that described by Lacan through his famous dictum that there is no such thing as a sexual relation. In this he was obviously not asserting that people do not make love, but that there is no single formula of sexuation that would absorb the masculine and feminine poles within a unified and complementary whole.[24] This is a radical outside which cannot be symbolically mastered. Heterogeneity is another name for the Real.[25] This fully explains why Žižek cannot understand the theoretical status of the Lacanian Real: if the mode of production was – as it is for him – a formal–transcendental matrix of the social, everything in society would have to be explained out of

Our Time (London: Verso, 1990), pp. 17–27; Laclau, *On Populist Reason*, pp. 139–56.

24 See on this subject the classical article of Joan Copjec, 'Sex and the Euthanasia of Reason', in Copjec, *Read my Desire* (Cambridge, MA: MIT Press, 1994).

25 This involves the representation of the unrepresentable leading to what Hans Blumenberg called 'the absolute metaphor'.

that matrix's own endogenous movements; ergo, there would be no place for heterogeneity (= the presence of a Real). Žižek's nonsensical attribution to the Real of a formal–transcendental content is at odds with the most elementary notions of Lacan's theory. It is interesting to observe that, within the Marxist tradition itself, the imperialistic epistemological ambitions of the category of 'mode of production' were downgraded a long time ago. To refer only to the Althusserian school, Étienne Balibar has demolished the essentialism of *Reading Capital* and shown that the unity of a social formation cannot be conceived out of a 'mode of production' matrix.[26]

But here is a still more important consequence of giving this constitutive role to heterogeneity, and it is that the category of 'class struggle' is overflown in all directions. Let us mention just the most important:

1. If antagonisms are not internal to the relations of production but take place *between* the relations of production and the way social agents are constituted *outside* them, it is impossible to determine the nature and pattern of an antagonism (at the limit: whether it is going to exist at all and its degree of intensity) merely from an analysis of the internal structure of the relations of production. We know that, empirically, groups of people can react in the most divergent ways to what are technically movements in the rate of exploitation. And we also know that, theoretically, it could not be otherwise, given the heterogeneity inherent in antagonisms. So there is no longer any room for that childish talk about 'false consciousness', which presupposes an enlightened elite whose possession of the truth makes it possible to determine what the 'true interests' of a class are.

2. But heterogeneity destabilizes working-class centrality in still another sense. Once it is accepted that antagonisms presuppose a radical outside, there is no reason to think that locations within the relations of production are going to be privileged points of their emergence. Contemporary capitalism generates all kinds of imbalances and critical areas: ecological crises, marginalization and

26   See Étienne Balibar, 'Sur la dialectique historique (Quelques remarques critiques à propos de *Lire le Capital*', in Balibar, *Cinq études du matérialisme historique* (Paris: Francois Maspero, 1984).

unemployment, unevenness in the development of different sectors of the economy, imperialist exploitation, and so on. This means that antagonistic points are going to be multiple, and that any construction of a popular subjectivity will have to start from this heterogeneity. No narrow class-based limitation will do the trick.

3. This has a third major consequence that I have discussed in detail in my book. The overflowing of any narrow class identity by equivalential logics has to take into account the fact that equivalences operate over a substratum of essentially heterogeneous demands. This means that the kind of unity that it is possible to constitute out of them is going to be *nominal* and not *conceptual*. As I have argued, the name is the ground of the thing. So popular identities are always historical *singularities*.

We now have all the tools to answer Žižek's objection concerning what he calls my reduction of the Real to the empirical determinations of the object. His target is a passage of my book where it is asserted that 'the opposition A–B will never fully become A–not A. The "B-ness" of B will be ultimately non-dialectizable. The "people" will always be something more than the pure opposition of power. There is a Real of the "people" which resists symbolic integration.'[27] Against this passage Žižek raises the following objection: there is an ambiguity in my formulation, for it oscillates between accepting a formal notion of the Real as antagonism and reducing it to those empirical determinations of the object that cannot be subsumed under a formal opposition. The crucial task, for Žižek, is to find out what in the 'people' exceeds being the pure opposite of power, because, if it were just a matter of a wealth of empirical determinations, 'then we are *not* dealing with a Real that resists symbolic integration, because the Real, in this case, is the antagonism A–non A, so that "that which is in B more than non–A" is not the real in B but B's symbolic determinations.'[28]

This objection is highly symptomatic, because it shows in the clearest possible way everything that Žižek does not understand concerning the Real, antagonisms and popular identities. To start with, there are for him only two options: *either* we have a dialectical

27 Laclau, *On Populist Reason*, p. 152.
28 Žižek, 'Against the Populist Temptation', p. 18.

contradiction (A–not A), or we have the ontic empiricity of two objects (A–B) – what Kant called *Realrepugnanz*. If that were an *exclusive* alternative, it is clear that any 'B-ness' in excess of 'not-A' could only be of an empirical nature, and Žižek would obviously have an easy ride in showing that, in that case, we would not be dealing with the Real but with the symbolic determination of the object. But Žižek has missed the essential point. The real issue is whether I have in 'A' everything that I need to move to its opposite (which, as a result, would be reduced to 'not A') – to return to our previous discussion: whether I find in the *form* of capital everything I need logically to deduce the antagonism with the worker. If that were the case, we would have a contradiction, but not an antagonistic one, because it would be fully representable within a unified symbolic space. And as it would be entirely symbolizable, we would not be in the least dealing with the Real. A space constructed around the opposition 'A–not A' is an entirely saturated space, which exhausts through that opposition all possible alternatives and does not tolerate any interruption. This is why the universe of Hegelian dialectics, with its ambition to obtain a complete overlap between the ontic and the ontological orders, is incapable of dealing with the Real of antagonism, which requires, precisely, the interruption of a saturated (symbolic) space. Our notion of antagonism as the limit of objectivity is another way of naming the Real, and its precondition is that we move away from any saturated 'A–not A' space.

Would we not be in the same situation, however – namely, within a saturated space – if we move to the second Žižekian alternative, asserting a non-dialectizable 'B-ness' of 'B'? We would, indeed, if that excess was identified with the empiricity of the object. That fully symbolized space would no longer be dialectical, but differential or semiotic; however, total objective representability would still be its defining dimension. But it is at this point that the full consequences of our analysis of heterogeneity can be adduced. I have asserted above that antagonism is not internal to the relations of production, but is established between the relations of production and the way social agents are constituted outside them. This means that capitalist exploitation has an *interruptive* effect. This effect is, as we have seen, the Real of antagonism. So the presence of antagonism denies to social agents the fullness of an identity; there is, as a result, a process of identification by which certain objects, aims, and so on, become the names of that absent fullness (they are 'elevated to the dignity of the Thing'). This is exactly what the 'B-ness of B' means: it is not simply an empirical object, but one that has been invested, cathected, with the function of representing a fullness overflowing its ontic particularity. So, as we can see, Žižek's alternative is entirely misconceived. Firstly, he conceives the Real of antagonism as a dialectical relation 'A–not A', in which the full representability of its two poles eliminates the interruptive nature of the Real. And, secondly, he reduces the 'B-ness of B' to the empirical determinations of the object, thus ignoring the whole logic of the *objet a*. There is not the slightest substance to Žižek's objection.

ON THE GENEALOGY OF THE 'PEOPLE'

Having reached this point in my argument, the next stage should be to say something about the way in which constitutive heterogeneity reflects itself in the structuration of social identities. Some dimensions of this reflection are already clear. In the first place, the dialectics between homogenization and heterogenization should be conceived under the primacy of the latter. There is no ultimate *substratum*, no *nature naturans*, out of which existing social articulations could be explained. Articulations are not the superstructure of anything but the primary terrain of constitution of social objectivity. This entails that they are essentially contingent, for they consist of relational ensembles that obey no inner logic other than that of their factually being together. This does not mean that they can move in any direction at any time. On the contrary, hegemonic formations can have a high degree of stability, but this stability is itself the result of a construction operating on a plurality of heterogeneous elements. Homogeneity is always achieved, never given. The work of Georges Bataille is highly relevant in this respect. A second dimension following from my previous analysis is that constitutive heterogeneity involves the primacy of the political in the establishment of the social link. It should be clear at this stage that by 'the political' I do not understand any kind of regional area of action, but the *contingent* construction of the social link. It is because of this that the category of 'hegemony' acquires its centrality in social analysis. The consequence is that the category of 'hegemonic formation' replaces the notion of 'mode of production' as the actual self-embracing totality. The reasons are obvious. If the mode of production does not out of itself provide its own conditions of existence – in other words, if the latter are *externally* provided and are not a superstructural effect of the economy – those conditions of existence are an internal determination of the primary social totality. This is even more clearly the case if we add that the links between various moments and components of the economic process are themselves the results of hegemonic articulations.

A third dimension to be taken into account is that, if heterogeneity is constitutive, the succession of hegemonic articulations will be structured as a narrative that is also constitutive, and is not the factual reverse of a logically determinable process. This means that the reflection of heterogeneity in the constitution of social identities will itself adopt the form of a disruption (again: the irruption of the Real) of the homogeneous by the heterogeneous. Since Marxism was, as we know, organized around the notion of 'necessary laws of history', it is worth considering for a moment the way in which a heterogeneous 'other' irrupted in the field of its discursivity and led to the re-emergence of the 'people' as a privileged historical actor.

The points at which classical Marxism as a homogeneous field of discursivity was interrupted by a heterogeneity unmasterable within its system of categories are legion. I will only refer, however, to the Leninist experience, both because of its centrality within the political imaginary of the Left, and because it shows, with paradigmatic clarity, the type of politico-theoretical crisis to which I want to refer. There were a few principles that organized classical Marxism as a homogeneous space of discursive representation. One was the postulate of the class nature of historical agents. A second was the vision of capitalism as an orderly succession of stages dominated by a unified and endogenously determined economic logic. A third, and the most important for our argument, was an outlook according to which the strategic aims of the working class were entirely dependent on the stages of capitalist development. Russia being in a process of transition to a fully-fledged capitalist society, the overthrowing of absolutism could only consist in a bourgeois-democratic revolution which, following the pattern of similar processes in the West, would open the way to a long period of capitalist expansion. All this was perfectly in tune with the political forecasts and the strategic vision of traditional Marxism. But there was a heterogeneous anomaly – an 'exceptionality', to use the vocabulary of the time – that complicated the picture: the Russian bourgeoisie had arrived too late to the capitalist world market and, as a result, it was weak and incapable of carrying out its own democratic revolution. This had been recognized since the first manifesto of Russian social-democracy, written by Peter Struve, and not even a diehard dogmatist like Plekhanov dared to attribute to the bourgeoisie a leading role in the revolution to come. In those circumstances, the democratic tasks had to be taken up by different classes (a workers' and peasants' alliance, according to Lenin; the working class, in Trotsky's vision). It is symptomatic that this taking up of a task by a class that is not its natural bearer was called by Russian social-democrats 'hegemony', thus introducing the term into political language. Here we already find a heterogeneity disrupting the smooth sequence of Marxist categories. The discourses of Lenin and Trotsky were a sustained attempt to keep those disruptive effects under control. It was not a question of the class identity of the working class changing as a result of its taking up the democratic tasks, or of the tasks themselves transforming in nature when the workers were their bearers. The Leninist conception of 'class alliances' is explicit in this respect: 'to strike together and to march separately'. And, for Trotsky, the whole logic of the 'permanent revolution' is based on a succession of revolutionary stages that only makes sense if the class nature of both the agents and the tasks remains what it was from the very beginning. Moreover, the 'exceptionality' of the situation was conceived as short-lived: the revolutionary power in Russia could only survive if a socialist victory took place in the advanced capitalist countries of the West. If that happened, the heterogeneous 'outside' would be reabsorbed by an orthodox, normal development.

The failure of the revolution in the West, important as it was in its dislocating effects, was not, however, the only determining factor in the collapse of the 'classism' of classical Marxism (its Russian variants included). In the Leninist vision of world politics, there were already some seeds foretelling such a collapse. World capitalism was, for Lenin, a political and not only an economic reality: it was an imperialist chain. As a result, crises in one of its links created imbalances in the relations of forces in other links. The chain was destined to be broken at its weakest link, and nothing guaranteed that such a link would be found in the most developed capitalist societies. The case was rather the opposite. The notion of 'combined and uneven development' was the clearest expression of this dislocation in the orderly succession of stages which was supposed to govern the history of any society. When, in the 1930s, Trotsky asserted that combined and uneven development was the terrain of all social struggles in our age, he was extending (without realizing it) a death certificate to the narrow classism of the Second and Third Internationals.

Why so? Because the more profoundly uneven and combined development dislocates the relation between tasks and agents, the less possible it is to assign the tasks to an aprioristically determined 'natural' agent, and the less the agents can be considered as having an identity independent of the tasks they take up. Thus we enter the terrain of what I have called 'contingent political articulations', and of the transition from strict 'classism' to broader popular identities. The aims of any group in a power struggle can only be achieved if this group operates hegemonically over forces broader than itself – which, in turn, will change its own subjectivity. It is in that sense that Gramsci spoke of 'collective wills'. This socialist 'populism' is present in all successful communist mobilizations of that period. Žižek's assertion that populism – understood in this sense – is incompatible with communism is utterly groundless. What was Mao doing in the Long March other than creating a wider popular identity, speaking even of 'contradictions within the people' – thus reintroducing a category, 'people', that was anathema for classical Marxism? And we can imagine the disastrous results that Tito, in Žižek's native Yugoslavia, would have obtained if he had made a narrow appeal to the workers instead of calling the vast popular masses to resist the foreign occupation. In a heterogeneous world, there is no possibility of meaningful political action unless sectoral identity is conceived as a nucleus and starting point in the constitution of a wider popular will.

On Further Criticisms

There are, finally, a few minor criticisms that Žižek makes of my work that I would not like to leave unanswered.

Concerning the distinction between my category of 'empty signifier' and Claude Lefort's notion of 'empty place of power', Žižek writes: 'The two emptinesses are simply not comparable: the emptiness of 'people' is the emptiness of the hegemonic signifier which totalises the chain of equivalences, i.e. whose particular content is "transubstantiated" into an embodiment of the social Whole, while the emptiness of the place of power is a distance which makes every empirical bearer of power "deficient", contingent and temporary.'[29] I would be the last person to deny that the distinction made by Žižek is correct. In fact, I have myself made it in the very passage from my book that Žižek quotes: 'For me, emptiness is a type of identity, not a structural location.'[30] Over several years I have resisted the tendency of people to assimilate my approach to that of Lefort, which largely results, I think, from the word 'empty' being used in both analyses. But that the notion of emptiness is different in each approach does not mean that no comparison between them is possible. What my book asserts is that if the notion of emptiness is restricted to a place of power that anybody can occupy, a vital aspect of the whole question is omitted – namely, that occupation of an empty place is not possible without the occupying force itself becoming, to some extent, the signifier of emptiness. What Žižek retains from the idea of 'every empirical bearer of power (being) "deficient", contingent and temporary' is only the possibility of being substituted by other bearers of power, but he totally disregards the question of the effects of that deficient, contingent and temporary condition on the identity of those bearers. Given Žižek's total blindness to the hegemonic dimension of politics, this is hardly surprising.

Regarding the anti-segregationist movement in the US, epitomized by Martin Luther King, Žižek asserts that 'although it endeavors to articulate a demand that was not properly met within the existing democratic institutions, it cannot be called populist in any meaningful sense of the term'.[31] Everything depends, of course, on the definition of populism that one gives. In the usual and narrow sense of the term, whose pejorative overtones associate it to sheer demagogy, no doubt the civil rights movement could not be considered populist. But that is the sense of the term that my whole book puts into question. My argument is that the construction of the 'people' as a collective actor entails extending the notion of 'populism' to many movements and phenomena that traditionally were not considered so.[32] And, from

---

29   Žižek, 'Against the Populist Temptation', p. 9.
30   Laclau, *On Populist Reason*, p. 166.
31   Žižek, 'Against the Populist Temptation', p. 10.
32   Whenever there is the definition of the ground organizing a certain area of subjectivity, the limits of the latter change and, as a result, the referents addressed by that discourse are substantially modified. See, for instance, the following passage from Freud: 'By demonstrating the part played by perverse impulses in the formation of

this viewpoint, there is no doubt that the American civil rights movement extended equivalential logics in a variety of new directions, and
made possible the incorporation of previously excluded underdogs
into the public sphere.

Finally, I want to refer to an anecdotal point, just because Žižek
has raised it. In an interview I gave in Buenos Aires,[33] I referred to
another interview with Žižek, also in Buenos Aires, in a different
newspaper,[34] in which he asserted that the problem of the US in world
politics is that it acts globally and thinks locally, and in this way cannot
properly act as universal policemen. From this call to the US to both
think and act globally, I drew the conclusion that Žižek was asking the
US to become the 'universal class' in the Hegelo-Marxist sense of the
term. In his *Critical Inquiry* article, Žižek reacts furiously to what he
calls my 'ridiculously malicious' interpretation, and asserts that what
he meant was 'that this gap between universality and particularity is
structurally necessary, which is why the US are in the long term
digging "their own grave"'.[35] Let us see exactly what Žižek said in that
interview. To the journalist's question ('Do you think that invading
Iraq was a correct decision from the United States?'), Žižek answers:
'I think that the point is different. Do you remember that ecologist
slogan which said "think globally, act locally"? Well, the problem is
that the United States does the opposite: they think locally and act
globally. Against the opinion of many left-wing intellectuals who are
always complaining about American imperialism, I think that this
country should intervene much more.' And, after giving the examples
of Rwanda and Iraq, he concludes: 'This is the tragedy of the United
States: in the short run they win wars, but in the long run they end up
aggravating the conflicts that they should resolve. The problem is that
they should represent more honestly their role of global policemen.
They don't do it and they pay the price for not doing it'.

---

symptoms in the psychoneurosis, we have quite remarkably increased the number of
people who might be regarded as perverts ... Thus the extraordinarily wide
dissemination of the perversions forces us to suppose that the disposition of perversion
itself is of no great rarity but must form a part of what passes as the normal constitution'
(Freud, *Standard Edition*, vol VII, p. 171). The same can be said about populism.

33 Ernesto Laclau, 'Las manos en la masa', *Radar*, 5 June 2005, p. 20.
34 'Žižek: Estados Unidos deberia intervenir màs y mejor en el mundo. Pide que
asuma su papel de policia global', *La Nación* (Buenos Aires), 10 March 2004.
35 Ibid., p. 14.

It is, of course, for the reader to decide whether I have been particularly ridiculous and malicious in not realizing that when Žižek called for the US to 'represent more honestly their role of global policemen', he meant to say that the gap between universality and particularity is *structurally necessary*, which is why the US would be in the long term digging its own grave. If so, the world is full of ridiculous and malicious people. I remember that, at the time of the publication of Žižek's interview, I commented on it to several people in Argentina, and I did not find a single person who had interpreted Žižek's words the way he is now saying they should be interpreted. Even the journalist interviewing him confesses to being puzzled by the fact that the one asking for the US to act as an international policeman is a Marxist philosopher. And the title of the interview is 'Žižek: The US Should Intervene More and Better in the World'. (What is the meaning of giving this advice if failure is considered 'structurally necessary'?)

But why is failure structurally necessary? Here Žižek calls upon Hegel's help: '*therein* resides my Hegelianism: the "motor" of the historico-dialectical process is precisely the gap between "acting" and "thinking"'.[36] But Hegel's remark does not particularly refer to international politics, because it applies to absolutely everything in the universe. So Žižek's answer to the question of whether the US was right or wrong in invading Iraq is that this is not the important question, for the real issue is that there is, in the structure of the real, a necessary gap between thinking and acting. Anyway, with a lot of goodwill, I am prepared to accept Žižek's interpretation of his own remarks. My friendly advice, however, is that, if he does not want to be utterly misunderstood, he should be more careful in choosing his words when making a public statement.

THE ULTRA-LEFTIST LIQUIDATION OF THE POLITICAL

We have brought into a close relationship a series of categories: the political, the 'people', empty signifiers, equivalence/difference, hegemony. Each of these terms requires the presence of the others. The dispersion of antagonisms and social demands, which are defining features of an era of globalized capitalism, requires the political construction of all social identity, something which is only possible if

---

36 Ibid.

equivalential relations between heterogeneous elements are established, and if the hegemonic dimension of naming is highlighted. That is the reason why *all* political identity is necessarily popular. But there is another factor that needs to be stressed. Antagonistic heterogeneity points, as we have shown, to the limits in the constitution of social objectivity, but, precisely because of that, it cannot be in a situation of *total* exteriority in relation to the system it is opposing. Total exteriority would mean a topological position definable by a precise location in relation to that system and, in that case, it would be part of it. Total exteriority is just one of the forms of interiority. A true political intervention is never merely oppositional; rather, it is one that displaces the terms of the debate, that rearticulates the situation in a new configuration. Chantal Mouffe has spoken about the agonism/antagonism duality, pointing out that political action has the responsibility not only of taking a position within a certain context, but also of structuring the very context in which a plurality of positions will express themselves.[37] This is the meaning of a 'war of position', a category that we have already discussed. This is what makes the ultra-leftist appeal to total exteriority synonymous with the eradication of the political as such.

It is difficult to find a more extreme example of this ultra-Leftism than the work of Žižek. Let us consider the following passage, which is worth quoting in full:

> There is a will to accomplish the 'leap of faith' and *step outside* the global circuit at work here, a will which was expressed in an extreme and terrifying manner in a well-known incident from the Vietnam War: after the US army occupied a local village, their doctors vaccinated the children on the left arm in order to demonstrate their humanitarian care; when, the day after, the village was retaken by the

---

37   It is some motive for celebration that Žižek, in his *Critical Inquiry* article, has for the first time made an effort to discuss separately my work and that of Chantal Mouffe, instead of attributing to each of us the assertions of the other. To refer to a particularly outrageous example: after a long quotation from a work by Mouffe, he comments: 'the problem here is that this translation of antagonism into agonism, into the regulated game of political competition, by definition involves a constitutive exclusion, and it is this exclusion that Laclau fails to thematize'. Slavoj Žižek, *Iraq: The Borrowed Kettle* (London: Verso, 2004), p. 90. The problem is not whether I agree or disagree with what Mouffe has said; the problem is that it is dishonest to criticize an author based on what another author has said.

Vietcong, they cut off the left arms of all the vaccinated children . . .
Although it is difficult to sustain as a literal model to follow, this
complete rejection of the enemy precisely in its caring 'humanitarian' aspect, no matter what the cost, has to be endorsed in its basic
intention. In a similar way, when Sendero Luminoso took over a
village, they did not focus on killing the soldiers or policemen
stationed there, but more on the UN or US agricultural consultants
or health workers trying to help the local peasants – after lecturing
them for hours, and then forcing them to confess their complicity
with imperialism publicly, they shot them. Brutal as this procedure
was, it was rooted in an acute insight: they, not the police or the army,
were the true danger, the enemy at its most perfidious, since they
were 'lying in the guise of truth' – the more they were 'innocent'
(they 'really' tried to help the peasants), the more they served as a
tool of the USA. It is only such a blow against the enemy at his best,
at the point where the enemy 'indeed helps us', that displays true
revolutionary autonomy and 'sovereignty'.[38]

Let us ignore the truculence of this passage and concentrate instead on
what matters: the vision of politics that underlies such a statement. One
feature is immediately visible: the whole notion of rearticulating
demands in a war of position is one hundred per cent absent. There is,
on the contrary, a clear attempt to consolidate the unity of the existing
power bloc. As usual, ultra-Leftism becomes the main source of support
of the existing hegemonic formation. The idea of trying to hegemonize
demands in a new popular bloc is rejected as a matter of principle. Only
a violent, head-on confrontation with the enemy as it is, is conceived as
legitimate action. Only a position of total exteriority with respect to the
present situation can guarantee revolutionary purity. There is only one
step from here to making exteriority *qua* exteriority the supreme political value, and to advocating violence for violence's sake. That there is
nothing 'ridiculously malicious' in my suggestion that Žižek is not far
from taking that step can be seen from the following passage:

The only 'realistic' prospect is to ground a new political universality
by opting for the impossible, fully assuming the place of the exception, with no taboos, no a priori norms ('human rights', 'democracy'),

---

38   Žižek, *Iraq*, pp 83–4.

respect for which would prevent us also from 'resignifying' terror, the ruthless exercise of power, the spirit of sacrifice . . . if this radical choice is decried by some bleeding-heart liberals as *Linksfaschismus*, so be it![39]

We might ask ourselves: What, for Žižek, are the political subjects of his *Linksfaschismus*? It is not easy to answer this question, because he is quite elusive when the question comes to the discussion of Left-wing strategies. So Žižek's book on Iraq is quite useful, because there he devotes a few pages to the protagonists of what he sees as true revolutionary action. He refers mainly to three: the workers' councils of the soviet tradition – which he himself recognizes have disappeared; Canudos – a millenarian movement in nineteenth-century Brazil; and the inhabitants of the Brazilian favelas. The connection between the last two is presented by Žižek in the following terms:

> The echoes of Canudos are clearly discernible in today's favelas in Latin American megalopolises: are they not, in some sense, the first 'liberated territories', the cells of future self-organised societies? . . . The liberated territory of Canudos in Bahia will remain for ever the model of a space of emancipation, of an alternative community which completely negates the existing space of the state. Everything is to be endorsed here, up to and including religious 'fanaticism'.[40]

This is pure delirium. The favelas are shanty towns of passive poverty submitted to the action of utterly non-political criminal gangs that keep the population terrified – to which one has to add the action of the police, who carry out executions regularly denounced by the press. As for the assertion that the favelas keep alive the memory of Canudos, it involves being so grotesquely misinformed that the only possible answer is 'go and do your homework'. There is not a single social movement in contemporary Brazil that establishes a link with the nineteenth-century millenarian tradition – let alone the inhabitants of the *favelas*, who have no idea of what Canudos was Žižek

39   Slavoj Žižek, 'Holding the Place', in Judith Butler, Ernesto Laclau and Slavoj Žižek, *Contingency, Hegemony, Universality: Contemporary Dialogues on the Left* (London: Verso, 2000), p. 326.
40   Žižek, *Iraq*, p. 82.

totally ignores what happened in Brazil today, yesterday or ever – which for him, of course, is no obstacle to making the most sweeping statements concerning Brazilian revolutionary strategies. This is the process of 'Martianization' I referred to before: attributing to actually existing subjects the most absurd characteristics, while keeping their names so that the illusion of a contact with reality is maintained. The people of the favelas have pressing enough problems without paying any attention to Žižek's eschatological injunctions. So what he needs are *real* Martians. But they are too clever to come down to our planet just to satisfy Žižek's truculent dreams.

CHAPTER 8

An Ethics of Militant Engagement

I

I find Alain Badiou's ethical reflections most congenial.[1] There are three aspects of them, in particular, that I find clearly appealing and close to my own theoretical approach. In the first place, his attempt to articulate ethics within an emancipatory project. Against the prevailing contemporary trend, which presents ethics as a purely *defensive* intervention – that is, as a reaction to the violation of human rights – Badiou roots his ethics in an essentially affirmative discourse. Secondly, the universality of the ethical address does not depend, for Badiou, on the presumed universality of its place of enunciation: on the contrary, ethics is constitutively linked to the fidelity to an event that is always concrete and situated. Finally, Badiou scrupulously avoids the temptation to derive the ensemble of moral norms from the ethical as such – the former belongs, for him, to what is countable within a situation that is strictly heterogeneous with respect to the latter.

My own theoretical approach is, from this point of view, at least comparable to Badiou's, and the fact has not gone unrecognized. Slavoj Žižek, for instance, writes:

> A series of obvious differences notwithstanding, the theoretical edifices of Laclau and Badiou are united by a deep homology. Against the Hegelian vision of the 'concrete universal', of the reconciliation between Universal and Particular (or between Being and Event) which is still clearly discernible in Marx, they both start by asserting a constitutive and irreducible gap that undermines the self-enclosed consistency of the ontological edifice: for Laclau, this gap is the gap between the Particular and the empty Universal, which necessitates the operation of hegemony (or the gap between the differential

---

1 I would like to thank Peter Hallward for his careful reading of the draft version of this article, and for his many comments which helped me to present my argument in a clearer and more precise way.

structure of the positive social order – the logic of *differences* – and properly political antagonism, which involves the logic of *equivalence*); for Badiou, it is the gap between Being and Event (between the order of Being – structure, state of situation, knowledge – and the event of Truth, Truth as Event). In both cases, the problem is how to break out of the self-enclosed field of ontology as a description of the positive universe; in both cases, the dimension which undermines the closure of ontology has an 'ethical' character – it concerns the contingent act of *decision* against the background of the 'undecidable' multiplicity of Being; consequently, both authors endeavour to conceptualise a new, post-Cartesian mode of *subjectivity* which cuts its links with ontology and hinges on a contingent act of decision.[2]

In spite of these many real points of convergence, there are also, however, several aspects on which our respective approaches fundamentally diverge, and it is these that I shall address in the following pages. The fact that our approaches are indeed comparable, however, has its advantages: opposite theoretical decisions can be presented as alternative routes whose divergence is thinkable out of what had been, up to that point, a relatively shared theoretical terrain. One last preliminary remark: I will mainly refer, in what follows, to Badiou's ethics, without any comprehensive discussion of his ontology – a task in which I hope to engage in the not too distant future.

Let us first recapitulate some basic categories of Badiou's theory. The main distinction, from his perspective, is that between *situation* and *event*. Situation is the terrain of a multiplicity corresponding to what can be called, in general terms, the field of objectivity. Being is not one – oneness is, for Badiou, a theological category – but multiple. Presentable or consistent multiplicity corresponds, essentially, with the field of knowledge, of the countable, of the distinct. The ensemble of objective distinctions corresponds to a structuring principle that Badiou calls the *state* of the situation. What we usually call morality – the normative order – is part of this state, and is organized by this structural principle. A distinction has to be established here between *presentation* of a situation in which structuration – order – shows itself as such, and *representation*, the moment in which not *structure* but

2   Slavoj Žižek, *The Ticklish Subject: The Absent Centre of Political Ontology* (London: Verso, 1999), pp. 172–3.

structuring comes to the fore. The event is grounded on that which is radically unrepresentable within the situation, that which constitutes its *void* (a category to which I will return below). The event is the actual declaring of that void, a radical break with the situation that makes visible what the situation itself can only conceal. While knowledge is the inscription of what happens within pre-given objective categories, *truth* – the series of implications sustained in the wake of an event – is *singular*: its eventual nature cannot be subsumed under any pre-existing rule. The event is, thus, incommensurable with the situation; its break with it is truly foundational. If we tried to define its relation with the situation, we could only say that it is a *subtraction* from it.

The ethical is intimately linked to the notion of event. Once the event takes place, the visibility that its advent makes possible opens an area of indeterminacy in relation to the ways of dealing with it: either we can stick to that visibility through what Badiou calls a *fidelity* to the event – which involves transforming the situation through a restructuring that takes the proclaimed truth as its point of departure – or we can negate the radically eventual character of the event. When it involves the perversion or corruption of a truth, this latter option is *evil*. In Badiou's account, evil can take one of three main forms: the form of *betrayal* (the abandonment of fidelity to the event), the form of the *simulacrum* (the replacement, through naming, of the void in the fullness of the community), and the form of a dogmatic *totalization* of a truth.

At this point we have to address a series of interrelated questions. Is an event, which defines itself exclusively through its ability to subtract itself from a situation, enough to ground an ethical alternative? Is the distinction void/fullness a solid enough criterion for discriminating between event and simulacrum? Is the opposition situation/event sufficiently clear-cut to ascribe to the eventual camp everything needed to formulate an ethical principle? My answer to all of these three questions will be negative.

It makes sense to start with a consideration of the three forms of evil to which Badiou refers. The main question is: To what extent does he smuggle into his argument something that he had formally excluded at its very beginning? As I said, the basic ontological opposition that he establishes is that between situation and event, whose only ground is given by the category of 'subtraction'. This also sets up the parameters within which the distinction is thinkable. We have to forget everything about the material, ontic contents of the situation, and reduce it to its purely formal defining principle (the organization of the countable, the differential, as such). In that case, however, the only possible content of the event as pure subtraction is the presentation or declaration of the unrepresentable. In other words, the event also can only have a purely *formal* content. As a result, the fidelity to the event (the exclusive content of the ethical act) has also to be an entirely formal ethical injunction. How, in that case, to differentiate the ethical from the simulacrum? As Badiou himself makes clear, the simulacrum – as one of the figures of evil – can only emerge in the terrain of truth. So if Badiou is going to be faithful to his theoretical premises, the distinction between event and simulacrum has also to be a formal one – in other words, it has to emerge from the form of the event as such, independently of its actual content.

Is Badiou true to his own theoretical presuppositions on this point? I do not think so. His answer to the question of the criterion distinguishing event from simulacrum is that the event addresses the *void* of a situation. 'What allows a genuine event to be at the origin of a truth – which is the only thing that can be for all, and can be eternally', he writes, 'is precisely the fact that it relates to the particularity of a situation only from the bias of its void. The void, the multiple-of-nothing, neither excludes nor constrains anyone. It is the absolute neutrality of being – such that the fidelity that originates in an event, although it is an immanent break within a singular situation, is nonetheless universally addressed.'[3] The simulacrum – Nazism, for instance – relates to the situation as plenitude or substance. According to the logic of a simulacrum, the pseudo-event 'is supposed to bring into being, and name, not the void of the earlier situation, but its plenitude – not the universality of that which is sustained, precisely, by no particular characteristic (no particular multiple), but the absolute particularity of a community, itself rooted in the characteristics of its soil, its blood, and its race'.[4] What is wrong with this solution? Several things – to which I will refer later – but especially one which, to some extent, anticipates the others: the distinction truth/simulacrum cannot ultimately be formulated, because it does not have any viable

---

    3   Alain Badiou, *Ethics: An Essay on the Understanding of Evil* (London: Verso, 2001), p. 73.
    4   Ibid.

place of enunciation within Badiou's theoretical edifice (at this stage of its elaboration, at least).[5] There are only two places of enunciation within Badiou's system: the situation and the event. Now, the situation is not a possible locus for a discourse discriminating between true and false events, between void and fullness, because the void is precisely that which the situation cannot think. But that place of enunciation cannot be constituted around the event either. The 'truth' that, over time, develops the implications of the event cannot contribute a discriminating capacity between true and false events that the event itself does not provide. All that the subjects engaged in a truth procedure can do, *once they accept the event as a true one*, is to be clear about what perverting an event would consist of – but this by itself does not establish a criterion for distinguishing truth from simulacrum. *It is only by appealing to a third discourse that is not itself easily integrated into Badiou's theoretical system that the distinction truth/ simulacrum can be maintained.* This is hardly surprising: if the event constitutes itself through a pure and simple subtraction from a situation conceived as a given contingent embodiment of the formal principle of counting (such that its concreteness has to be strictly ignored), there is no way for the subjects affirming that event to discriminate between types of interruption of that situation – let alone of attributing a differential ethical value to those types.

It is clear that, on the basis of the asserted premises, we cannot advance beyond establishing the formal components of a militant ethics, and that we cannot legislate anything concerning the content of the latter – except by smuggling a third (as yet untheorized) discourse into the argument. This appeal to a third discourse as a sort of *deus ex machina* is not peculiar to Badiou. Žižek's analysis of Nazism proceeds along similar lines. It starts by subscribing to Badiou's distinction:

> In contrast to this authentic act which intervenes in the constitutive void, point of failure – or what Alain Badiou has called the 'symptomal torsion' of a given constellation – the inauthentic act legitimises itself through reference to the point of substantial fullness of a given

---

5 I have been told that, in his courses of the late 1990s, Badiou partially addressed this objection through his reference to 'reactionary' and 'obscure' subject positions. I can only refer, however, to his published material.

constellation: Race, True Religion, Nation . . . it aims precisely at obliterating the last traces of the 'symptomal torsion' which disturbs the balance of that constellation.[6]

The analysis of Nazism that follows from these premises offers few surprises:

> The so-called 'Nazi revolution', with its disavowal/displacement of the fundamental social antagonism ('class struggle' that divides the social edifice from within) – with its projection/externalisation of the cause of social antagonisms into the figure of the Jew, and the consequent reassertion of the corporatist notion of society as an organic Whole – clearly *avoids* confrontation with social antagonism: the 'Nazi revolution' is the exemplary case of a pseudo-change, of a frenetic activity in the course of which many things did change – 'something was going on all the time' – so that, precisely, something – that which *really* matters – would *not* change; so that things would fundamentally 'remain the same'.[7]

The advantage of Žižek's over Badiou's formulations is that they make quite explicit that third silent discourse which is present in Badiou's texts only through its theoretical effects. Žižek makes no bones about the nature of his exercise: he robustly asserts a crude theory of 'false consciousness', which enables him to detect the fundamental social antagonisms, what 'really matters' in society, and how things could change without any meaningful change taking place.[8] What is wrong

---

6   Slavoj Žižek, 'Class Struggle or Postmodernism? Yes, Please', in Judith Butler, Ernesto Laclau and Slavoj Žižek, *Contingency, Hegemony, Universality: Contemporary Dialogues on the Left* (London: Verso, 2000), p. 125.

7   Ibid., pp. 124–5.

8   The fact that Žižek makes more explicit than Badiou what I have called the 'third discourse' does not mean that his theoretical stance is more consistent. He constantly oscillates between grounding his ethico-political options in a Marxist theoretical approach (even an *ad usum Delphini* Marxism, as in the passage that I have just quoted) and the exaltation of the purely formal virtues of *vivere pericolosamente*. And when it is a matter of opting for the latter – of being anti-system for the sake of being so – he can be quite relaxed concerning ideological constraints. He suggests, for instance, that 'the only "realistic" prospect is to ground a new political universality by opting for the *impossible*, fully assuming the place of exception, with no taboos, no a priori norms ("human rights", "democracy"), respect for which would prevent us also from "resignifying" terror, the ruthless exercise of power, the spirit of sacrifice . . . if this

with all this? Not, obviously, the concrete content of his assertions – I agree with most of it – but the role that those assertions play in his theory and, in a more subtle way, also in Badiou's theory. For they are a set of ontic assertions whose ambition is to establish distinctions between *ontological* categories. 'Situation', 'event', 'truth', 'generic procedure', have an ontological status in Badiou's discourses.[9] Likewise the 'void' and its opposite – namely, a full particularity convoked as the substance of a situation. So, in that case, how are we to determine which is the true void of a concrete situation? There are only two possibilities: either to reabsorb, in a Hegelian fashion, the ontic into the ontological – a solution that Žižek flirts with but that Badiou most scrupulously tries to avoid; or to name the void through the axiomatic postulation inherent to a truth procedure – in which case there seem to be no available means of discriminating between true and false events, and the principle of the distinction between event and simulacrum collapses.

A third solution is conceivable: that the *marks* of a true event are already ontologically determined (or, if you like, transcendentally preconstituted). For Badiou these marks exist and are inscribed in the *exclusive* alternative of either relating to a particular situation from the bias of its void, or naming the presumed 'fullness' of a certain situation. If we could demonstrate that such an alternative is truly exclusive, and that it is constitutively inherent to any possible concrete situation, our problem would have been solved.

This demonstration is, however, impossible. Let us look at the matter from the two sides of this potential polarity – from the void, in the first place. What figures as void is always, for Badiou, the void of a situation. Whatever counts as void, or as nothing, is scattered throughout a situation and is necessarily included in every subset of a situation; since there is nothing 'in' the void that might serve to identify or locate it, any such operation is impossible. But each situation contains a minimally identifiable element, a group or individual located on the 'edge' of whatever counts as nothing for the situation – an element

<hr />

radical choice is decried by some bleeding-heart liberals as *Linkfaschismus*, so be it!'. 'Holding the Place', in Judith Butler, Ernesto Laclau and Slavoj Žižek, *Contingency, Hegemony, Universality*, p. 326. Slightly truculent, isn't it?

9 The term 'ontology' has a particular meaning in Badiou's theoretical approach, different in some respects from the current philosophical use. I am employing it in the latter sense. The ontic/ontological opposition comes, of course, from Heidegger.

that counts only as an indiscernible 'something', with no other identifying characteristics. This element, for Badiou, has no elements of its own in common with the situation – in other words, no elements that the situation itself can recognize or discern. The inhabitants of this liminal space are presentable in two very different ways, whose articulation is crucial for the question we are discussing. Firstly, they can be *named* in a *referential* way: the *sans-papiers* in today's France, the working class in capitalist society, the death of Christ in Saint Paul's discourse in its opposition to Hebrew Law and Greek wisdom, and so on. In the second place, however, that name remains *empty* because what it designates, and proclaims through the event, does not correspond to anything that is representable within the counting of the situation – it would be, to use a different terminology, a signifier without a signified.

The problem that immediately arises concerns the precise way in which these two dimensions are to be linked. If referential designation and non-representabilty within the situation did exactly overlap with each other, there would be no problem: the edge of the void would be precisely located in a site defined by the parameters of the situation. But there are neither logical nor historical reasons to make this simplifying assumption. Let us suppose that a society is experiencing what Gramsci called an *organic crisis*: what confronts us, in that case, are not particular sites defining (delimiting) what is unrepresentable within the general field of representation, but rather the fact that the very logic of representation has lost its structural abilities. This transforms the role of the event: it does not simply have to proclaim the centrality of an exception with respect to a highly structured situation, but also to reconstruct the principle of situationality as such around a new core.

This, in my view, radically changes the void/situation relationship. It is precisely at this point that my approach begins to differ from Badiou's. Within Badiou's system, there is no way in which the void can be given any content, as it is and remains empty by definition. The 'evental site', on the other hand, always has a certain content. This is what I call 'referential designation'. This distinction makes perfect sense within the set theory approach within which Badiou operates. The possibility that I have raised, however – that the logic of representation might lose its structuring abilities – raises questions that can hardly be answered within Badiou's system. For, in that case, what becomes uncountable in the situation is the principle of countability as such. So the truth procedure in which its subjects engage consists, in one of its basic dimensions, in reconstructing the situation around a new core. The consequence is that there is no longer any question of a linear development of the implications of the event: the latter has to show its articulating abilities *by going beyond itself*, so that the drastic separation between evental site and void must necessarily be put into question. Consequently some filling of the void – of a special kind that requires theoretical description – becomes necessary. (Needless to say, the very idea of such a filling is an anathema for Badiou: any filling of the void is, for him, evil.)

How might this filling proceed? Badiou thinks that the void, having no members of its own (in the situation presented by set theory it figures as the empty set) does not belong to any particular situation – which means that it belongs to them – but that, as far as human situations are concerned, the subjects of a truth that affirms the event addresses pure and simple universality. This means indistinct humanity – in the sense that Marx, for instance, asserted that the proletariat has only his chains. I can only go halfway with Badiou in this argument. There are two insurmountable difficulties. The first is that the category of void – of the empty set: Æ – is only empty when it operates within mathematics. When it is transposed to social analysis it is filled with certain contents – thinking, freedom/consciousness, only chains, and so on – which are far from being empty. What we have here is a hopelessly metaphorical exercise by which emptiness is equated with universality. But it only takes two seconds to realize that the universal content is not empty. We are simply confronted with an attempt at an ethical defence of universality which proceeds through an illegitimate appeal to set theory. So much for Badiou's claim that any filling of the void is evil. In the second place, we are sometimes presented with the argument that the subjects of a truth have means of differentiating between truth and simulacrum – criteria such as strict equality, universality, indifference to all qualities and values, and so on. But it is clear that the validity of these criteria entirely depends on accepting as a starting point the equation between void and universality. So the argument is perfectly circular.

Let me be clear: mine is not an objection to universality as such, but to Badiou's way of constructing it theoretically. In one sense, it is true that a radical interruption of a given situation will interpellate people across and beyond particularisms and differences. Every revolutionary break has, in that respect, universalizing effects. People live for a moment the illusion that, because an oppressive regime has been overthrown, what has been overthrown is oppression *as such*. It is in those terms that the void, in Badiou's sense, not having any distinctive content, addresses something which is beyond all particularity *as particularity*. But the other side of the picture, the moment of referential designation, is still there, doing its job. For – and at this point I definitely disagree with Badiou – I do not think that the particularism inherent in that local reference can be simply eliminated from the picture as a site having only relations of exteriority with the void. The *sans-papiers*, as an indiscernible element within their situation, *may* come to articulate a position that holds true for all members of that situation (for example, 'Everyone who is here is from here'); but they are also constituted as political subjects through a series of particular demands that could be granted by an expansive hegemony of the existing situation and, in that sense, individual *sans-papiers* may come to be counted in their turn – to become normal members of the situation.

The conclusion is obvious: the frontiers between the countable and the uncountable are essentially unstable. But this means that there is no locus, no site within the situation, which has inscribed a priori within itself the guarantees of universality – that is, there is *no natural name* for the void. Conversely, no name is a priori excluded from naming it. Let us give an example. The Solidarność movement began as a set of particular demands of a group of workers in Gdansk. However, as those demands were formulated in a particularly repressive context, they became the symbols and the surface of inscription of a plurality of other demands that were uncountable within the situation defined by the bureaucratic regime. That is, it was through the articulation between themselves that these demands constructed a certain universalism that transcended all particularities. This especially applies to the central symbols of Solidarność: a certain remnant of particularism cannot be eliminated from them, but because those symbols served to represent a large set of democratic equivalential demands, they became the embodiment of universality as such. It is through this equivalence/transcendence between particularities that something like the name of the void can be constructed. This is what in my work I have called hegemony: the process by which a particularity assumes the representation of a universality that is essentially incommensurable with it.

Two principal conclusions follow from this argument: first, universality has no a priori sites of emergence, but is the result of the displacement of the frontier between the countable and the uncountable – of the construction of an expansive hegemony; second, if articulation is given its proper, central role, naming the void is constitutively linked to the process of its filling, but this filling can only proceed through an uneasy balance between universality and particularity – a balance which, by definition, can never be broken through the exclusive domination of either of its two poles. To fill a void is not simply to assign to it a particular content, but to make of that content the nodal point of an equivalential universality transcending it. Now, from the point of view of our original problem, which was the determination of a true event (whose precondition was the naming of a pure void – a universality not contaminated by particularity), this means that such a pure universality is impossible. Its place is always going to be occupied/embodied by something that is less than itself.

Let us now move to the other side of the polarity: the particularistic filling of the void that Badiou and Žižek discuss in connection with Nazism. Let us remain within that example which, being extreme, presents the best possible terrain for Badiou to argue his case. Badiou cannot be accused of trying to make his case easy: on the contrary, he stresses without concessions the structural parallels between event and simulacrum. ' "Simulacrum" must be understood here in the strong sense', he admits:

> all the formal traits of a truth are at work in the simulacrum. Not only a universal nomination of the event, inducing the power of a radical break, but also the 'obligation' of a fidelity, and the promotion of a *simulacrum of the subject*, erected – without the advent of any Immortal – above the human animality of the others, of those who are arbitrarily declared to belong to the communitarian substance whose promotion and domination the simulacrum–event is designed to assure.[10]

How does Badiou establish, on these premises, the distinction between event and simulacrum? Not surprisingly, through a drastic

10   Badiou, *Ethics*, p. 74.

192 THE RHETORICAL FOUNDATIONS OF SOCIETY

opposition between the *void* and what stands as the *substance* of the community – precisely the distinction that I tried to undermine. 'Fidelity to a simulacrum – unlike fidelity to an event – regulates its break with the situation not by the universality of the void, but by the close particularity of an abstract set (the "Germans" or the "Aryans")'.[11] To assess the viability of Badiou's solution, we have to ask ourselves some questions that are the opposite of those we were dealing with in the case of the void: To what extent is the particularism of the Nazi discourse incompatible with any appeal to the universal (to the void)? And to what extent does the abstract set that regulates the break with the situation (the 'Germans', the 'Aryans', and so on) function in the Nazi discourse as a particularistic instance?

Let us consider these two questions in turn. Regarding the first, there can be no doubt at all: the void is as much addressed in the Nazi discourse as in any socialist one. Let us remember that the void is not in our view universality in the strict sense of the term, but that which is uncountable in a given situation. As I have argued, and I think Badiou would agree, it does not have a single and precise site in a critical situation, when the very principles of counting are threatened and the reconstruction of the community as a whole around a new core comes to the fore as a fundamental social need. That was exactly the situation that prevailed in the crisis of the Weimar Republic. There was not, then, a clash between an uncountable presence and a well-structured situation (between a proclaimed event and the state of the situation), but a fundamental destructuring of the community which required that the named event became, from its very inception, a principle of restructuration. It was not a matter of substituting a fully-fledged existing situation with a different one deriving from a new principle subversive of the status quo, but of a hegemonic struggle between rival principles, between different ways of naming the uncountable to see which one was more capable of *articulating a situation* against the alternative of anomie and chaos. In this sense, there is no doubt that the void as such was clearly addressed in Nazi discourse.

But what about the particular set (blood, race, and so on) that Nazism convoked as the event breaking with the situation? Is this particular communitarian substance not incompatible with the

---

11 Ibid.

universality of the void (of the empty set)? We have to consider the matter carefully. In my discussion of the naming of the void I have distinguished between the referential designation of the edge of the void and the universality of the content that site embodies. I have also argued that that universality will depend on the extension of the chain of equivalences expressed through that name. This means that no name having a certain political centrality will ever have a univocal, particular reference. Terms that formally name a particularity will acquire, through equivalential chains, a far more universal reference, while, conversely, others whose denotation is apparently universal can become, in certain discursive articulations, the name of extremely particularistic meanings. This means, first, that there is no name of a pure, uncontaminated universality (of a pure void); and, second, that a purely particular name is also impossible.[12] What I have earlier called hegemony consists precisely in this undecidable game between universality and particularity. In that case, however, the distinction between true event and simulacrum collapses: it is simply impossible to conceive evil as a result of a particularistic invocation against the universality of truth. For the same reason, neither can the sharp distinction between generic set and constructible set be maintained, as far as society is concerned.

Does this mean that the very notion of evil has to be abandoned, that anything goes, and that it is not possible to pass an ethical judgement about phenomena such as Nazism? Obviously not. The only thing that *does* follow from my previous argument is that it is impossible to ground ethical options at the abstract level of a theory dominated by the situation/event duality, and that these categories

---

12 My basic assumption is that the central terms of a discursive formation universalize themselves by operating as nodal points (as master signifiers, in the Lacanian sense) of an equivalential chain. I have mentioned before the example of Solidarność, but this universalization through equivalence is always present. Let us just think of the demands of 'peace, bread and land' in the Russian Revolution, which condensed a plurality of other demands, or of the role of the 'market' in Eastern European discourse after 1989. My argument is that the construction of Nazi hegemony operated exactly in the same way and that, as a result, the central symbols of its discourse – those that named the void – cannot be conceived as having a purely particularistic reference. Of course, the universal function of those names weakens but does not eliminate their particular content, but that happens with all hegemonic discourses. It is not possible for the universal to speak in a direct way, without the mediation of some particularity.

– whatever their validity in other spheres – do not provide criteria for moral choice. This also means that the terrain on which these criteria can emerge is going to be a much more concrete one. This much Badiou himself would be ready to accept: truth for him is always the truth of a situation. In that case, however, what I have called the silent third discourse implicit in his approach – the one that would actually provide him with a legitimate position of enunciation for his discourse on evil – needs explicitly to be brought to the fore. But this operation is not possible without introducing some changes into Badiou's theoretical apparatus. This is the question I will address next.

II

Let us summarise our argument so far. Badiou, quite correctly, refuses to ground ethics in any a priori normativism – the latter belonging, by definition, to the situation as a countable *given*. The source of ethical commitment should be found in the implications or consequences drawn from the event conceived as *subtraction* from that situation. In that case, however, any distinction between true and false events cannot be based on what events actually proclaim – firstly, because that would smuggle into the argument the normativism that was axiomatically excluded, and, secondly, because it would require a judging instance external to both situation and event (what we have called a 'third discourse'). The latter is what makes Žižek's argument hopelessly eclectic, and it is what Badiou tries to avoid. That being so, the only course open to him is to attempt to ground the event/simulacrum distinction in the very structural differentiations that his dualistic ontology has established. He finds this ground in the void/plenum duality. This does not entirely eliminate the problem of the third discourse, for Badiou has still to explain why giving expression to the void is good while giving it to the plenum is bad – but at least a step in the right direction has been taken. The cornerstone of the argument thus relies on the void/plenum distinction being unambiguous. But, as we have seen, Badiou's distinction is untenable: firstly, because, as I argued above, the void – insofar as the category is applicable to a human situation – is not for Badiou really empty, but has already a certain content: the universal; and, secondly, because the arrangement of the elements of the situation brought about by the subject out of the generic inconsistency revealed by the event requires, if the notion of 'arrangement' is going to make any sense, some consistency between the universality *shown* by the event and the new arrangement resulting from the subject's intervention. Of what does this 'consistency' consist? One possibility is that it is a logical consistency. But Badiou – and I, too – would reject this possibility because, in that case, the gap between event and situation would be cancelled, and the notion of an ontology grounded in multiplicity would no longer make any sense. The *only* other alternative is that the consistency between event and new arrangement results from a contingent construction – and it necessarily has to be so, given that it starts from the terrain of a primordial inconsistency. This simply means that the consistency of the new arrangement is going to be, through and through, a constructed one. Ergo 'truth procedure' and 'contingent construction' are interchangeable terms. Now, what else is this but *filling in* the void? If my argument is correct, the void/plenum distinction falls – or at least establishes between its two poles a far more complex system of mutual displacements than Badiou's sharp dichotomy allows.

What I will now go on to argue is that, paradoxically, the blind alley we are discussing is not unconnected to what is perhaps the most valuable feature of Badiou's ethics: his refusal to postulate any kind of a priori normativism. This refusal, however, has been accompanied by the *assertion* of some ontological presuppositions that are the very source of the difficulties we are dealing with. Let us make one last remark before embarking on this discussion. Of the three figures of evil to which Badiou refers, only the first – the distinction between truth and simulacrum – intends to discriminate between true and false events. The second, as Badiou himself recognizes, would be seen as evil not only from the perspective of the true event, but from that of the simulacrum (a fascist as much as a revolutionary would consider evil any kind of weakening of the revolutionary will). As for the third figure, it presents problems of its own that I will discuss presently.

As I said at the beginning, I do not intend in this chapter to discuss in any detail the complex – and in many respects fascinating – ontology developed by Badiou. But some reference to it is necessary, given that his ethics strictly depend on his ontological distinctions. The most important categories structuring the latter are as follows. Situation and event, void and plenum, we have already explained. Let us add that, the situation being essentially multiple, a new category – the 'state of the situation' – has to be introduced to bring about a principle of internal stabilization: the possibility that the structuring resources of the situation can themselves be counted as *one*. The borders between the situation and its void are conceived in terms of 'edges' – that is, 'sites of the event'. The latter, although belonging to the situation, will provide a certain degree of infrastructure to an event, should one take place; I am calling it 'infrastructure' in a purely topographical sense without, obviously, any kind of causal connotation.

I have already raised the possibility of some displacements within Badiou's categories which could, I think, go some way in the direction of solving some of the difficulties that his ethical theory presents at the moment. I will now review, in sequence: first, the precise nature of those displacements; second, the extent to which they put the ethical argument on firmer ground; third, the consequences that they would have – if accepted – for Badiou's ontological perspective.

I have attempted an initial deconstruction of the stark void/plenum opposition. I have suggested that the edge of the void is not a precise place within an otherwise fully ordered (countable) situation, but something whose very presence makes it impossible for a situation to be entirely structured as such. (It is like the Lacanian Real, which is not something that exists *alongside* the Symbolic, but is *within* the Symbolic in such a way as to prevent the Symbolic from being fully constituted). In that case, however, a distinction has to be introduced between the *situation* and what we could designate with the neologism *situationness* – the former being the actually ontic existing order, and the latter the ontological principle of *ordering* as such. These two dimensions never fully overlap with each other. This being the case, the *event* – whose unpredictability within the situation, asserted by Badiou, I fully accept – has from its very inception the two roles that I mentioned earlier: on the one hand, to subvert the existing state of the situation by naming the unnameable; on the other, I would add, to restructure a new state around a new core. Mao's Long March succeeded because it was not only the destruction of an old order but also the reconstruction of the nation around a new core. And Gramsci's notion of a 'becoming state' of the working class – against any simplistic notion of 'seizure of power' – moves in the same direction. In that case, however, situation and event contaminate each other: they are not separate locations within a social topography, but

constitutive dimensions of any social identity. (One central consequence of this assertion is, as we will see, that the event loses, in some
respects, the exceptional character attributed to it by Badiou.)

The same goes for the duality event/site of the event. (The site
would be, for instance, in Christian discourse, Christ's mortality,
while the event would be his resurrection.) For Badiou there is an
essential heterogeneity between the two. It is only at that price that the
event can be truly universal – in other words, it can reveal the void
that does not belong in any part of the situation, although it is necessarily included in all of them. In the Christian notion of incarnation,
again, no physical quality anticipated, in the particular body of Mary,
that she was going to be the mother of God. I cannot accept this logic.
As in the previous case, the relationship between event and site of the
event has to be conceived as one of mutual contamination. The
demands of the *sans-papiers* are clearly, *in the first instance*, particular
and not universal demands. So how can any kind of universality
emerge out of them? Only insofar as people excluded from many
other sites within a situation (who are unnameable within it) perceive
their common nature as excluded and live their struggles – in their
particularity – as part of a larger emancipatory struggle. But this
means that any event of universal significance is constructed out of a
plurality of sites whose particularity is equivalentially articulated but
definitely not eliminated. As I tried to show earlier with the example
of Solidarność, one particular site can acquire a special relevance as
locus of a universal equivalent, but even at that site, the tension
between universality and particularity is constitutive of the emancipatory struggle.

The consequence of this is clear: a hegemonic universality is the
only one that any society can achieve. The infinity of the emancipatory task is very much present – it is not a question of denying it in the
name of a pure particularism – for the struggle against an oppressive
regime can be constructed, through equivalential chains, as a struggle
against oppression in general, but the particularism of the hegemonic
force (however diluted that particularity might be) is still there
producing its limiting effects. It is like gold, whose function as general
equivalent (as money) does not cancel the oscillations inherent to its
nature as a particular commodity. There is a moment in Badiou's analysis in which he almost approaches the hegemonico-equivalential
logic that I am describing: it is when he refers to 'investigations'

(*enquêtes*) as militant attempts to win over elements of the situation to the event.[13] But his attempt is rather limited: it is not conceived by him as the *construction* of a wider evental site through the expansion of equivalential chains, but as a process of total conversion in which there is either 'connection' or 'disconnection', without possibility of any middle. Although the result of this piece-by-piece construction is as much for Badiou as for me a widening of the evental site, there is not in his account any deepening of the mechanisms underlying the operations of 'connection' and 'disconnection'. In the end, the process of conversion, seen at its purest in the case of religion, remains, for Badiou, the model paradigm for any description of the process of winning over.

So where are we left, as far as our ethical question is concerned, if we accept this set of displacements of Badiou's categories (and I am sure Badiou would not accept them)? Firstly, it is clear that all ground for the distinction between truth and simulacrum has collapsed. That ground – in Badiou's discourse – was given by the possibility of a radical differentiation between void and plenum. But it is precisely that distinction that does not stand once the filling of the void and the naming of it have become indistinguishable from each other. However, this very collapse of the distinction opens the way to other possibilities that Badiou's stark dichotomy had closed. For the edge of the void not only has no precise location (if it had it would have a proper, unambiguous name), but names the absent fullness of the situation – it is, if you like, the presence of an absence, something that can be *named* but not *counted* (in other words, which cannot be represented as an objective difference). If, on top of that, we accept that the void is constitutively included in any situation – and this is something I very much agree with, from a different theoretical perspective – the possibility of *naming* it, which Badiou quite rightly sees as its only possibility of discursive inscription, would be that of *attributing to a particular difference the role of naming something entirely incommensurable with itself – namely, the absent fullness of the situation.*[14] In that case, naming the void and naming the plenum

---

13   Alain Badiou, *L'être et l'événement* (Paris: Éditions du Seuil, 1988), p. 334.

14   The notion of 'absent fullness' is mine and not Badiou's. See my essay 'Why Do Empty Signifiers Matter to Politics?', *Emancipation(s)* (London: Verso, 1996). It has no exact equivalent in Badiou's system because it is based in my different way of conceiving the process of naming.

become indistinguishable from each other. The only other possibility – that the site of the event *qua* site determines what the event can name – is excluded de jure by Badiou's argument; and, anyway, it would again raise the spectre of the 'third discourse'. In that case, however, blood, race, the nation, the proletarian revolution, or communism – all are indifferent ways of naming the void/plenum. Let us be clear: from a political viewpoint, of course, it makes all difference which signifier will name the void. The problem, however, is how to construct such a political differentiation discursively. Badiou's implicit answer would be that – *malgré lui* – the void has potentially a certain content: the universal. For me, given the subversion I have attempted at the ontological level of the truth/simulacrum distinction, this solution is not available. In what follows, I will present an outline of what is, for me, the right way of dealing with this problem.

How to get out of this impasse? In my view the answer requires two steps. The first is the full recognition that, under the label of the 'ethical', two different things have been put together that do not necessarily overlap – in fact they usually do not. The first is the search for the unconditioned – for that which would fill the gap between what society is and what it ought to be. The second is the moral evaluation of the various ways of carrying out this filling role – as long, of course, as this filling operation is accepted as a legitimate one (which is not the case for Badiou). How do these two different tasks interact with each other? A first possibility is that the distinction between the two is denied. Plato's search for the 'good society' is at one and the same time the description of a society that is both without gaps, or holes, and morally good. Aristotle's *Nicomachean Ethics* pursues a similar conjunction of spheres. The problem emerges when it is perceived that the filling function can operate through many different fillers, and that there is no way of determining the latter through the mere logical analysis of the former. To return to my previous terminology: the void undermines the principle of countability in society (what I have called the *situationness* of the situation), but does not anticipate how to choose between different states of the situation. In a society experiencing an organic crisis, the need for *some kind of order*, whether conservative or revolutionary, becomes more important than the concrete order fulfilling this need. In other words, the search for the unconditioned prevails over the evaluation of the ways of achieving it. Hobbes's sovereign drew its legitimacy from the fact that it could bring about *some* order, regardless of its content, against the chaos of the state of nature. In other words, what in those cases is the object of ethical investment is not the ontic content of a certain *order*, but the principle of *ordering as such*.

It is not difficult to realize that a militant ethics of the event, as opposed to the situationally determined normative order, has to priv- ilege this moment of rupture over the ordering resources of the situational dimension. But, with implacable logic, this leads to a total uncertainty about the normative content of the ethical act. We can easily end in Žižek's exaltation of the ruthlessness of power and the spirit of sacrifice as values in themselves.[15] Badiou tries to avoid this pitfall through a strict distinction between void and plenum; but, as we have shown, this is an untenable distinction. In order to avoid this cul-de-sac we have to perform a first ascetic operation, and strictly separate the two meanings that the label 'ethics' embraces in an unhappy symbiosis: 'ordering' as a positive value beyond any ontic determination, and the concrete systems of social norms to which we give our moral approval. I suggest that we should restrict the term 'ethics' to the first dimension. This means that, from an ethical point of view, fascism and communism are indistinguishable – but, of course, ethics no longer has anything to do with moral evaluation. So how can we move from one level to the other?

It is here that our second step has to be taken. The ethical as such, as we have seen, cannot have any differentiating ontic content as its defining feature. Its meaning is exhausted in the pure declaring/filling of a void/plenum. This is the point, however, at which the theoretical effects of deconstructing Badiou's dualisms can be brought into oper- ation. I have already explained the basic pattern of that deconstruction: the contamination of each pole of the dichotomies by the other. Let us go to the ontic/ontological distinction that we have established between situation and situationness. There is no event that is exhausted, as far as its meaning is concerned, in its pure breaking with

---

15   This does not mean, of course, that I am reducing Žižek's approach to these questions to assertions of that type. Žižek has the virtue of his own eclecticism, so many times he develops political analyses of much higher interest, and his whole approach to the politico-ideological field is complex and, in several respects, potentially fruitful. Those assertions remain, however – and not without producing some sterilizing theoretical and political effects.

the situation – in other words, there is no event which, in the very movement of this break, does not present itself as a potential bearer of a new order, of situationness as such. This implies that the meaning of the event per se is suspended between its ontic content and its ontological role, or, in other words, *that there is nothing which can proceed as a pure subtraction*. The breaking moment involved in an event – in a radical decision – is still there, *but the site of the event is not purely passive*; going back to Saint Paul, there would have been no resurrection without death.

Where does this leave us as far as ethical theory is concerned? At this point: the ethical as such – as I have defined it – has no normative content, but the subject that constitutes itself through an ethical act is not a pure, unencumbered subject, but one whose site of constitution, and the lack inherent in it, are not done away with by that ethical act (the event). That is, the moment of the ethical involves a *radical investment*, and in this formula its two terms have to be given equal weight. Its radicalism means that the act of investment is not explained by its object (as far as its object is concerned, the act proceeds truly *ex nihilo*). But the object of the investment is not a purely transparent medium, either: it has a situational opaqueness that the event can twist but not eliminate. To use a Heideggerian formulation, we are *thrown* into the normative order (as part of our being thrown into the world) so that the subject who constitutes him- or herself through an ethical investment is already part of a situation and of the lack inherent in it. Every situation deploys a symbolic framework without which even the event would have no meaning; the lack implies that, since the symbolic order can never be saturated, it cannot explain the event out of its own resources. 'Events' in Badiou's sense are moments in which the state of the situation is *radically* put into question; but it is wrong to think that we have purely situational periods interrupted by purely evental interventions: the contamination between the evental and the situational is the very fabric of social life.

So the answer to the question of how we can move from the ethical to the normative, from the unconditional assertion inherent in any event to the level of moral choice and evaluation, is that such a choice and evaluation has largely been already made, before the event, with the symbolic resources of the situation itself. The subject is only partially the subject inspired by the event; the naming of the unrepresentable in which the event consists involves reference to an unrepresented within

202 THE RHETORICAL FOUNDATIONS OF SOCIETY

a situation, and can only proceed through the displacement of elements already present in that situation. This is what I have called the mutual contamination between situation and event. Without it any winning over by the event of elements of the situation would be impossible, except through a totally irrational act of conversion.

This gives us, I think, the intellectual tools to solve what would otherwise be an aporia in Badiou's analysis. I am referring to the issues related to what is, for him, the third form of evil – the attempt to totalize a truth, to eradicate all elements of the situation that are foreign to its implications. That this totalitarian attempt is evil is something I am fully prepared to accept. The difficulty lies in the fact that, in Badiou's system, there are no adequate theoretical resources to deal with this form of evil and, especially, with the alternative social arrangement in which situation and event are not in a relation of mutual exclusion. What does it exactly mean for a truth not to attempt to be total? Badiou's partial answer in terms of a necessary recognition of human animality is certainly less than convincing. For what a truth which is less than total will be confronted with is other opinions, views, ideas, and so on – and if the truth is *permanently* non-total it will have to incorporate into its form this element of confrontation, which involves collective deliberation. Peter Hallward has quite rightly pointed out, in his introduction to the English edition of Badiou's *Ethics*, that it is difficult, given Badiou's notion of an event, to see how this element of deliberation can be incorporated into his theoretical framework. I would add: it is not difficult; it is strictly impossible. For if the proclaimed truth is self-grounded, and if its relation with the situation is one of pure subtraction, no deliberation is possible. The only real alternatives, as far as the elements of the situation are concerned, are total rejection of the truth (disconnection) or what I have called conversion (connection), whose mechanisms are not specified. In these circumstances, that the truth does not attempt to be total can only mean that deliberation is a dialogue of the deaf in which the truth just reiterates itself in the expectation that, as a result of some miracle, radical conversion will take place.

Now, if we move to our own perspective, which involves the contamination between situation and event, the difficulty disappears. First, social agents share, at the level of a situation, values, ideas, beliefs, and so on, that the truth, not being total, does not put entirely into question. Thus, a process of argumentation can take place that justifies the situational rearrangements in terms of those situational factors that the truth procedure does not subvert. Second, the void requires, in my view, a filling, but the filler is not a necessary one – that is why the event is irreducible to the situation. In that case the process of connection ceases to be irrational as far as it presupposes an identification that proceeds out of a constitutive lack. This already involves deliberation. But, third, the edges of the void are, as we have seen, multiple, and the event is only constructed through chains of equivalences linking a plurality of sites. This necessarily involves deliberation conceived in a wide sense (involving partial conversions, dialogues, negotiations, struggles, and so on). If the event only takes place through this process of collective construction, we can see that deliberation is not something added to it externally, but something belonging to its inherent nature. The aspiration to make of truth a total one is evil as far as it interrupts this process of equivalential construction and turns a single site into an absolute location of the enunciation of truth.

There is a last point we have to deal with. I have suggested a series of displacements of the categories informing Badiou's analysis. Can these displacements take place within the general framework of Badiou's ontology – in other words, within his attribution to set theory of a grounding role in the discourse concerning being as being? The answer is clearly negative. Let us frame our question in a transcendental fashion: How must an object be so that the type of relation that we have subsumed under the general label of 'contamination' becomes possible? Or, what amounts to the same thing: What are the conditions of possibility of such a relation? Let me be clear that we are not speaking about any regional ontology; if something such as an 'articulation', or an 'equivalential relation', or the 'construction of the universal through its hegemonic taking up by some particularity' is going to take place at all, the very possibility has to be given at the level of an ontology dealing with being *qua* being – especially if, as I think, these operations are not superstructural expressions of a hidden deeper reality, but the primary terrain of constitution of objects.

Now, it should be clear that set theory would find serious difficulties in dealing with something such as a relation of articulation, especially if it is grounded in the postulate of extensionality. Needless to say, I am not advocating the return to any kind of 'intensional' grounding, which would present all the difficulties that have been well-known since Russell's paradox. As far as set theory is concerned, extensionality is fine. What I am questioning is that set theory could play the role of a fundamental ontology that Badiou attributes to it. I think that set theory is just one way of constituting entities within a much wider field of ontological possibilities. If we take the equivalential relation, for instance, it involves an articulation between universality and particularity that is only conceivable in terms of *analogy*. But such a relation cannot be properly conceived of within the framework of Badiou's mathematical ontology. The same happens with the ensemble of phenomena known in psychoanalysis as 'overdetermination'. And I insist that it is not possible to sidestep this incompatibility by attributing it to the level of abstraction at which we are working[16] (set theory operating at such a level that all the distinctions on which our theoretical approach is based would not be pertinent or representable). The true issue is that the emergence of any new field of objectivity presupposes ontological possibilities that it is philosophy's task to uncover.

Is there a field more primary than that uncovered by set theory which would allow us to properly, *ontologically* account for the type of relations that we are exploring? I think there is, and it is *linguistics*. The relations of analogy through which the aggregation constructing an evental site are established are relations of *substitution*, and the differential relations constituting the area of objective distinctions (which define the 'situation', in Badiou's terms) constitute the field of *combinations*. Now, substitutions and combinations are the only possible forms of objectivity in a Saussurean universe, and if they are extracted from their anchorage in speech and writing – that is, if the separation of form from substance is made in a more consequent and radical way than Saussure's – we are not in the field of a regional but of a general or fundamental ontology.

I would even add something more. This ontology cannot remain within the straitjacket of classical structuralism, which privileged the syntagmatic over the paradigmatic pole of language. On the contrary, once equivalential relations are recognized as constitutive of objectivity as such – once the paradigmatic pole of substitutions is given its

---

16   And it would not be possible either to restrict set-theoretical analysis to the situation, given that the contamination between situation and event is a more fundamental ground than their distinction.

proper weight in ontological description – we are not only in the terrain of a linguistic ontology, but also of a rhetorical one. In my previous example of Solidarność, the 'event' took place through the aggregation of a plurality of 'sites' on the basis of their *analogy* in the common opposition to an oppressive regime. And what is this substitution through analogy but a metaphorical aggregation? Metaphor, metonymy, synecdoche (and especially catachresis, as their common denominator) are not categories describing adornments of language, as classical philosophy had it, but ontological categories describing the constitution of objectivity as such. It is important to see that this does not involve any kind of theoretical nihilism or anti-philosophy,[17] because it is the result of a critique that is fully internal to the conceptual medium as such – and is, in that sense, a strictly philosophical enterprise. Many consequences follow from taking this path, including the ability to describe in more precise conceptual terms what I have called the contamination (a better term might perhaps be overdetermination) between the evental and the situational.[18]

The huge question that remains is the following: Could the ensemble of relations that I have described as rhetorical be absorbed and

---

17   I find the whole distinction between philosophy and anti-philosophy a red herring. I do not deny that there are cases in which the notion of anti-philosophy would be pertinent – such as Nietzsche – but I find the generalization of the distinction, to the point of transforming it into a *ligne de partage* crossing the whole of the Western tradition, a rather naive and sterile exercise. To detect a Platonic gesture as a founding moment separating conceptual thought from its 'other' is simply to ignore that the Platonic dualism is itself grounded in an army of metaphors that make the theory of forms deeply ambiguous. And, closer to home, to claim that the *Philosophical Investigations* or *La voix et le phénomène* are anti-philosophical works does not make any sense to me. It is one thing to deny the validity of conceptual thought; it is another to show, through a conceptual critique, that the conceptual medium is unable to ground itself without appealing to something different from itself. To reduce the latter to the former is not a defence of the concept but just conceptual ethnocentrism.

18   As I have repeatedly asserted in this chapter, the overdetermination between the situational and the evental supposes that the event cannot *just* be the exceptional kind of break that Badiou has in mind. Those breaks no doubt take place, and it is in them that the duality between the state of the situation and what I have called 'situationness' becomes fully visible. But the important point is that, if the event is the decision that escapes determination by what is countable within a situation, any kind of social action is dominated by the situation/event distinction. It is simply wrong to think that, apart from revolutionary breaks, social life is dominated by the purely programmed logic of what is countable within a situation. (Wittgenstein's critique of the notion of applying a rule is highly relevant for this discussion.)

described as a special case within the wider categories of set theory, so that the latter would retain their ontological priority? Or, rather, could set theory itself be described as an internal possibility – admittedly an extreme one – within the field of a generalized rhetoric? I am convinced that the right answer implies the second alternative, but a demonstration of this will have to await another occasion.

CHAPTER 9

Bare Life or Social Indeterminacy?

I have great admiration for the work of Giorgio Agamben. I particularly appreciate his dazzling classical erudition, his skill – both intuitive and analytical – in dealing with theoretical categories, and his ability to relate systems of thought whose connections are not immediately obvious. This appreciation does not go, however, without some deep reservations concerning his theoretical conclusions, and it is on these reservations that I want to elaborate in the following pages. If I had to put them in a nutshell, I would assert that Agamben has – inverting the usual saying – the vices of his virtues. Reading his texts, one often has the feeling that he jumps too quickly from having established the *genealogy* of a term, a concept or an institution, to determine its actual working in a contemporary context, that in some sense the *origin* has a secret determining priority over what follows from it. I am not, of course, claiming that Agamben makes the naive mistake of assuming that etymology provides the cipher or clue to what follows from it, but I would argue that his discourse often remains uneasily undecided between genealogical and structural explanation. Let us take an example from Saussurean linguistics: the Latin term *necare* ('to kill') has become in modern French *noyer* ('to drown'), and we can examine this diachronic change in the relation between signifier and signified as much as we want, and we will still not find in it any explanation of the meaning resulting from its last articulation – signification depends entirely on a *value* context that is strictly singular, and that no diachronic genealogy is able to capture. This is the perspective from which I want to question Agamben's theoretical approach: his genealogy is not sensitive enough to structural diversity and, in the end, it risks ending in sheer teleology.

Let us start by considering the three theses in which Agamben summarises his argument towards the end of *Homo Sacer*:

1. The original political relation is the ban (the state of exception as zone of indistinction between outside and inside, exclusion and inclusion).

2. The fundamental activity of sovereign power is the production of bare life as originary political element and as threshold of articulation between nature and culture, between *zoē* and *bios*.

3. Today it is not the city but rather the camp that is the fundamental biopolitical paradigm of the West.[1]

Let me start with the first thesis. According to Agamben, who is quoting Cavalca, 'to ban' someone is to say that anybody may harm him.[2] That is why the 'sacred man' can be killed but not sacrificed – the sacrifice is still a figure representable within the legal order of the city. The life of the bandit clearly shows the kind of exteriority belonging to the sacred man:

> The life of the bandit, like that of the sacred man, is not a piece of animal nature without any relation to law and the city. It is, rather, a threshold of indistinction and of passage between animal and man, *physis* and *nomos*, exclusion and inclusion: the life of the bandit is the life of the *loup garou*, the werewolf, who is precisely *neither man nor beast*, and who dwells paradoxically within both while belonging to neither.[3]

Sovereignty is at the source of the ban, but it requires an extension of the territory within which the ban applies, for if we were only to deal with the exteriority to law of the *loup garou* we would still be able to establish a clear line of division between the 'inside' and the 'outside' of the community. Agamben is very much aware of the complexity of the relation between outside and inside. For that reason, speaking about Hobbes's 'state of nature', he indicates that it is not a primitive condition that has been eradicated once the covenant has transferred sovereignty to the Leviathan, but a constant possibility within the communitarian order, which arises whenever the city is seen as *tamquam dissoluta*. In that sense, we are not dealing with a pure, pre-social nature, but with a 'naturalization' that maintains its reference to the social order insofar as the latter ceases to work. This explains how

---

1 Giorgio Agamben, *Homo Sacer: Sovereign Power and Bare Life* (Stanford, CA: Stanford University Press, 1998), p. 181.

2 Ibid., pp. 104–5.

3 Ibid., p. 105.

the state of exception emerges. Carl Schmitt had asserted that there is no rule applicable to chaos, and that the state of exception is required whenever the agreement between the legal order and the wider communitarian order has been broken:

> Far from being a prejuridical condition that is indifferent to the law of the city, the Hobbesian state of nature is the exception and the threshold that constitutes and dwells within it. It is not so much a war of all against all as, more precisely, a condition in which everyone is thus *wargus, gerit caput lupinum*. And this lupization of man and humanization of the wolf is at every moment possible in the *dissolutio civitatis* inaugurated by the state of exception. This threshold alone, which is neither simple natural life nor social life but rather bare life or sacred life, is the always present and always operative presupposition of sovereignty.[4]

This explains why sovereign power cannot have a contractual origin: 'This is why in Hobbes, the foundation of sovereign power is to be thought not in the subjects' free renunciation of their natural right but in the sovereign's preservation of his natural right to do anything to anyone, which now appears as the right to punish.'[5]

Thus, the ban holds together bare life and sovereignty. And it is important for Agamben to point out that the ban is not simply a sanction – which as such would still be representable within the order of the city – but that it involves *abandonment* of the *homo sacer*, and the other figures that Agamben associates with him are simply left outside any communitarian order. That is why he can be killed but not sacrificed. In that sense, the ban is non-relational: its victims are left to their own separatedness. This, for Agamben, is the originary political relation, linked to sovereignty. It is a more originary extraneousness than that of the foreigner, who still has an assigned place within the legal order. 'We must learn to recognise this structure of the ban in the political relations and public spaces in which we will live. *In the city the banishment of sacred life is more internal than every interiority and more external than every extraneousness*.'[6] The ban has thus been at the

---

4   Ibid., p. 106.
5   Ibid.
6   Ibid., p. 111. Italics as in original.

source of sovereign power. The state of exception, which reduces the citizens to bare life (he has in mind Foucault's biopolitics) has determined modernity from its very beginning.

Agamben has, no doubt, touched with the category of the ban something crucially important concerning the political. There is certainly, within the political, a moment of negativity that requires the construction of an inside/outside relation, and requires that sovereignty is in an ambiguous position with respect to the juridical order. The problem, however, is the following: Does the articulation of dimensions through which Agamben conceives of the structure of the ban exhaust the system of possibilities that such a structure opens? In other words: Has not Agamben chosen just one of those possibilities and hypostatized it so that it assumes a unique character? Let us consider the matter carefully. The essence of a ban is given by its effects – namely, to place somebody outside the system of differences constituting the legal order. But in order to assimilate *all* situations of being outside the law to that of *homo sacer* as described by Agamben, some extra presuppositions have to be added. In the first place, the sheer separatedness – absence of relation – of the outside involved that the banned person is a naked individuality, dispossessed of any kind of collective identity. But, secondly, it also entails that the situation of the outsider is one of radical defencelessness, wholly exposed to the violence of those inside the city. Only at that price can sovereign power be absolute. But are these two extra presuppositions justified? Do they logically emerge from the mere category of 'being outside the law'? Obviously not. The outsider does not need to be outside *any* law; what is inherent to the category is only the fact of being outside the law *of the city*. Abandonment comes only from the latter. Let us consider the following passage from Frantz Fanon, which I have discussed in another context:

> The *lumpenproletariat*, once it is constituted, brings all its forces to endanger the 'security' of the town, and is the sign of the irrevocable decay, the gangrene ever present at the heart of colonial domination. So the pimps, the hooligans, the unemployed, and the petty criminals . . . throw themselves into the struggle like stout working men. These classless idlers will by militant and decisive action discover the path that leads to nationhood . . . The prostitutes too, and the maids who are paid two pounds a month, all who turn in

circles between suicide and madness, will recover their balance, once more go forward and march proudly in the great procession of the awakened nation.[7]

Here we have actors who are entirely outside the law of the city, who cannot be inscribed in any of the categories of the latter, but such an exteriority is the starting point for a new collective identification *opposed* to the law of the city. We do not have lawlessness as against law, but two laws that do not recognize each other. In another work,[8] Agamben discusses the notion of 'necessity' as elaborated by the Italian jurist Santi Romano, and points out that, for the latter, revolutionary forces which, according to the state juridical order would be, strictly speaking, outside the law, nevertheless give themselves a new law. The passage from Romano quoted by Agamben is most revealing: after having recognized the anti-juridical nature of the revolutionary forces, he adds that this is only the case

> with respect to the positive law of the state against which it is directed, but that does not mean that, from the very different point of view from which it defines itself, it is not a movement ordered and regulated by its own law. This also means that it is an order that must be classified in the category of originary juridical orders, in the now well-known sense given to this expression. In this sense, and within the limits of the sphere we have indicated, we can thus speak of a law of revolution.

So we have two incompatible laws. What remains as valid from the notion of the ban as defined by Agamben is the idea of an uninscribable exteriority, but the range of situations to which it applies is much wider than those subsumable under the category of *homo sacer*. I think that Agamben has not seen the problem of the inscribable/uninscribable, of inside/outside, in its true universality. In fact, what the mutual ban between opposed laws describes is the constitutive nature of any radical antagonism – radical in the sense that its two poles cannot be reduced to any super-game that would be recognized by them as an objective meaning to which both would be submitted.

---

7 Frantz Fanon, *The Wretched of the Earth* (New York: Grove, 1968), p. 130.
8 Giorgio Agamben, *State of Exception* (Chicago/London: University of Chicago Press, 2005), pp. 28–9.

Now, I would argue that only when the ban is mutual do we have, *stricto sensu*, a *political* relation, for it is only in that case that we have a radical opposition between social forces and, as a result, a constant renegotiation and re-grounding of the social bond. This can be seen most clearly if we go back for a moment to Agamben's analysis of Hobbes. As we have seen, he asserts that, contrary to the counterculturalist view, the sovereign is the only one that preserves his natural right to do anything to anybody – in other words, the subjects become bare life. The opposition between these two dimensions, however, does not stand. In order for the sovereign to preserve his natural right, he needs such a right to be recognized by his subjects, and such a recognition, as Agamben himself points out, finds some limits:

> Corresponding to this particular state of the 'right of Punishing' which takes the form of a survival of the state of nature at the very heart of the state, is the subjects' capacity not to disobey but to resist violence exercised on their own person, 'for . . . no man is supposed bound by Covenant, not to resist violence; and consequently it cannot be intended, that he gave any right to another to lay violent hands upon his person'. Sovereign violence is in truth founded not on a pact but on the exclusive inclusion of bare life in the state.[9]

Agamben draws from the minimal nature of the notion of a right to resist violence against one's person a further proof of his argument concerning the interconnections between bare life, sovereignty and the modern state. It is true that the Hobbesian view invites such a reading, but only if a conclusion is derived from it: that it amounts to a radical elimination of the political. When a supreme will within the community is not confronted by anything, politics necessarily disappears. From this viewpoint the Hobbesian project can be compared with another that is its opposite but, at the same time, identical in its anti-political effects: the Marxian notion of the withering away of the state. For Hobbes, society is incapable of giving itself its own law and, as a result, the total concentration of power in the hands of the sovereign is the prerequisite of any communitarian order. For Marx, a classless society has realised full universality, and that makes politics superfluous. But it is enough that we introduce some *souplesse* within

9   Ibid., pp. 106–7.

the Hobbesian scheme – that we accept that society is capable of *some partial* self-regulation, to see immediately that its demands are going to be more than those deriving from bare life, and that they are going to have a variety and specificity that no 'sovereign' power can simply ignore. When we arrive at that point, however, the notion of 'sovereignty' starts shading into that of 'hegemony'. This means that, in my view, Agamben has clouded the issue, for he has presented as a political moment what actually amounts to a radical elimination of the political: a sovereign power that reduces the social bond to bare life.

I have spoken of social self-regulation as being partial. By this I mean that social and political demands emerge from a variety of quarters, not all of which move in the same direction. This means that society requires constant efforts at re-grounding. Schmitt, as we have seen, asserted that the function of the sovereign – in the state of exception – is to establish the coherence between law and the wider communitarian order (one cannot apply law to chaos). If this is so, however, and if the plurality of demands requires a constant process of legal transformation and revision, the state of emergency ceases to be exceptional and becomes an integral part of the political construction of the social bond. According to Wittgenstein, to apply a rule requires a second rule specifying how the first one should be applied, a third one explaining how the second will be applied, and so on. From this he drew the conclusion that the instance of application is part of the rule itself. In Kantian terms – as Agamben points out – this means that in the construction of the social bond we are dealing with reflective rather than determinative judgements. Vico's remarks – also quoted by Agamben – about the superiority of the exception over the rule are also highly pertinent in this context. This explains why I see the history of the state of exception through different lenses than Agamben. While he draws a picture in which the becoming rule of the exception represents the unavoidable advance towards a totalitarian society, I also try to determine, with the generalization of the 'exceptional', countertendencies that make it possible to think about the future in more optimistic terms. I discussed earlier what Santi Romano said concerning revolutionary laws. Now, that does not only apply to periods of radical revolutionary breaks – what Gramsci called 'organic crises' – but also to a variety of situations in which social movements constitute particularistic political spaces and give themselves their own 'law' (which is partially internal and partially external to the legal system of the state). There is a molecular process of partial transformations that is absolutely vital as an accumulation of forces whose potential becomes visible when a more radical transformation of a whole hegemonic formation becomes possible.

What we have so far already make clear that, in my view, the second thesis of Agamben concerning bare life as resulting from the activity of sovereign power does not fare any better. To start with, the distinction between *zoē* and *bios* cannot play the central role in historical explanation to which Agamben assigns it. As he himself asserts at the beginning of *Homo Sacer*, the Greeks used two terms to refer to life: '*zoē*, which expressed the simple fact of living common to all living beings (animals, men or gods), and *bios*, which indicated the form or way of living proper to an individual or a group'.[10] This means that living beings are not distributed between two categories – those who have exclusively *bios* and those who have exclusively *zoē* – for those who have *bios* obviously have *zoē* as well. So *zoē* is primarily an abstraction. Even the *oikos*, whose aim was merely concerned with reproductive life, has its own internal structure, based on a hierarchical distribution of functions, so that although its aims are not political, it is far from being bare life, since it has its own configuration and system of rules. Ergo, if Agamben's thesis is to hold, he would have to prove that, in some circumstances, bare life ceases to be an abstraction and becomes a concrete referent.

It is at this point that Agamben brings into the picture Foucault's *biopolitics*: 'According to Foucault, a society's "threshold of biological modernity is situated at the point at which the species and the individual as a simple living body become what is at stake in a society's political strategies".'[11] It is most revealing that Agamben links Foucault's biopolitical hypothesis to the earlier work of Hannah Arendt: 'Hannah Arendt had already analyzed the process that brings *homo laborans* – and, with it, biological life as such – gradually to occupy the very centre of the political scene of modernity. In *The Human Condition*, Arendt attributes the transformation and decadence of the political realm in modern societies to this primacy of natural life over political action.'[12] Of course, to present the argument in these terms is grotesquely biased. One could more plausibly make

---

10   Ibid., p. 1.
11   Ibid., p. 3.
12   Ibid., p. 4.

the opposite argument – namely, that in modernity there is no primacy of natural life over political action, but rather a politicization of a terrain previously occupied by 'natural' life (and it is already to concede too much to assume that that life was merely 'natural'). What, in any case, is wrong with the argument about a rigid opposition between political sovereignty and bare life is the assumption that it necessarily involves increasing control by an over-powerful state. All the notion of a politicization of 'natural' life involves is that increasing areas of social life are submitted to processes of human control and regulation – but it is a non sequitur to assume that such control must crystallize around a tendentially totalitarian instance.

Given Agamben's assertion of a strict correlation between the ban and sovereignty, the postulation of an *ad quem* totalitarian trend was, of course, to be expected. The result is that he equates human situations whose nature is entirely dissimilar. In order to have a 'bare life', as we have seen, the receiving end of the ban has to be entirely defence-less and fully submitted to the 'abandonment' dictated by the sovereign power. Some of the situations that Agamben describes in fact approach the state of bare life that is the mere object of a political intervention. Thus he refers to the figure of 'der Musselmann', an inhabitant of the concentration camps, 'a being from whom humiliation, horror and fear had so taken away all consciousness and all personality as to make him absolutely apathetic';[13] or to a biochemist suffering from leukaemia who decides to transform his body into a laboratory: 'His body is no longer private, since it has been transformed into a labora-tory; but neither is it public, since only insofar as it is his own body can he transgress the limits that morality and law put into experimen-tation . . . It is a *bios* that has, in every particular sense, so concentrated itself in its own *zoē* as to become indistinguishable from it';[14] or to the body of Karen Quinlan, a comatose person whose organs are going to be transplanted: 'Here biological life – which the machines are keep-ing functional by artificial respiration, pumping blood into the arteries, and regulating the blood temperature – has been entirely separated from the form of life that bore the name Karen Quinlan: here life becomes (or at least seems to become) pure *zoē*.'[15]

---

13 Ibid., p. 185.
14 Ibid., p. 186.
15 Ibid.

Up to this point, Agamben's argument concerning 'bare life' would be just plausible, although one could wonder about its political relevance. But later on he tries to extend it into entirely different situations. From the comatose we move to the bandit:

> his entire existence is reduced to a bare life stripped of every right by virtue of the fact that anyone can kill him without committing homicide; he can save himself only in perpetual flight or a foreign land . . . He is pure *zoē*, but his *zoē* is as such caught in the sovereign ban and must reckon with it at every moment, finding the best way to elude or deceive it. In this sense, no life, as exiles and bandits know well, is more 'political' than his.[16]

The life of the bandit or the exile can be entirely political, but they are so in an entirely other sense than that of Karen Quinlan, because they, unlike Quinlan, are capable of engaging in antagonistic social practices. They have, in that sense, their own law, and their conflict with the law of the city is a conflict between laws, not between law and bare life. Agamben is aware of a potential criticism of the extreme and marginal character of his examples of bare life, and he tries to answer in anticipation with examples that he calls 'no less extreme and still more familiar': 'the Bosnian woman at Omarska, a perfect threshold of indistinction between biology and politics, or – in an apparently opposite, yet analogous, sense – military interventions on humanitarian grounds, in which war efforts are carried out for the sake of biological ends such as nutrition or the care of epidemics.'[17] At this point, however, we no longer know what is the issue under discussion: the care for the biological survival of populations or the reduction of people to *zoē*, entirely stripped of any *bios*? Agamben, in his argument, constantly mixes both levels.

If the example of the bandit already shows a displacement of the logic of exclusion to something that clearly exceeds the notion of 'bare life', this excess is only more visible when Agamben tries to expand the logic of sovereignty/bare life into a general theory of modernity. He starts by pointing out an undeniable fact – namely, that in most languages the notion of 'the people' is ambiguous: on the one hand it

---

16   Ibid., pp. 183–4.
17   Ibid., p. 187.

refers to the community as a whole (*populus*), on the other to the underdog (*plebs*). His reading of this ambiguity, however, is that the community is sharply divided and that the totalitarian logic of modernity is an attempt to overcome that division:

> In this sense, our age is nothing but the implacable and methodical attempt to overcome the division dividing the people, to eliminate radically the people that is excluded. This attempt brings together, according to different modalities and horizons, Right and Left, capitalist countries and socialist countries, which are united in the project – which is in the last analysis futile but which has been partially realized in all industrialized countries – of producing a single and undivided people.[18]

There is something basically wrong with this analysis. In the first place, division is perfectly compatible with the status quo, as long as the differences resulting from social diversity are not constructed in an antagonistic way. Hierarchy means, precisely, social differentiation, so that the elimination of division, conceived as multiplicity, is not something that the dominant groups are systematically aiming at. But, in the second place, if we are speaking about an antagonistic division, one that constructs 'the people' as an underdog, the plebs that this division creates does not perpetuate but attempts to supersede the original division. We are dealing with a part that attempts to incarnate the whole, with a heterogeneity aspiring to be reabsorbed into a new homogeneity. So the dialectic between part and whole, between homogeneity and heterogeneity, is far more complex than what Agamben's simplistic alternative of either 'division' or 'undivided people' allows us to think. The Gramscian distinction between 'corporative' and 'hegemonic' class allows for more complex strategic moves than Agamben's mechanical teleology. Differences can be partialities within a whole – as the plebs was for patrician eyes – or the names of alternative totalities (requiring the investment of the whole within the part, as in Lacan's *objet a*). Homogenizing logics can be, *reductio ad absurdum*, thoroughly totalitarian, but they can equally be emancipatory, as when they link, in an equivalential chain, a plurality of unsatisfied demands. Sovereignty, finally, can also be totalitarian in

---

18   Ibid., p. 179.

the extreme case in which it involves a *total* concentration of power; but it can also be profoundly democratic, if it involves an articulating rather than a determining power – in other words, when it 'empowers' the underdog. In that case, as I have already pointed out, sovereignty should be conceived as hegemony.

Needless to say, I fully reject Agamben's third thesis, according to which the concentration camp is the *nomos* or fundamental biopolitical paradigm of the West. He asserts:

> the birth of the camp in our time appears as an event that decisively signals the political space of modernity itself. It is produced at the point at which the political system of the modem nation-state, which was founded on the functional nexus between a determinate localization (land) and a determinate order (the State) and mediated by automatic rules for the inscription of life (birth or the nation), enters into a lasting crisis, and the State decides to assume directly the care of the nation's biological life as one of its proper tasks . . . Something can no longer function within the traditional mechanisms that regulated this inscription, and the camp is the new, hidden regulator of the inscription of life in the order – or, rather, the sign of the system's inability to function without being transformed into a lethal machine.[19]

This series of wild statements would only hold if the following set of rather dubious premises were accepted:

1. the crisis of the functional nexus between land, state and the automatic rules for the inscription of life has freed an entity called 'biological – or bare – life';
2. the regulation of that freed entity has been assumed by a single and unified entity called the state;
3. the inner logic of that entity necessarily leads it to treat the freed entities as entirely malleable objects whose archetypical form would be the ban.

Needless to say, none of these presuppositions can be accepted as they stand. Agamben, who has presented a rather compelling analysis of the way in which an ontology of potentiality should be structured,

---

19   Ibid., p. 175.

nevertheless doses his argument with a naive teleologism in which potentiality appears as entirely subordinated to a pre-given actuality. This teleologism is, as a matter of fact, the symmetrical *pendant* of the 'etymologism' I referred to at the beginning of this chapter. Their combined effect is to divert Agamben's attention from the really relevant issue, which is the system of structural possibilities that each *new* situation opens. The most summary examination of that system would have revealed, first, that the crisis of the 'automatic rules for the inscription of life' has freed many more entities than 'bare life', and that the reduction of the latter to the former takes place only in some extreme circumstances that cannot in the least be considered as a hidden pattern of modernity; second, that the process of social regulation to which the dissolution of the 'automatic rules of inscription' opens the way has involved a plurality of instances that were far from unified in a single unity called 'the state'; and, third, that the process of state-building in modernity has involved a far more complex dialectic between homogeneity and heterogeneity than the one that Agamben's 'camp-based' paradigm reflects. By unifying the whole process of modern political construction around the extreme and absurd paradigm of the concentration camp, Agamben does more than present a distorted history: he blocks any possible exploration of the emancipatory possibilities opened by our modern heritage.

Let me conclude with a reference to the question of the future as it can be conceived from Agamben's perspective. He asserts:

> Only if it is possible to think the Being of abandonment beyond every idea of law (even that of the empty form of laws being in force without significance) will we have moved out of the paradox of sovereignty towards a politics freed from every ban. A pure form of law is only the empty form of relation. Yet the empty form of relation is no longer a law but a zone of indistinguishability between law and life, which is to say, a state of exception.[20]

We have not been told anything about what a movement out of the paradox of sovereignty and 'towards a politics freed from every ban' would imply. But we do not need to be told: the formulation of the problem already entails its own answer. To be beyond any ban and any

---

20   Ibid. p. 59.

sovereignty means, simply, to be beyond politics. The myth of a fully reconciled society is what governs the (non-)political discourse of Agamben. And it is also what allows him to dismiss all political options in our societies and to unify them in the concentration camp as their secret destiny. Instead of deconstructing the logic of political institutions, showing areas in which forms of struggle and resistance are possible, he forecloses them through an essentialist unification. Political nihilism is his ultimate message.

Acknowledgements

Chapter 1 first appeared as 'The Death and Resurrection of the Theory of Ideology', in *Journal of Political Ideologies*, 1996, 1(3), pp. 201–20.

Chapter 2 first appeared as 'On the Names of God', in Sue Golding, ed., *The Eight Technologies of Otherness* (New York: Routledge, 1997).

Chapter 3 first appeared as 'Articulation and the Limits of Metaphor', in Ewa Plonowska Ziarek, James Bono and James Dean, eds, *A Time for the Humanities: Futurity and the Limits of Autonomy* (New York: Fordham, 2008), pp. 61–83.

Chapter 4 first appeared as 'The Politics of Rhetoric', in Tom Cohen, J. Hillis Miller, Andrzej Warminski and Barbara Cohen, eds, *Material Events: Paul de Man and the Afterlife of Theory* (Minneapolis: Minnesota University Press, 2001), pp. 229–53.

Chapter 5 first appeared as 'Antagonismo, subjetividad y política', in *Debates y Combates*, 2(3), June–July 2012.

Chapter 6 first appeared as 'Ethics, Normativity and the Heteronomy of the Law', in Sinkwan Cheng, ed., *Law, Justice and Power: Between Reason and Will* (Palo Alto, CA: Stanford University Press, 2004).

Chapter 7 first appeared as 'Why Constructing a "People" Is the Main Task of Radical Politics', in *Critical Inquiry*, 32, Summer 2006.

Chapter 8 first appeared as 'An Ethics of Militant Engagement', in Peter Hallward, ed., *Think Again: Alain Badiou and the Future of Philosophy* (London: Continuum, 2004).

Chapter 9 first appeared as 'Bare Life or Social Indeterminacy', in Matthew Calarco and Steven DeCaroli, eds, *Giorgio Agamben: On Sovereignty and Life* (Palo Alto, CA: Stanford University Press, 2007).

Index